MONTREAL 2010

FACING MULTIPLICITY: PSYCHE, NATURE, CULTURE

PROCEEDINGS OF THE XVIIITH CONGRESS
OF THE INTERNATIONAL ASSOCIATION
FOR ANALYTICAL PSYCHOLOGY

Montreal 2010

Facing Multiplicity:
Psyche, Nature, Culture

Proceedings of the XVIIIth Congress
of the International Association
for Analytical Psychology

Edited by Pramila Bennett

DAIMON
VERLAG

The articles in this publication (CD included) were edited and compiled to provide as true as possible a record of the Proceedings of the Eighteenth Congress of the IAAP held in Montreal in August 2010. The views expressed in them are those of the authors and are neither endorsed nor necessarily held by the Editor or the Publishers; they are meant to promote scholarship.

We are grateful to the Art Gallery of Greater Victoria for use of the painting by Emily Carr, 'Totem Walk at Sitka', 1907, watercolour, from their collection as a cover illustration for this volume.

Contents

Thursday, 26 August 2010

Friday, 27 August 2010

Programme Committee

Axel Capriles (SVAJ, AGAP)
Grazia Cerbo (AIPA)
Kusum Dhar Prabhu (AGAP)
François Martin-Vallas (SFPA)
Judith Pickering (ANZSJA)
Joe Cambray (NESJA, JPA)
Paul Kugler (PSJA, IRSJA)
Jörg Rasche (DGAP)
Hester Solomon (*ex officio*)
Tom Kelly, Chair

Executive Committee:
Society Representatives

Walter Fonseca Boechat (AJB)
Angela Connolly (CIPA)
JoAnn Culbert-Koehn (CGJILA)
Toshio Kawai (AJAJ)
Tamar Kron (IIJP)
Marianne Müller (SGAP)
Marjorie Nathanson (CGJISF)
Denise Ramos (SBrPA)
Jan Wiener (SAP)

Ethics committee

Chair, Richard Willetts, United States, CGJISF
Honorary Secretary, Ann Casement, United Kingdom, BAP
Henry Abramovitch, Israel, IIJP
Mariana Arancibia, Chile, IM
Christian Gaillard, France, SFPA
Dong-Hyuck Suh, Korea, KAJA
Ellen Kandoian Sweeney, United States, OVAJA
Carole Beebe Tarantelli, Italy, CIPA
Ursula Wirtz, Switzerland, SGAP

Secretary to the President
Mariuccia Tresoldi

IAAP Secretariat
Yvonne Trüeb

Webmaster
Don Williams (IRSJA)

Local Organizing Committee

Jan Bauer, Chair (IRSJA, AGAP)
Denis Charrier-Adams (IRSJA)
Daniel Bordeleau (IRSJA)
Françoise Cloutier (AGAP)
Guy Corneau (IRSJA, AGAP)
Marcel Gaumond (AGAP)
Rosemary Murray-Lachapelle (OAJA)
Yvon Rivière (AGAP)
Tom Kelly (IRSJA, AGAP)

IAAP Officers

Hester Solomon, President
Joe Cambray, President-Elect
Tom Kelly, Vice-President
Jörg Rasche, Vice-President
Paul Kugler, Honorary Secretary

Editor's Note

In this record of the Montreal Congress Proceedings, the titles of several of the papers presented were altered by their authors (while the text remained the same); these adjustments were made after the programme was printed.

Some who had been scheduled to make a presentation were unable to attend; their papers were read on their behalf. In a few cases, though the papers were not read, they are included here because they were submitted.

Many papers had illustrations; however it was not possible to use all of these images in this publication for reasons of 1) copyright 2) the sheer number of them. Those that are included will appear in colour on the CD-rom.

Papers that were presented in a language different from English are to be found in the Appendix. These are published verbatim.

The Posters which are recorded and listed in a section by themselves are based on the original proposals.

Acknowledgements

As Wotan says in *Das Rheingold:* 'Vollendet das ewige Werk'.

The proceedings of the Montreal Congress are the work of many hands. Assembling and editing the papers, a number of them written by analysts whose first language is not English, has been a long haul. I would like to thank everyone who contributed, the authors themselves for their prompt response and patience, and particularly Bob Hinshaw and Tom Kelly for their generous support and understanding. I am especially indebted to Marcus West and Jean Knox for their incisive contribution and advice and to Alessandra Cavalli for her practical assistance. My thanks also go to Angela Connolly for her constructive comments and to Asha Ramgulam and Anya Smart who worked alongside me. I very much value Jan Wiener's and JoAnn Culbert-Koehn's friendship and continued interest. I am particularly grateful to Robert Imhoff of Daimon Verlag for his invaluable input in the preparation of this publication and, finally, to my husband George for putting up with my many hours of absence from the domestic hearth.

Pramila Bennett

Foreword

Tom Kelly

It is with great pleasure that, in these Proceedings, we present you with a collection of the papers given at the XVIII International Congress of the IAAP in Montreal in August 2010. The Proceedings serve a number of purposes: for one, they are a record of the presentations given at the Congress and are made available to all members of the IAAP so that those who could not attend may nevertheless access the material. In addition, the Proceedings provide a record of the intellectual history of Jungian thought and development over the years. Our Congress Proceedings allow us to trace where we are in relation to the foundations of analytical psychology and indicate possible directions for future developments. They are important for the present in that they provide a record of the presentations but also for the future in that they mark a chapter in the history of the development of Analytical Psychology. The presentations during the Montreal Congress expanded the boundaries of analytical psychology by reaching beyond the familiar into new domains. Contrasts and comparisons of our concepts with those of other disciplines contributed to putting into question established ways of thinking and challenged each participant to go beyond what is taken for granted. Among the many seeds planted at the Montreal Congress, only the future will tell how many of these will have taken root and in which direction they will have developed.

The excitement of the Congress itself as colleagues from around the world gathered, where old friends met up again and new acquaintances and friendships were forged, belies the arduous work and detailed organization required to make this occasion a successful event. We owe a large measure of gratitude to the members of the Programme Committee composed of Axel Capriles (SVAJ, AGAP), Grazia Cerbo (AIPA), Kusum Dhar Prabhu (AGAP), Farnçois Martin-Vallas (SFPA), Judith Pickering (ANZSJA), Joe Cambray (NESJA, JPA), Paul Kugler (PSJA, IRSJA), Jörg Rasche (DGAP), Hester Solomon (ex officio) and Tom Kelly, Chair.

In February 2008, the Programme Committee first met in Zürich to establish a theme for the Montreal Congress. Each member of the Committee came to the table prepared with ideas after having asked the members of their society for input and suggestions about a theme that would ignite the interest and enthusiasm of their members. Under constraints of time and with pressure to give birth to a theme, the members of the Committee worked assiduously, sharing ideas and suggestions, exploring avenues of interest and of potential, holding the inevitable and visibly palpable tension till eventually a theme emerged that was inclusive and multifaceted: Facing Multiplicity: Psyche Nature Culture. This theme, it was felt, would allow us to explore the multifarious and novel expressions of the self in an ever changing world. In response to the Call for Participation in the Congress, the Programme Committee received well over 300 proposals. In February 2009, the Committee met for a second time in Montreal for the arduous task of making a selection from the many worthwhile submissions. It was with great regret that we could not accept each and every proposal. Constraints of time and space at the congress venue forced us to make very difficult choices.

Over the five days of the Congress, participants were treated to twelve plenary presentations in the morning, including three panel presentations, and one hundred and five break-out sessions in the afternoons. It was an honour and a pleasure to work with such an accomplished group of colleagues and I am thankful to each of them for their invaluable contribution and participation. The record number of participants at the Congress testifies to the accomplishment of the Programme Committee in sculpting a stimulating and innovative program.

The local Organizing Committee, composed of Jan Bauer (Chair), Daniel Bordeleau, Denis Charrier-Adams, Françoise Cloutier, Guy Corneau, Marcel Gaumond, Rosemary Murray-Lachappelle and Yvon Rivière did a masterful job of organizing the welcome reception on Sunday evening which mirrored the warmth, openness and creativity of the local group of analysts. Evening events throughout the week included a presentation on the Red Book, a musical concert in a local church, a guided visit to an art gallery, a film presentation by a Quebec producer, a performance of the Jung-White letters, several book launches and, on Friday evening, the closing banquet. To each of my colleagues, my heartfelt thanks for their constant support, creative ideas, and especially for their enthusiasm and playfulness throughout the lengthy preparations to host our colleagues from around the globe. The joy we had working together to make this a memorable congress was palpable, I believe, in the warm and hearty welcome offered to the participants throughout the week of the congress.

I would also like to thank Conference Groups and Incentives for their help with the minutiae of organizational details, particularly Yee Fun Wong who worked tirelessly to make this Congress a success and who managed to handle things behind the scenes during the Congress with admirable patience and calm.

I am indebted to Pramila Bennett, editor of these Congress Proceedings, for her tireless energy and sensitive care in preparing the texts for these Proceedings. Pramila's sharp eye for and attention to detail, her well honed sense of organization and the quality of her work have made working with her a real pleasure. We are privileged to have her edit these Congress Proceedings and I am most grateful to her for her efficient collaboration throughout the preparation of the Proceedings.

On behalf of the IAAP, I would like to extend my thanks and appreciation to Daimon Verlag, publishers of these Congress Proceedings. Robert Hinshaw and Daimon Verlag have been stalwarts for the publication of IAAP Congress Proceedings. Their help and collaboration in publishing Jungian authors is well known and we are deeply appreciative of our collaboration with them.

Finally, in name of the Programme Committee and the Organizing Committee, I would like to extend our thanks to all the presenters and participants of the Congress. We hope the Montreal Congress left an indelible impression on the participants and that they were able to come away from the Congress enriched by the content of the presentations and with a taste of the 'joie de vivre' of Montreal.

We now look forward to the next gathering of the Jungian clan at the IAAP Congress in Copenhagen in 2013! We hope to have the pleasure of seeing many of you there.

Tom Kelly
Chair, Programme Committee

Opening Address

Joe Cambray
President-Elect

Dear Colleagues, Esteemed Guests and Friends,

It is a great honour, privilege and pleasure to open and welcome you to this, the IAAP's 18th International Congress, *Facing Multiplicity: Psyche, Nature,Culture*. In gazing out at you, I see that together we will indeed have the opportunity this week to put faces onto the multiplicity within our community; this impression is bolstered by the registrations which highlight the diversity of those present: over *668* people coming from *45* countries spanning 6 continents – we still do not have anyone from Antarctica, unless there is a new application I don't know about – this includes representatives from *49* Group Member Societies of the IAAP and 43 members of our Developing Groups including, 10 Provisional Members, 32 routers, as well as members from our Allied Organizations.

Our congresses have travelled widely in recent year, moving sites across cultures, languages and countries, a reflection, I believe, of the vibrancy of analytical psychology to speak to the soul of the modern world. As C. G. Jung had many North American analysands, colleagues and followers, it is not surprising that his psychology took root here early on and has grown greatly over the years, with more than 20 societies from Canada to Mexico. However, it has been 18 years since an IAAP congress was last in North America, when Chicago was the host site of the 12th International Congress in 1992. Thus it is timely, fitting and appropriate that we have the chance to return to this continent, and to come to Montreal, a North American city rich in history, with many layers of multiplicity (in languages, cultures, and traditions) as you will discover this week, if you do not already know it.

At the last congress in Cape Town, South Africa, following the delegates' choice of Montreal as the next congress site, the then newly formed Programme Committee began with an awareness of the need for inclusion of the worldwide community. Members of the Programme Committee hail from 5 continents, representing all the official languages of the IAAP along with a few more, with Tom Kelly serving as an excellent, dedicated chair as well as local resident. The importance of Canada as the host country was one of the first items to be considered. The committee learned that the country's name has been traced by scholars to the expedition of the explorer Jacques Cartier up the St. Lawrence River in 1535. On August 13th of that year two Iroquois youths pointed out to Cartier the route to the village of Stadacona, the future site of Quebec City, using the word 'kanata', the Huron-Iroquois word for village, settlement, or the Programme Committee's favourite, a 'cluster of dwellings'. Cartier subsequently employed the word 'Canada' referring both to the settlement of Stadacona and the land surrounding it, subject to the local Chief Donnacona. The name stuck and was soon applied to a much larger area: by 1547 world maps were designating everything north of the St. Lawrence River as 'Canada'. So, this place whose name comes from the First Nation peoples of the area with their habitable 'cluster of dwellings' has metaphoric resonance for the clustering of IAAP groups at this congress.

Traditionally living close to nature, many First Nation peoples have not only actualized but have also come to symbolize an ecological mindedness, with 'green' values, themes that were particularly present in the many proposals for this congress. Canada seems the ideal place for bringing these principles into dialogue with Jungian theory and practice, especially in the year 2010. Consider, next month the World Energy Council will hold *its* triennial congress here in Montreal, just a couple months after the G8 and G20 held their summits in Canada, which included discussions, at times controversial, on the environment and climate change. There are clearly many environmental problems which challenge all of our futures; so how might we best seek meaning in these events? Where is the place of spirit and soul in proposed solutions so often lacking in attempts at technological fixes? – I feel the programme we have this week will provide ample opportunities to begin such reflections.

2010 is also a significant anniversary year in the analytic world; 100 years ago the Second Psychoanalytic Congress took place in Nuremberg. At that congress Sigmund Freud had Sandor Ferenczi propose the establishment of an official international psychoanalytic association, which was approved and so the IPA was born. At the same time Freud also had Ferenczi nominate Jung as President for life! which due to the protests of the Viennese had to be scaled down to a term as president (he was actually re-elected for a second term but resigned during this); the headquarters of psychoanalysis also shifted to Zürich with his presidency. Thus in 1910 Jung at age 35 became the first president of the IPA in one of history's little ironies. Recently I have also been informed by Jörg Rasche that a commemorative plaque to celebrate the 100 anniversary of the IPA has just this year been placed at the Grand-Hotel in Nuremberg, site of the Nuremberg Congress: Freud, Jung and Adler are all mentioned as are the organizations that have carried on their work, including the IAAP[1]. In 1910 Jung was also working on Mithraism and in late August he wrote to Freud playfully suggesting the motto for the newly formed IPA be taken from a Mithraic ritual 'Give what thou hast, then shall thou receive'; perhaps we should consider reviving it!

Back to the present, for this Congress, in addition to topics of environmentalism and history, including the fascinating popularity of the newly published *Red Book*, the programme offers a great variety of ways in which the contemporary world is being engaged by our members and colleagues. Thus, for example, you will find papers commenting on the renewed interest in matters of the spirit in the cultures of the world; this even includes the neurosciences and the broader analytic community. At the same time Jungian analytic theory and practice are undergoing their own reflective processes, incorporating ideas from attachment theory, the neurosciences, new developments in biological understanding, as well as new trends in the humanities and the arts; these can all be found here. Furthermore the application of analytical psychology in disaster relief, as in China, points to new directions that can emerge when we bring ourselves fully to collisions of psyche, nature and culture. This congress is a tribute to our multiplicity, of interests, passions, engagements and practices.

Before concluding I note the evolving tradition at these congresses has been to have the President-elect of the Association make the opening remarks. This trend seems to ritually solidify the continuity between administrations through democratic processes, with an eye towards the future; it is now built into the fabric of our congresses. So a few words towards the future are in order: as a living organization

---

1 Jörg Rasche has generously translated the plaque from the German as follows: In this building on March 30, 1910 the International Psychoanalytic Association (IPV/ IPA) was founded by Sigmund Freud, Carl Gustav Jung, Alfred Adler and other psychoanalysts. From this foundation of the 'like-minded' different psychoanalytic movements emerged and founded their own organizational form:
The International Association for Individual Psychology (IVIP/IAIP) (Alfred Adler, founded 1954),
The International Association for Analytical Psychology (IGAP/IAAP) (Carl Gustav Jung, founded 1955),
The International Federation of Psychoanalytic Societies (IFPS) (Erich Fromm, founded 1962).

Today the German Psychoanalytic Association (DPV) and the German Psychoanalytic Society (DPG) are the two representatives of IPV/IPA in Germany.

This Memorial Plate is sponsored by the German Association for Analytical Psychology (DGAP).

Nuremberg, March 20, 2010

The plate information has been published in Metzner, Elke, and Schimkus, Martin (Ed.): *Die Gründung der Internationalen Psychoanalytischen Vereinigung durch Freud und Jung*. Psychosozial-Verlag, Gießen 2011, p. 265.

the IAAP continues to undergo maturational and transformative processes, tended to by the Executive Committee at the behest of the delegates. For example, our constitution and by-laws are, as we will hear, in need of revision; a proposal to bring this forward will be presented at the delegates' meeting. The Developing Groups and Individual Membership router programmes have expanded and changed over the years and now are in need of consolidation and some restructuring; so an Education Sub-Committee is being considered. Previous questions from the delegates about the breadth and depth of training have caused the current Executive Committee to explore our models of training and to consider the role of child analysis in our profession. How these findings will be integrated into the IAAP remains an open question for the next administration. The Society Applications Sub-Committee has worked out and implemented procedures for groups wishing to join the IAAP but a multidimensional consultative service to assist in such matters has not yet been fully formulated; hopefully we will bring this to the next congress along with a study on Jungian forms of organization and leadership. The important and necessary work of the Academic Sub-Committee on research and grants will continue and perhaps we will be able to look more closely at the IAAP's intellectual history, how key ideas have been introduced at congresses such as this one and how they have developed over the years. With the growth of communication technology, the IAAP will seek with the help of the Publications and Communications Sub-Committee and our webmaster, Don Williams, to broaden and open up more channels for engagement with and among our membership.

It is now time for the scientific portion of the congress to begin; I wish all of you a wonderful week as you attend the various sessions and enjoy the planned events, thanks to our Organization Committee chaired by Jan Bauer and the Programme Committee chaired by Tom Kelly. May you take great pleasure in the multiplicity of offerings.

Monday, 23 August 2010

From Einstein's God to the God of the Amerindians[1]

Jacques Languirand

Canada (Guest Speaker)

I am a communicator, a writer and journalist for the print media, television and radio. Among other things, this will be my fortieth year as the host of a four-hour weekly radio show. Over time, I have also become an observer of the movements of our society. This has made me aware of the evolution of values in the field of religion, and, like you yourselves, perhaps, I find that Western society has become alienated from certain religious beliefs of the past.

And I've also noticed that certain believers now feel uncomfortable with beliefs they had never questioned before. That's what happened to me.

The realization spurred me to embark on an endeavour (for myself, initially) to seek out and clarify my own values. In the course of my search, I explored pantheism. Later, this discovery would result in my writing two books, in collaboration with a philosopher friend; the first was on Einstein, the second, on the spiritual heritage of the Amerindians. Our goal was to find the lowest common denominator of belief in God (if you'll allow me to use the expression!).

There are several forms of pantheism in the world. I believe the most appropriate to be the pantheism suggested by Spinoza, who defined it succinctly in these terms: '*Deus sive Natura*' – 'God or Nature'.

Our research showed us that a number of contemporary scientists had also become pantheists. One can cite the Nobel laureate in medicine, Christian de Duve, quantum physicist David Bohm, astrophysicist Trinh Xuan Thuan, and many others, including Einstein's colleague Erwin Schrödinger, animal behaviourist Konrad Lorenz, and many more. Our studies focused on Albert Einstein, in particular. The following year, we explored another form of belief in a pantheistic God, again according to Spinoza: that of our fellow Canadians, the Native Americans.

---

1 Translated by Anita Conrade. The French version of this text can be found in the Appendix (CD).

A Rational Pantheism: Spinoza, the Free Thinker

The philosopher Baruch Spinoza was born in 1632 in Amsterdam's Jewish community. However, he gradually wandered from Judaism, associating with free thinkers and liberal Christians, and recommending the Bible be replaced with the Light of Reason. Excommunicated from the Amsterdam synagogue and accused of atheism, he went into exile, travelling around Northern Europe. He became friends with Leibniz, refused a position at Heidelberg University, and earned his living grinding optical lenses. When he died in 1677 at the age of 45, he had already published his major works, with the exception of the one that is best known today, *Ethics*, considered by today's scholars to be his most important book. It contains the most complete vision of the God in whom Spinoza believed, and the religion he recommended.

Spinoza gives us the representation of his God in a three-word brief that is now famous: 'God or Nature' (*Deus sive Natura*). The word 'or' signifies equivalence: God is Nature, imagined in the form of a Great Creature or infinite, self-regenerating life force. It is the very Being or Universal Spirit animating the cosmos, a little like the Soul of the World Giordano Bruno had described nearly a century earlier.

Einstein defined himself as a rational pantheist along the lines of Spinoza, according to a perception of the immanence of the Divine in the great cosmic whole. Understood literally, pantheism means the All is God.

> When I make a judgment about a theory, I wonder whether I'd have arranged the world that way, if I were God.

And also:

> For me, higher reason being revealed in the world of experience expresses the idea of God. In simple language, like Spinoza, we would express it with the term pantheism. ... The individual feels [...] the sublimity and marvelous order which reveal themselves in nature [...] and he wants to experience the universe as a single significant whole.
>
> (Einstein, *How I See the World*)

The universe is envisioned as an orderly cosmos; the world, conceived as a Great Creature, and omnipresent Reason is the very stuff of which everything is made. The Stoics saw the universe as the visible body of the Deity and the Deity as the invisible soul of the world. Marcus Aurelius sums up his beliefs in *Thoughts for Myself*:

> Whatever suits thee suits me, O World! Nothing comes to me earlier or later than what is for thee ripeness. For me, all that thy

seasons produce, O Nature, is my fruit. Everything comes from thee, everything dwells in thee, and everything returns in thee.

The concept of the Deity as 'One and All' (*Hen kai Pan,* a Greek phrase) has a pantheistic flavour. During the Renaissance, the epithet was taken up by philosopher Giordano Bruno, burned at the stake in 1600 after having been pursued by the Holy Inquisition, in particular for his pantheistic and heliocentric opinions.

Yes, before Spinoza, Giordano Bruno gave the pantheistic god a creative nature, shaping the world. An Artist-God, Universal Reason prefiguring Einstein's God, like the very sap of the great cosmic tree; in other words, 'the Soul of the world' mentioned by many philosophers since Pythagoras, Plato, the Stoics, and Plotinus.

Although Einstein was aware of the thinkers of Ancient Greece and the Renaissance, he associated his rational pantheism with that of Spinoza. Einstein's God, like that of Spinoza, Giordano Bruno, the Stoics, Parmenides, and the ancient Greek cults, was far from being a great old man with a long beard, intervening arbitrarily in human business from the heavens. Einstein conceived of God as impersonal higher Reason, a universal, immanent force in the cosmos, as had been discussed by the Stoics. This God is what aroused in Einstein what he called his 'cosmic religious feeling'.

In the same vein as Einstein, Rupert Sheldrake, an internationally known British scientist and specialist in biochemistry and cellular biology, thinks of the universe as a Super-organism that is alive and developing. In his eyes, the primordial 'unified field' of the universe, the theory Einstein searched for until the end of his life, can be compared to the idea of 'the Soul of Nature', the ancient cosmotheistic version of 'the Soul of the World'. Sheldrake hints at his cosmotheistic and perhaps pantheistic vision of the Divine in the title he gave one of his recent books about the universe: *The Soul of Nature.*

Could the ancient god Pan be in the process of returning under the aegis of a new science? Perhaps the mechanistic, fragmentary and materialistic vision of yesteryear is being replaced by an organic, spiritualist, holistic one. And the inspiration and intuition of instinctive pantheism may also be quickening again today, in modern science and philosophy, in an entirely new form: rational pantheism.

In the wake of Einstein's rational pantheism, 20th century physicists and biologists clearly and openly speak of something that might be called the incarnation of the Spirit in matter, and even the presence of the Divine in the cosmos. Through the lens of the cosmotheistic, pantheistic vision, they show us the face of a cosmic God who is supposedly One and Everything, all at once.

Like Spinoza, Einstein was always careful to state that he was not an atheist. Instead, he defined himself as 'a profoundly religious man'. He writes:

> We disciples of Spinoza see our God in the marvellous order and regularity of what exists. It's quite another question to know if the belief in a personal God should be opposed.

Spinoza's God is Nature in its power to create (*Natura naturans*), an active, productive, dynamic Nature, the source of the variety and multiplicity of the beings she contains. This 'All is One' engenders its own parts. All creatures, both multiple and united, are therefore presented as an effect or product existing only thanks to the continuous creative activity of this immanent God. This is what Spinoza calls 'Nature already created' (*Natura naturata*). As the product of creative Nature, it is the temple of God, from one end to the other.

> God is the immanent cause of all things. […] He acts in himself and not outside himself, because nothing exists outside himself.
>
> (Baruch Spinoza, *Ethics*[1])

The Spinozan Being does not play dice any more than Einstein's God. Creative Nature is a perfect Thought in which all of the essences that are created exist. They are all existing ideas that result from Nature, naturally and necessarily. In other words, Nature in its creative power is an intelligible cause, producing all substance according to the needs of its own Thought; and the substances created express some aspect of the universal, divine Reason. Like glass (Spinoza might have noted), the creatures are penetrated by this divine light. Like Einstein's, Spinoza's pantheism is rational.

> My belief, related to a profound feeling of a higher Reason being revealed in the world of experience, expresses the idea of God for me. In simple language, like Spinoza, it would be expressed by the term pantheism.
>
> (Albert Einstein)

Spinoza uses another fundamental concept to name his God: that of Substance. This idea serves as a counterweight to the too-human, too-anthropomorphic vision of a personal God, who would intervene arbitrarily in human affairs. God is thus seen as the single cosmic Substance who is the whole and perfect Being. This infinite Substance, which is its own cause, contains its essence, which itself contains its existence. This unique Substance, which is God, creates and sums up, in its very being, the multiplicity and variety of all that exists.

As Spinoza sees it, this cosmic, divine Substance is expressed and revealed in a multitude of infinite attributes, even though only two of

---

1 Spinoza, B. (2005). *Ethics*. Trans. E. Curley. London: Penguin Classics.

them are visible to us: the extent (the order of bodies and matter) and thought (the order of ideas and the mind). Sometimes the Substance is seen as the source, unity, and totality of material bodies, entities, or organisms; at others as the source, unity, and totality of essences, souls, or ideas of these material bodies.

Spinoza's God appears as a purely immanent, cosmic God, naturally connected to the product of the act of creation. He alone exists as the source; everything else exists only by and in Him. And all of these creatures necessarily result from the essence of God, which created them according to a sublime and harmonious order. Spinoza's pantheism points to the essence of Einstein's rational pantheism.

True Religion

How does someone unite with the Cosmic God, seemingly so remote from the personal God of all the monotheistic religions? According to Spinoza, in this unity lies salvation – what could it be? Venturing to answer these questions leads us towards the path of a natural religiosity. This natural religiosity is rooted in a person's profound desire to be. Spinoza believed that the primal fibre of the human being, and any other living creature, in fact, is this desire, this effort to persevere in being (see Alain's *Spinoza*, 1946[1]): 'Before I desire anything at all, I desire to be. Any desire which is not contained in that one comes not from me.'

> Since there is an inner revelation, we need nothing other than to use our reason properly to attain true religion and true happiness. [...] By seeking the spirit of God, we are saved. Philosophy is what will save us. Philosophy is the truth of all religion.
>
> Wherever there is a reasonable man, there is already the sprout of the happy city. [...] The man led by reason is happier in the city, where he obeys laws, than in a desert, where he would obey only himself.
>
> To act in compliance with virtue is therefore to act in compliance with reason, to act according to the laws of one's own nature, to take actions of which one is the sufficient and adequate cause. Therefore, reason cannot lead us to anything other than understanding, and it is in the act of understanding that our effort to persevere in being is most completely fulfilled.
>
> The soul's feelings bring us back to two large sorts: pleasant feelings and unpleasant ones; that is, joy and sorrow. Hence, it is obvious that joy is the feeling of transition to a greater perfection, and sorrow the feeling of transition to a lesser perfection.

---

1 Alain (Emile Chartier) (1946). *Spinoza*. Paris: Éditions Gallimard, 1949.

Spinozan natural religion resides in knowledge and, more precisely, in the use of the reason dwelling in the heart of our being. In this philosophy, God is ultimate Reason, the repository and the source of all the ideas defining the essences of things and creatures in this world. Thought is an attribute of God.

At this stage of knowledge, the better we understand ourselves and the better we understand singular creatures, the better we understand God (Creative Nature or Cosmic Substance) and the more we love God, with a love penetrated with intelligence. Since human reason is an expression of Divine Reason, the reasonable and virtuous man is the home of the true natural religion; and the most noble form of worship is to honour God from within. The virtuous and reasonable man knows freedom, which is much more than simply free will. He who acts according to the inner necessity or requirement of his being is free. He in whom the thought of God is expressed is free.

The psalmody of the soul is also joy: the feeling of attaining perfection and certain accomplishment of one's being. Joy is the sign that the creature is fulfilled according to his deepest nature. Joy is part of our salvation, making us feel our participation in eternity and divinity.

Spinoza's pantheism can be recognized by its cosmic God, the unique, universal Substance and immanent creative Nature of the universe. This natural religiosity flows along three inseparable paths: the desire to be, intuitive reason, and the joy that accompanies virtue and freedom. Cosmic religious feeling expresses a grandeur, perfection, beauty, and wisdom too rarely encountered, for, as Spinoza writes in the last line of his *Ethics*: 'Everything excellent is as difficult as it is rare.'

On the same theme of pantheism, I now offer you a glimpse of the spirituality of the Amerindians. You will notice that even though the Amerindians are also speaking of pantheism, the language is somewhat different from Einstein's description. It's almost as though Einstein's pantheism were masculine and Amerindian spirituality were feminine. Like two sides of a coin.

An Intuitive Pantheism

The pantheistic vision of the Divine is shared by human groups or societies close to their early roots. In parts of the world where communities have not been too severely affected by Western civilization or the proselytizing religions, a vision infused with animist elements still exists.

This form of animistic pantheism contains an immediate perception of the cosmic mystery, a compound mingling the human, Nature, and the Divine. Divine transcendence is spontaneously intuited in the pure human and cosmic immanence. In truth, the human being is perceived as being profoundly rooted in nature, inhabited by the Divine in all of its elements and all of its events. Everything and every being are like prisms refracting the divine light shining in the cosmos.

> I see the white man chop down a tree without a prayer, without a fast, without respect of any kind, and yet the tree can tell him how to live, and so can the spider, the snake, the raccoon, the bear, the salmon, and the eagle! The peoples who live on this planet have to get over the narrow idea of human freedom, and begin to see that extended to the whole of the natural world. What we need is the freedom of all the things that maintain life: air, the waters, all things that support the sacred weave of life. The original instructions order that we, who walk on the earth, show great respect, affection, and gratitude to all the spirits that create and maintain life. We greet and thank the many allies of our own existence: wheat, beans, squash, the winds, the sun. […]
> We think that all living things are spiritual beings. The spirits can be expressed in the form of energy translated into matter: a blade of grass is a form of energy manifested as matter.
>
> (Excerpts from *Voix indiennes*[1], statements by Russell Means)

Something of this pantheistic, animistic vision can be recognized in Amerindian societies who have preserved their profound spiritual tradition. Their spirituality is an assertion of the human's symbiotic participation in nature, a stream flowing in the river of cosmic energy inseparable from the Great Spirit, or communion with all things – animal, vegetable, or mineral – seen as a spiritual creature and child of the Earth Mother. All Nature herself is infused with this psalmody of souls, which is nothing other than the singing of the immanent God. In the magnificent Amerindian, pantheistic, animistic text below, note the kinship with certain Oriental holy writings, particularly those of Hinduism, Buddhism, or Taoism. The feelings it expresses also reverberate with the discourse of deep ecology, and even with that of 20th century physics.

> Man has lost sight of the teachings of our mother the earth. That is why our waters and our sky are so polluted. We must remember the need for harmony in all things with nature and of all things together. Our future is in our past. Future is only an illusion. We have never raped our mother earth. For us, the earth is sacred.
> (Excerpts from *Voix indiennes*[2], statements by Selo)

Sun and sky are seen as carrying the active divine principle, which gives light, heat, rain, and wind, bringing the earth to life and bringing new life out of her. The earth contains the receptive divine principle,

---

1 Graugnard, M. (1979). *Voix indiennes*.
2 Ibid.

an inner gift of ripening and latency, promising and bearing the gift of
life.

In the Sioux story of creation, the great Mysterious One is not
brought directly upon the scene or conceived in anthropomorphic
fashion, but remains sublimely in the background. The Sun and
the Earth, representing the male and female principles, are the
main elements in his creation, the other planets being subsidiary.
The enkindling warmth of the Sun entered into the bosom of our
mother, the Earth, and forthwith she conceived and brought forth
life, both vegetable and animal.

(Charles Eastman, *The Soul of the Indian*[1])

In the traditional Amerindian spiritual path Sun and Earth are truly
archetypal images, attributes of the Divine. They were also found in
Egyptian worship, in the representations of Ra (the Sun, the masculine
principle) or Osiris (the Sun reappearing and beginning a new cycle
when night is over) and Isis (the universal mother). The Greeks
represented them as Zeus (the masculine principle, celestial light) and
Demeter (the feminine principle, the abundant earth); the Romans, in
the figures of Jupiter (a masculine principle, the sky, and daylight) and
Ceres (a feminine principle, and fertility). All this attests to the deep
roots and significant attention the Amerindian spiritual path deserves,
alongside other religious traditions.

The Protective, Nourishing Mother

Earth-Mother is filled with divine compassion: she generously and
graciously gives what she produces to the creatures living upon her,
satisfying their needs. To feed us, she causes corn, beans, and squash
to grow, and later wheat; to cook the food, she offers herself in the
form of wood; for the sacred pipe, she provides tobacco. When seeds
are planted in her soil, she takes it upon herself to make them grow.
Her fertile body enfolds the embryos that will become nutritive and
medicinal plants.

For the Amerindian, the first mother is Earth. The procreator
of life, source of every form of life, the Earth-Mother embodies
fertility and fecundity, the effect of a union with the Sky-Father. It
is Earth-Mother who causes the foetus to grow in a woman's belly.

(Rodolphe Gagnon, *Lettres amérindiennes*[2])

Earth-Mother is truly the infinite womb, the beneficent origin and

---

1   Eastman, C. *The Soul of an Indian and Other Writings from Ohiyesa*. San Rafael, CA: New
    World Library, 1993. Also as etext, the Electronic Text Center, University of Virginia
    Library.
2   Gagnon, R. (2008). *Lettres amérindiennes*. Ed. Louise Courteau.

source of all vegetation, which for both animal and man, provides food, shelter, or medicine, according to the need. The protective Mother: this is her sacred song, and this is her divine calling. For this reason, the Amerindian composes hymns to her glory, hymns in which human gratitude is also expressed.

Moreover, all of us, each and every one, are children of Earth-Mother; we were all born from her body; we are all brothers and sisters. She is the Mother shared by all living things; she is the Substance of which everything is made: *Mater/Materia*. We are directly related to her as sons and daughters. Everything she produces is animated: in other words, everything contains a 'soul', even the stone. Nevertheless, the Earth-Mother is subject to changing moods: in her, days alternate with nights, joys with suffering, summers with winters. We must not forget that in the infinite and sacred cycle of the alternation between life and death, she gives Life to one of her children, takes it back, and then gives it again, to the children of the next generation. This is the law of Nature, the primal law, and the human being is bound to respect it, by learning the wisdom of the Ancestors.

> The Earth does not belong to man; it is man who belongs to the Earth. The Earth is therefore the mother of us all. As sons of the same mother, are we not all brothers and sisters, regardless of our race, the colour of our skin, or what we believe?
>
> (Ancient Amerindian text)

The Earth-Mother is woman. She testifies to the holiness of the feminine acknowledged by Amerindian spiritual tradition. In return, the Amerindian woman testifies to the holiness of the Earth-Mother. A deep and mysterious bond, a sort of mystical solidarity, links the woman to the earth or nature. The ripening of the foetus in the woman's womb reflects the emergence into the sunlight of a seed buried in the soil. Earth or woman, each is a carrier of life, a protective container for it, responsible for its awakening and accomplishment. Both offer the most precious gift: the future of life, renewal in the sacred Circle of death and life.

The Living Earth

The Earth-Mother is like an immense living organism. And all the creatures who dwell upon her, from the hardest rock to the most spiritual man, live in and by her, being integral parts of her. All of them are her own children, bound together by this relationship. In other words, the Earth-Mother possesses a body and soul. The currents of her great, vital, sacred energy flow through her meridians. He who lends an attentive ear can perceive the beating of her heart, can listen to the cycle of her breathing, in and out. Especially, he can hear the

very voice of her soul: her motherly teachings, her cries of pain, and
how she sings with delight when creating beauty.

The Lakota was filled with compassion and love for nature ... The
elders were literally in love with the ground, and whenever they sat
or lay down directly upon it, they could feel the maternal strength
emanating from it. The ground was smooth to the skin, and they
liked to take off their moccasins and walk barefoot on the sacred
Earth.

(*Pieds nus sur la Terre sacrée* [Barefoot on Sacred Earth:
writings collected by T.C. McLuhan])

The energy of the Earth-Mother flows through every living creature.
Every beating heart is united with the universal heart of the Earth.
Rain and wind, rivers and forests, natural wonders like crystalline
clarity and birdsong are in each one of us. All of these things, which
are gifts from the Earth-Mother and share her generous breath,
are interrelated, and each one belongs to all the others. Everything
is connected to everything else. And so nothing can be owned by
anyone, because everything belongs to the Creator. In sum, each of us
is merely taking care of what the Earth-Mother has temporarily lent
to him, in the name of the Great Spirit. 'We owe all our relatives the
greatest respect', the Amerindian sage always declared!

A Cosmic God

How can we characterize the Amerindian perception and representations of God in greater detail? What fundamental experience of
the Divine does this spiritual heritage reflect? The deity is a 'cosmic
God' similar in some respects to the 'cosmic God' of Spinoza, Einstein,
and certain 20th century scientists and philosophers, but in others
obviously quite different.

The Invisible Dimension of the Cosmos

Nature is an immense living organism open to the Divine. The
Great Mystery could be compared to the invisible Soul of the visible
world. Each entity, as an inseparable fragment or cell linked to the rest
of the great natural creature, the universe, is a unique expression of
the Great Mystery, and perhaps even an irreplaceable divine blessing.
Hidden within, the Divine is revealed to all those who take the time
to open their heart. In this sense, nature as seen by Amerindian
spirituality is enchanted; that is, it is inhabited by the divine mystery.
Deep within, every physical object has an invisible, spiritual dimension. The waterfall is the audible song of the inaudible divine melody

inhabiting it; the distant heavenly fires, the stars in the sky, attest to the invisible divine light kindling them; the flight of the eagle is the majestic movement contained in immaterial divine energy. All that lives on Earth is a messenger from the Great Mystery, which remains far too vast and profound to be spoken.

When we decipher the language of things, we realize that each is a mirror of the immeasurable span of the universe. God can be tasted in all things. Thus, the spiritual is concealed in materiality; thus, what is on high is hidden in what is below; thus, the elsewhere can be found in the here. In other words, the Divine is sealed into the cosmic. These are the reasons for characterizing the Amerindian spiritual path as something certain believers call 'a mystique of nature'. Others describe it as 'primal pantheism', and still others as a form of 'cosmotheism'.

Regardless of the differences in appellation, the point is that they always bespeak a deep bond between the Divine and the cosmic. In fact, the two are virtually one. The universe emanates constantly from God the creator, who acts by, for, and upon the universe. If there is no world without God, there is no God without the world. The invisible bond between every creature and God is simultaneously the inner, mysterious soul where God dwells. God is the spirituality infusing all the matter of this world and illuminating it. It is the Great Universal Being, or even the Great Cosmic Mystery.

Divine Omnipresence

At the very heart of the Amerindian spiritual experience, we discover a vision of the universe as a creation of God, twinned with an image of this creation as God's home. The Amerindian God inhabits the entire universe. He is its breath, its motion, its vibration. In sum, God is the Spirit of the universe, a creative spirit that penetrates, vitalizes, and animates all of nature from inside, channelling innate spiritual powers that are sometimes feminine (the Earth Mother) and sometimes masculine (the Sky and its Sun).

We could say that God is revealed as the invisible substance of all visible appearance, as the permanent essence of all that changes in this world. The universe is driven by this supra-personal, divine, infinite force. Its mysterious creative energy is expressed everywhere: in the glint of a chip of quartz and in the human being himself. This cosmic God is a spiritual power with neither beginning nor end, in perpetual renewal within the universe.

This Amerindian version is essentially rooted in the cosmic manifestation of the divine Great Mystery. In other words, Amerindian 'cosmology' is basically a 'theophany'. It is comparable to the Einsteinian and Spinozan approaches in that divine transcendence is manifested as cosmic immanence, while remaining partially hidden.

> We believe that the spirit pervades all creation and that every creature possesses a soul in some degree, though not necessarily a soul conscious of itself.
>
> (Charles Eastman, *The Soul of the Indian*[1])

God is immanent to each creature and present in the whole world by his Spirit, the Great Spirit of the universe. He is the mysterious inhabitant of the world he created and steers, with goodness and wisdom. Therefore, in a way, the cosmic space is also a divine space. This is why Amerindian spirituality perceives and asserts so strongly the sacred character of nature, of all the life and energy it contains, and the whole natural order of which the human himself is an integral part.

> Most tribes acknowledged the existence of a Great Spirit who had created everything ... But their beliefs are mingled with a strong dose of pantheism: in fire, water, air, and all of the immensity of nature whose Mystery surrounds them, they sense the presence of invisible and generally beneficial forces ... honoured without fail by the Indian at every opportunity.
>
> (R. Thévenin & P. Coze, *Mœurs et histoire des Indiens d'Amérique du Nord* [*Customs and History of the North American Indians*][2])

The divine teachings, called the original Instructions, are inscribed everywhere in Nature and can therefore be read in Nature. An encounter with God is also possible in the ultimate depths of the human heart, or along the paths that lead to the silent summit of the mountain, in the blowing of the winds from the four directions, in the gentle light of the sky at night or the majesty of the eagle's flight. Each cosmic entity, even the most modest, has an inner reason for existing, for it is deeply impregnated by one of the characteristics of the power and infinite goodness of the Creator. In this sense, in its own way, it takes on sacred attributes, attesting to a divine Presence in this world.

The Divine Bond of All Things

The universe, or nature, is a whole system, like an immense living organism. It encompasses everything, and all of its parts are linked by indissoluble bonds. All the world's creatures are the children of the sole Great Spirit; all of them, from the most humble to the human, are therefore brothers and sisters. This is why the Amerindian often

---

1 ibid.
2 Thévenin, R. & Coze, P. (2004). *Mœurs et histoire des Indiens d'Amérique du Nord*. Paris: Payot et Rivages.

ends his prayers or spiritual statements with the sentence, 'To all my relations'.

A Cosmic Religious Feeling

Because the Amerindian God is revealed in the form of a profoundly immanent cosmic divinity, the approach or path a person must follow to become closer to the Divine and converse with it is also deeply impregnated with a cosmic dimension. But what is contained in this cosmic religious sentiment?

Awe-inspiring Nature

A spiritual path was blazed by the Ancestors and handed down from generation to generation, chiefly by oral and ritual means. It is wholly steeped in a feeling of the presence of the Divine in the heart of Nature, of which the human being is a fundamental part. To embark on the journey to the Divine, a man must be aware of the Great Mystery which simultaneously envelopes and pervades the Cosmic Whole, and the quest for intense unity with the ineffable cosmic Principle of all life. For this reason, the awe inspired by Nature and its mysteries is at the core of traditional Amerindian spirituality.

The cosmos and man are deeply mingled in this mystical religiosity. Man experiences the existence of an invisible Power radically immersed in the visible world, of a luminous Transcendence revealed only in the shadowy lines of the cosmos. Each reality of this world is perceived in reference to the Great Mystery, participating in it according to its own being. Each is imbued with an aspect of the mystery's majesty, and conveys it. Actually, God is already present in a cosmos that is still fully 'magical'. The idea is to learn to see and hear God in all that is living. Man is capable of almost literally breathing the divine presence in nature, thereby merging with it. Lastly, man must accept a shift in the centre of gravity from himself to the vast, invisible world.

Like each of the creatures inhabiting it, the cosmos is pregnant with the Great Mystery of its origin, source, and destiny. He who contemplates creation from the deepest part of his soul can find a gateway to the invisible reaches, the passage to the Other World mysteriously hidden in this one. In a mystical silence on a mountain peak, a person may commune with the spirit of the mountain; or perhaps one may lose oneself infinitely in the spirit of the night sky as one stares into the starry vault. In a sublime act of compassion, one may even become the spirit of consolation that soothes suffering. When a child is born, does one not also relearn to drink in the spirit of all that is born in the world?

A Natural Religion

In Amerindian spiritual tradition, human beings have an organic relationship to the natural environment surrounding them. The relationship is never imagined to be purely functional and utilitarian. The bond with plants and animals is measured by satisfaction of the human's legitimate needs, the possibilities of the natural environment, and concern for the generations to come. And this attitude is much more than simply ecological. It also clearly contains a spiritual dimension, precisely because the cosmic Great Spirit is believed to be present in the plants and animals, mediated by the spirits representing it. For the same reason, the hunter begs the animal he has killed to forgive him, and the gardener thanks Earth Mother for feeding her children with corn, beans, and squash.

Listening to the Original Instructions

Nature speaks to the human being. She tells him to preserve the natural order, reminding him that he is an integral part of it. A sacred alliance binds the two of them. If men fail to respect the divine order of things, if they damage some part of the environment, nature helps man become aware that ultimately he is hurting himself. 'Listen to the signals I send you', Nature says. 'Follow the natural path.'

In the Amerindian spiritual path, because the whole universe is sensed as a creation of the Great Spirit, it is also perceived as where the Spirit dwells. This Spirit's active and continuous presence is assured by the myriad spirits of each of the links of the great chain of life. Speaking through the spirit of stones and great stars, or that of plants and animals, or again by that of the four seasons and four directions, the Great Spirit offers a glimpse of the secrets of his wisdom, to be seen, smelled, tasted, and heard. This cosmic wisdom is there to help every human being as he or she travels through the cycle of his or her life.

> God transmits his Precepts to all living creatures, according to his plan, drawn up for the whole world. He gave these precepts to each element in Nature.
>
> (Harvey Arden, *Noble Red Man Mathew King*, A Lakota Sage[1])

One of the human being's most important tasks is precisely to decipher the sacred wisdom, using his senses, his intelligence, and his heart; to gather the fruit of insight offered up to us by all the voiceless inhabitants of the cosmos. For in its spiritual depth, each cosmic reality is a note in the eternal song of the Great Mystery. What does

---

1 Arden, H. (1995). *Noble Red Man: Lakota Wisdomkeeper Matthew King*. Hillsboro, Oregon: Beyond Words Publishing.

the salmon tell us? That from our innermost souls each of us is called to go home, all the way to the Source. What does the eagle teach? That the only values worthy of the name are the loftiest, those that give wings to our Humanity, elevating it to the mountaintops where the spirits fly.

The Sense of the Sacred

In Amerindian spiritual tradition, the sense of the sacred is expressed both in ceremonial rituals and in day to day life. Therefore, many special places — boulders, streams, mountains, burial grounds, or ancestral lands — must be preserved as sanctuaries for the spirits, the nexus where their world touches ours. Likewise, many natural phenomena, like the winds coming from the four directions, the light from the sky, the breathing of the Earth Mother, and even men's dreams — should be recognized as special moments when the human is touched by the Divine. A number of different objects — rattles, pipes, eagle feathers — take on a sacred character when they are associated with rituals.

Thoreau, a white American, spent years living in the forest, absorbing Nature and Amerindian Philosophy:

> On the morning of May 6, 1862, Henry David Thoreau's breathing grew faint ...
>
> He murmured the words 'Moose' [in Algonquian] and 'Indian', and at nine o'clock, without the least resistance he died. In his Journal, he'd written, 'My profession is always to be alert to find God in Nature ... Nature ... These movements everywhere in Nature are certainly the divine pulsation. When the sail swells, or the brook flows, the tree rustles, the wind wanders, where else would they derive this excellence and infinite freedom?
>
> (Gilles Farcet, *Henry David Thoreau, L'éveillé du Nouveau Monde*[1])

Visible reality is made sacred by the invisible dimension it contains in its deepest core. This invisible element is what fills something with sense and intensifies its being. Everything that exists is sacralized by a spiritual space rooted in its materiality, a space where an ineffable encounter can occur between the Great Mystery and human consciousness, a consciousness that becomes open and transparent to the presence of the Divine in this world. Reality can then be a sacrament: that is, truly a sacred sign testifying to the presence of the Divine.

---

1 Farcet, G. (1998). *Henry David Thoreau, L'éveillé du Nouveau Monde*. Paris: Editions sang de la terre.

Conclusion

Let me tell you a little more about Amerindians, but from a lighter side: Many years ago, in the 1950s, French president Vincent Auriol paid an official visit to Quebec. After he gave a speech, he was interviewed by a reporter from Radio-Canada. A few minutes later, Mr. Auriol discreetly asked one of the Quebec hosts if they would be kind enough to introduce him to an Indian. It was then that they whispered cautiously to him that he had just been interviewed by a real Amerindian, who was a tribal chief to boot. That simply shows that these days you can't tell a man by his suit.

One Home, Many Homes: Translating Heritages of Containment

John Hill
Switzerland (AGAP)

In this paper[1] I am going to approach the topic of home from four perspectives: home as individuation, home in the consulting room, home in the global world, home as a many-storied house.

Facing Multiplicity, there is no better place to start than with home. We encounter multiplicity when we consider the many ways people have transformed environment into home. For most of us home is nourished from memories of intimate attachments to parents, caretakers, family, or loved ones. But we also find traces of home in affiliation to a clan, community, profession, nation, or favourite landscape. The soul's hunger to belong reveals a remarkable plasticity, extending beyond a particular person, family, or nation. Some people find home in attachment to a forest, garden or favourite animal. For one woman home was the stable. She had a closer connection with her horse than with her parents. There are narratives in which home is neither place nor person but the way something gets expressed. Home becomes a beautiful piece of music, a painting, an icon, a myth, an embrace, a moment of deep emotional rapport, a body, the inner life, or a space in which to create. Other home narratives are about being on the move. For one woman home became her suitcase. She was the daughter of a diplomat. Her family constantly changed dwellings. Every time a move was imminent, she would pack her treasures in a little suitcase, which she still takes with her today wherever she goes. Home may take on the significance of a place of exile, a pilgrimage, being a nomad – a frame of mind so aptly expressed in the words of a Native American: 'I can place my tepee anywhere in the world because my soul is at one with the earth.' Some will say that home is not of this earth. Home is connection with the ancestors or with loved ones who have gone before us. Home as heaven; home as God.

---

1 Several passages in this paper are to be found in my book, *At Home in the World, Sounds and Symmetries of Belonging* (New Orleans: Spring Journal Books, 2010); it was published at the same time as the IAAP congress in Montreal.

Home as Individuation

If we adopt Jung's individuation process as a model for ongoing life, care is needed that it does not become an ideology, or worse still, a power-programme, dividing the sheep from the goats; those who can individuate from those who cannot. Life itself, in all its fullness, is individuation, as implied in the first chapters of *The Red Book*. Life is far too complex to follow an itinerary, which expects everyone to fulfil the biological needs in the first half of life and the spiritual in the second half. If the necessary conditions are given, an individual life evolves of its own accord. A child who gains a sense of self and of being at home in the world at the end of the first three years of life can reasonably expect his or her life to unfold in an authentic way. The purpose of home is to provide a foundation to survive a gain or loss of any particular home, which is to be expected throughout the course of a lifetime. Plasticity has become a key biological and psychological term, denoting an inherent resilience in all living beings to survive loss and adapt to new environments.

We first encounter home in those compelling memories of child-hood that hit us on a sensory level: an image, a smell, a sound, or the taste of a favourite food. These are not just fleeting impressions, but are embedded in special circumstances, which constantly repeat themselves, thus binding us to our family and social history. We remember a world we trusted and felt secure. Christian von Krockow (1992, pp. 8-10) feels we never forget our childhood home because it was a world that remained the same. Eva Hoffman (1990, pp. 5-6) describes her lost childhood home in Poland. She remembers the hum of the Cracow trams, a home in which everything was unchanging and predictable.

Yet the opposite is also true. We already experience exile, when banished from the comforting waters of the womb. Another phase of exile may be experienced in the weaning process from the mother's breast. This is followed by the child's separation-reunion process, as outlined by Mahler (1985, pp. 109-11). Once able to tolerate contradictory self-images of being dependent on and independent of caregivers, a consolidation of lifelong individuality and the internalized image of the caretaker – personality formation and object constancy – can be achieved.

Children who survive exile from the mother, without loss of identity, indicate a precursory stage of coping with later homesickness. Should however this stage of the child's individuation fail, later transitional phases may be complicated. When the adult is faced with forced separation from an old home, loss of home may become unbearable. Conflicts of the present become confluent with earlier experiences of insecure and unpredictable relationships. In difficult transition phases an otherwise coherent identity, held together by a collective, local, and relatively stable environment, begins to fragment. Isolation, withdrawal, or nostalgic idealization emerges, should adaptation to the new home prove to be disappointing.

Children in the post-Oedipal phase of development still live in a world of fantasy that becomes just as real as the concrete world. They not only absorb the objective world, but also its hidden magic waiting to be discovered in the womb of that same world. Still living in fantasy, children explore ways to establish kinship with the non-human environment. For James Hillman (1983, p. 129) such a personified world is not just a 'what' but a 'who'. Children know very well that the hunger to belong cannot be stilled in the shelter of non-empathetic parents. Already at an early age they experience exile. They pour out their aching heart to trees, embrace domestic animals with their unloved bodies, or build a secret shelter in a loft or garden to protect their vulnerable souls. If their imagination has not been strangled, they weave all kinds of narratives around pet animals, rivers, lakes and caves. Their new friends are their new home, which moulds their nomadic soul and helps them survive later transitional phases.

Have we forgotten that phase of our childhood? Do we treat nature in the same way today? Abundant are the tales of its exploitation (Swiss National Radio, 2009), as witnessed in the case of the Komoro people of West Papua. They regard the mountains as the head of the great mother and the rivers as milk flowing from her breasts. Recently a multi-national mining concern quarried the mountains and polluted the rivers in search of gold and copper. For the Komoro people this meant their mother's head was decapitated and the milk from her breasts poisoned. Their home and culture were destroyed. Their exiled souls when not able to adapt to urban life, inevitably found an outlet in drugs and criminality.

In the post-Oedipal stage of a child's development we witness the foundation of an attitude sensitized to ecological issues. The Native Americans can help us remember that phase of life. When the Lakota people smoke the peace pipe, they make a connection with the Great Spirit above and the Earth Mother below. Nationhood for the Lakota is founded on a spirituality, embracing a wholeness that respects the sacredness of all life. Less burdened by the conflicts of European civilization, their voices still sing the song of the universe, a home common to all humanity. Those who perceive the universe as home will love it, take care of it, enjoy it, defend it.

As the latency period advances there is a shift in the child's interest from the realm of fantasy to the objective world. The child identifies with people and objects outside the family home, making them an integral part of its social and moral standards. As the ethno-psychoanalyst Mario Erdheim (1993, p. 134; my translation) points out:

In the latency period, the child internalizes a relationship to objects that is specific to his ethnic heritage; what is determined in this period is the way one moves and behaves, what trend or taste to follow, what kind of food is disgusting and which children to play with and which not.

He interprets divisive forms of nationalism and racism as an inability of the adolescent to put into perspective and achieve critical distance to an ethnic identity defined by family and society during this latency stage of a child's development. Such conventional behaviour patterns may also, however, lead to a suppression of one's cultural identity. Living in permanent exile, the parents of the renowned intellectual, Edward Said, suppressed the loss of Palestine by adopting a Western standard of life, thus preventing their son from having access to a deeper cultural identity connected with his nation and people (2000, p. 165).

Already in late puberty a young man or woman can no longer identify with the parental world and start looking for a new home in a partner, profession, family, or creed. In midlife, the glamour of outer success begins to fade. One may no longer have the same energy to repair or improve the house, buy more furniture for rooms that are already overcrowded, struggle for the next level of promotion, or continue a partnership that has gone dead. For some the reality of the soul may then become a focus of attention, manifesting as an inner voice, or in an encounter with another person who bears a different message than those of previous relationships. The energies released from such encounters can either renew the faded life of the old home or signal the foundation of a new home, partnership, or profession, perhaps liberating one from the urge to hoard and possess.

During the final stages of life we have to relinquish everything: all the attachments that we have made, all the homes we have experienced. But sometimes the soul attaches itself so deeply to some object that it won't let go of it until one understands its hidden purpose. I once saw an exquisite Kelim carpet on a visit to Turkey. At the time, I did not want to buy a rug; my home was already cluttered, and I had no idea what I could do with it. However, as I looked closer, I became so enthralled with it that I started bargaining in the accustomed oriental manner. Finally we had reached a price that might still have been too high, but was reasonable for this object of beauty. I hesitated, and muttered doubts about its being too heavy to carry. The owner immediately dispelled them, promising to pack the rug in a light bag – all included in the price! I could no longer avoid making a decision. I ruminated back and forth until I finally decided not to buy it. I walked back to the boat about to depart for Greece, fully convinced I had made the right choice. On the long journey back, belief in my ability to make a reasonable decision began to fall apart. I could not let go of the image of the rug. I was obsessed with it. It became for me the most beautiful carpet in the world. Worse still, I was convinced this was my carpet; I had made an awful mistake in not buying it. I kept 'seeing' its simple design: green patterns in the centre and around its fringes on a background of light beige, all beautifully woven in intricate ways. The restlessness continued until the following morning.

I decided I would have to resolve this issue, and spent the rest of the day meditating on what to do. Why was the rug so important? Why could I not let go? After all, it was only a rug. I focused on its colours and simple pattern, which caught me on a deeper level. The light beige was the colour of the Aegean Islands; the green was that of Ireland, my original homeland. My soul belongs to those two places in profound ways. I could not let go of the rug until I understood what my soul was trying to say. In a kind of daze, a voice called out: 'I am at home in these lands, in the rocks of the Aegean and the green fields of Ireland. I love this carpet because it is me, your soul, that you must take with you wherever you go.' Emerging from this reverie, the obsession to buy the carpet disappeared. The artist who had made this thing of beauty had also to let it go. I knew too well that I could not possess the threads of my identity as I would possess a material object. In the last phases of life, letting go can be a way of opening up to new horizons.

Home in the Consulting Room

Most of us have had several homes. Each home has its own story. Each story reveals an identity, formed and fashioned by the circumstances of that dwelling place. We may try to link the various homes, our various identities, described in tales of deterioration, tales of repetition, tales of development, as we attempt to grasp what holds our life together.

Psychotherapists encounter moving home narratives in the symptoms, sufferings, and aspirations of their clients. Analysis can help people find roots, create new meaningful relationships, and initiate authentic understanding of what it means to be at home in one's self and the world. Therapists cannot provide home as a material substitute for all that was missing in childhood, but they can provide a context in which the meaning of our first homes may be re-appraised. In therapy one listens to scenes of unacknowledged violence and abuse that have devastated young lives. Often the narratives do not hang together and are told in a confused or fragmented way. If analysts attempt to intervene, they may find themselves shut out by a defensive system, which was erected to protect a core self that has long retreated into a world of silence. Home can be a nightmare. Images or dreams reveal what it feels like to live in such a home – a dungeon, a dwelling place without windows, a tower in a frozen landscape. Images of not having skin, being turned to stone, or buried alive give visual form to the inner torment of those who fear their uncontained identity is continually threatened.

It is not easy to enter such an abode, but once invited in, the analyst can embody the empathic presence of a supportive witness, crucial to a healing process. We may find it difficult to appreciate the hospitality of the host's inner home. One analysand required that I always speak in a low voice. Another wanted to play games, but insisted that he would have to win.

In the first hour of therapy the analyst may recognize an epiphany of homecoming when a client comes into the office, looks around and wonders if he/she can feel comfortable in the room. One of my clients did just that for several sessions. She had to interiorize everything about my office so that she could connect with it, and ultimately with me. Sometimes the first signs of attachment can manifest in the client's concern about any changes in the office or the therapist's attire. One client was upset when I wore a tie. She felt my whole identity had changed and I was no longer the same person whom she could trust. I had become a 'Swiss bank manager', someone just out to get her money, like most men she knew. I had to approach the 'bank manager' in a non-defensive way, in order to help her understand why such a figure should be constellated. Negative projections cannot be discarded, even a 'Swiss bank manager' may need to participate in the 'home' space of analysis.

Within the framework of transference, we encounter the multiple faces of home as we respond to the maturation process of the inner child. We may find we are becoming a mother or father to this child. Timing the parental role is crucial: when to mirror, when to elucidate, when to set limits. Within this interactive space, imaginative, mutual, and deeply involved kinship narratives take place. They convey to the client what it means to be familiar in the presence of another, reconstructing the image of self in and through a relationship with the analyst.

This is no easy process. Having once been abandoned, the inner child feels doubly let down when the analyst goes away on holiday, or when a process is suddenly interrupted because the hour is over, or when the analyst gives more attention to his/her 'other' family than to the 'adopted' child in analysis. Empathy cannot enact an ideal parent-child relationship. According to Joseph Lichtenberg (1983, p. 226), it serves primarily as a means of registering, understanding and communicating the meaning of such experiences to the adult client and, I might add, especially when the analyst fails to meet the client's expectations. Here the dyad is triangulated within the context of the analyst's professional skills, standards, and collegial affiliations. An analyst may provide a home in analysis, but that home is embedded in the context of a professional community.

At Home in Analysis?

Analysis as home is difficult, ambiguous and controversial, especially in view of the fact that it will all have to end. Clearly home in analysis is not an option for everyone. Indeed it might be only for the few whose early development has been so impaired that they have been unable to form lasting attachments or to know what a good enough home can be. Home in analysis activates a kinship bonding, which transcends the analytic context and may even outlast it. The origins of kinship emerge from personal biography, but they also have a collective, cultural significance. Diane Bell (1990, p. 25), in her book *Daughters of Dreaming,* describes the waiting period needed before she could begin her research on the tribal secrets of the Australian Aboriginal woman. Only after she had been incorporated into the so-called skin relationships − as mother to A., daughter to B., aunt to C. − could the women talk about their tribal mysteries. One may ask if the analyst's attempt to relate with clients in the context of transference represents a modern version of a Stone Age pattern of kinship, as Jung once implied. We discover again and again that people in analysis are ready to speak about their deepest secrets only after some form of authentic attachment has been established.

When analysis has been a home, termination can be extraordinarily difficult. Disappointment, mistrust, betrayal can complicate a good ending. Clients experience the analyst as a father, mother, friend, helper, or companion, and in the end they may feel it has no substance. There is no one solution to the problems that arise in such a situation. Obviously an abrupt end should be avoided. Occasionally an ending has to be negotiated over a long period of time. It may happen that the relationship after analysis consists of discussions about how the years in therapy have changed one's life, what one has learnt from analysis, or what could have been done better.

Home in the Global Society?

Today's global movements have compelled many to re-think their sense of home. In 2008 it was estimated by the UN that there were approximately 190 million voluntary migrants worldwide. Not included in that number were 42 million people uprooted by force, of which 26 million were internally displaced in their own country (Koser 2007, p. 17). Despite the plight of millions each tale about the loss of home is unique. Within millions of unhappy narratives, the significance of home remains an inimitable personal experience, echoing Tolstoy's opening passage of *Anna Karenina*. Narratives about happy families are very similar, but unhappy ones are always different.

In today's global world, cities have now become a home for most people. As home is intimately connected with security and identity, home in a city can no longer be separated from the notion of citizenship. With the waning of the older, cohesive forces of nationality, the political and social rights of citizenship have become increasingly an anchor of security for inhabitants of contemporary urban life. Many questions arise concerning the conditions of granting citizenship to the multi-cultural inhabitants of today's mega cities. Yet how can those who are denied the basic rights of citizenship maintain any sense of home as a secure base in such places? How can citizenship take into consideration the cultural values of different nations and peoples without granting exclusivity to any one culture or nation? How can the lawmakers inspire the holders of citizenship to see beyond themselves and act in service of a greater whole? Citizenship is not simply a status, but a responsibility, even a way of life. Contemporary humanity will hardly be convinced of its significance without internalizing its value and making conscious its psychological meaning.

If citizenship is to reflect something of Jung's idea of the Self in today's world of fragmented communities, it must be open to the entirety of creation as an arena of multiple dimensions. It can no longer ignore questions concerning cultural rights, the rights of the marginalized, the rights of women and the rights of children. As cities or nations no longer exist as isolated entities in this global age, citizenship must be extended to include responsibility for the preservation of animal and plant species and the natural resources of Planet Earth. Added to the list of rights are so-called 'collective rights' – the rights of indigenous peoples, and rights concerning the protection of land, water, and language.

Sociologists remind us that cosmopolitanism is not identical with globalization, corporate society, or the values of a secular state. According to Gerard Delanty (2002, pp. 73-78), cosmopolitan citizenship must reflect the root meaning of the word 'cosmopolitan', implying a sense of belonging to 'cosmos' and 'polis', to the universal and the local. Cosmopolitan citizenship, as a symbol of a newly emerging identity, is in the process of incarnating in the individual psyche, structuring affinities within a particular community, or nation. Representing transnational values, it also implies an opening to citizens of other nations in matters concerning humanity as a whole, such as justice, equality, peace and the preservation of creation.

Motivated by the inner symbolic meaning of citizenship, we learn to recognize that we are serving home as a greater whole, one that requires loyalty, trust, endurance and responsibility. It is a way of serving the Self, which seeks affinities not only in a family, society, or nation, but through an identity, which transcends individual or group consciousness, embracing a reality, which is all-inclusive, even if only grasped in rare moments of inspiration. Once citizenship takes on a broader symbolic significance, a whole range of privileges, responsibilities, and community participation opens new horizons of being at home in the world, even preventing images of Divinity becoming the exclusive property of one race, nation, or culture. Cosmopolitan citizenship happens in those moments when, according to Delanty (ibid., p. 145) 'context bound cultures encounter each other and undergo transformation as a result'. In other words the newly emerging identity of contemporary humanity happens in a space between divergent social and cultural realities and is often achieved in a translation of one containing heritage in terms of another. Embracing the unfamiliar, a transformation of consciousness may occur, creating attitudes that connect hitherto irreconcilable differences.

'Polis', representing the city, a community, or a society where human exchanges take place, opens itself up to 'cosmos' representing the other, the stranger, the unknown, the entirety. Regarded from a symbolic point of view, this model of social development corresponds to some of Jung's basic tenets concerning the individuation process, as a continual creative exchange between ego and self or ego and shadow. 'Polis' represents much of ego activity. Cities, communities, or societies are the realms where most of our daily interactions with the outside world occur and are usually contained within a manageable, familiar or local space. 'Cosmos' approximates more to an experience of the self. Encountering the universe of the unknown, either in a person or an event, is experienced as ruptures in daily life, which appear threatening or inspiring, causing us to take flight, or stand firm and discover what the mystery is all about.

To belong or not to belong, that is the question when facing encounters with strangeness in today's world of multiple identities. The meeting of 'cosmos' and 'polis' correlates with the creative process in every human psyche. They are the moments when the ego encounters the unconscious, within or without; when it can let go of rigid defences, allowing space for the unexpected, which in turn can activate the unconscious to produce images and perspectives, leading to the formation of a new attitude. Jung's transcendent function provides a psychological model of a 'mid-point personality', a point between I and the unknown other. Such moments are a far cry from a sentimental embrace of everyone, but must, according to Richard Sennett (1998, p. 143), also include solid 'ground rules of engagement' to deal with the inevitable conflicts.

Jung's Many-Storied House

Jung's own individuation process can be traced from the remarkable number of dwelling places he inhabited. First a parental home, then an inner home, peopled by all kinds of strange figures as now witnessed in *The Red Book*. He created a professional and family home in Küsnacht. In Bollingen we witness the expression of his life work in masonry, a dwelling place to converse with nature and the spirits of the dead. In primeval Africa while beholding the dawn lighting up the world in all its magnificence, home became kinship with the entire universe. Finally in his vision of 1944 Jung experienced a home definitely not of this world, described as a rock temple, representing an historical matrix that would ultimately satisfy his hunger to belong. Jung's long, rich and intensive life permitted him to gain a rare insight into the multiple significance of home and, the multiple ramifications of human existence.

Perhaps the roots of Jung's ability to create multiple homes can be traced to a dream, dating from 1912 (Jung 1912/1931, para. 54), in which he likens the human psyche to a many-storied house that embraces the entirety of evolution, and which is still in the process of being built. The top floor would symbolize the conscious personality, but as one descends, one discovers other stories containing relics of an historical consciousness.

> It is … a building whose upper story was erected in the nineteenth century, the ground floor dates back to the sixteenth century, and careful examination of the masonry reveals that it was reconstructed from … the eleventh century. In the cellar we come upon Roman foundations and under the cellar a choked-up cave with Neolithic tools … That would be the picture of our psychic structure …

Whereas the dream views home from an inner, vertical perspective, one must not forget that Jung's extensions to that building involved a huge amount of work on the outer horizontal plane, including many personal and professional encounters, intensive research, travel, artistic expression, intricate masonry.

Journeying through psyche's many-storied house, I began this talk on the ground floor. Here we encounter home as a physical, sensuous, and emotional reality in the intimacy of family relations, helpful or harmful for later development. From the ground flour we discover worlds outside of the parental home. We learn to create homes of our own as we explore the invisible spaces between self and other. We may find home in a partnership, family, creed, or profession, as we build extensions to psyche's many-storied house to embrace the complexity of the world around us. When we move to the upper floors in search of meaning and spirituality we realize the roots of identity reach down far below the cellar. We discover that all the levels and extensions of the psyche, all the identities we have created, have been held together by a collective history of which we are scarcely conscious. Our parents and teachers convey to us a set of cultural canons that often determine our most fundamental attitudes to life as we absorb the ideals of prophets, priests, or political leaders. The Biblical exile, the search for the Promised Land, the Wanderings of Ulysses – all bear witness to joy and grief over homes gained or lost. The Hebraic 'Never forget' is an example of the power of a cultural memory which has bonded a people over thousands of years.

This view approximates to Hans Georg Gadamer's 'consciousness of effective history' (*wirkungsgeschichtliches Bewusstsein*), which, according to Jerald Wallulis (1990, p. 5), involves 'the recognition that we are part of a larger effective history that happens to us beyond our willing and doing more than it is guided by our conscious direction'. Rooted in history, we gain assurance that the homes we are building have solid foundations, crucial if we are to add one more story to a house that will survive life's vicissitudes. We do not choose our history, and we can only partially invent identity. Living in the tension between the familiar and the strange, we find ways of appropriating new experiences. Appropriation – implying making something one's own in an authentic way – is not to be understood as an act of possession, or as an achievement of the solitary ego, but as an expression of kinship, re-created according to life's changing circumstances.

As we move out from the ground floor, we discover psyche's many-storied house is situated in a wider context. Not only does it have a vertical axis, its horizontal significance and sustenance depends on other psyches and other homes. Home is not just an inner reality, but is created between people. Relying on the work of Norbert Elias, Steph Lawler (2008, p. 8) exclaims:

'"Without you I'm nothing": without a nexus of others, none of us could be "who we are".' New narratives about home emerge into consciousness in the space between self and the other. The old 'inner/outer' split is only too likely to create rigid ideologies and favour alienation by casting away those unwanted parts of the self on to the stranger through the mechanisms of projection, displacement, or scapegoating. The creative imagery that lies dormant in the cellars of psyche's many-storied house invites us to discover the world as an interim realm of multiple meanings. Exploring those in-between spaces we learn to appreciate the mysterious threads that weave 'polis' and 'cosmos' into new patterns, threads that anticipate an innovative understanding of identity and citizenship.

Home also emerges into consciousness in the reciprocal interaction between the human and non-human environment. Why can't we invest living symbolic forms in the objects of our surroundings?

Material objects do not have to be reduced to signs devoid of meaning in a world that has become purely functional. Why can't the objects, made by the human hand, gain an excess meaning, creating a world that invites play and imagination? We do not have to be ashamed of myth-creating languages, which may not achieve the clarity of scientific discourse, but can inspire people to create objects of beauty. Inspired by soul images, the objects of the world become open-ended, wombs of inexhaustible potentiality. The sounds and symmetries of this unfinished language can be compared to the polymorphous linguistic landscape of a James Joyce, the purposefully incomplete paintings of a Cezanne, the metaphysical voids in a Giacometti sculpture, or the daring asymmetry of Frank Gehry's deconstructive aesthetic. With this language we may see and hear again the mysterious and beautiful intentionality of all natural phenomena, including the human, a vision that now can be enriched with knowledge of its material complexity. We can inspire architects to invest buildings with metaphysical intention that would include the technical and functional achievements of our times. We can support political, social and educational institutions guided by individuals whose norms and values are not just conditioned by power, production, or profit, but account for the indefinable potentiality in every human to live a symbolic life.

Opening the doors and windows of psyche's many-storied house I have tried to elucidate the sounds and symmetries of belonging in nature, family, community, nation, and culture. Home for me has become an experience, born from a sense of belonging to my family of origin, matured through the family I created, devastated in leaving that family, reborn in encounters that helped me find space for those exiled parts of myself, which never had been appropriately housed. Home has been a profession. In the work with clients I have been challenged, humbled and inspired. Crucial to the work is the support and criticism of colleagues. My home would never have been possible without others: parents, wife, children, friends, clients, and colleagues. The list is long, and it would also include animals, plants, objects, and all the events that I have loved, and sometimes hated. By enduring the trials of my personal and professional life, I have added one more story to a house, the origins and future I can only dimly perceive in the penumbra of the dawn and dusk of life.

Home remains a paradox, a word that everyone understands in different ways, depending on one's life story. Seen from a horizontal perspective, home is formed in and through relationships. Identities have emerged from attachments to the diverse homes we have created and interiorized in that space between self and other. Home serves as a containing vessel, which preserves a sense of continuity, as we find ourselves thrown into a world that can be alien and unpredictable. Home is also about boundaries, the windows and walls of the realms of privacy, which allow us to gain perspectives on the world outside. Home, as an expression of the self, represents the way we hold worlds together, the way we can relate to others and the way we can protect, care and fight for the living universe.

Seen from a vertical perspective, home reveals a quest for selfhood which transcends the fleeting experiences of time. In the beginning of life those of us who have had good homes presumed that they would never change. At the end of life many hope they will visit a home that will last forever. That is an ideal of the spirit which is continually subject to the seasons and the cyclic patterns of life, death and rebirth. Most of us gain or lose several homes as we proceed through life. Despite loss or gain, something in us never seems to give up the hope that we belong to somebody, some event, or something, as we continue to build psyche's many-storied house. Home has a spiritual significance, which is not confined to a particular confession. Home becomes a trusted shelter in those moments when we take in worlds and make them our own, not as a possession, more as gifts that require respect and gratitude, gifts from a source unknown.

References

Bell, D. (1990). *Daughters of the Dreaming.* Sydney: Allen & Unwin.

Delanty, G. (2002). *Citizenship in a Global Age: Society, Culture, Politics.* Buckingham, UK: Open University Press, 2000.

Erdheim, M. (1992). 'Spätadoleszenz und Kultur'. In *Phantasie und Realität in der Spätadolezenz.* Opladen: Westdeutscher Verlag.

Hillman, J. with Pozzo, L. (1983). *Inter Views.* Dallas: Spring Publications.

Hoffman, E. (1990). *Lost in Translation: A Life in a New Language.* New York: Penguin.

Jung, C.G. (1912/1931). 'Mind and earth'. *CW* 10.

Koser, K. (2007). *International Migration, A Very Short Introduction.* Oxford: Oxford University Press.

Lawler, S. (2008). *Identity: Sociological Perspectives.* Cambridge: Polity Press.

Lichtenberg, J. (1983). *Psychoanalysis and Infant Research.* Hillsdale, NJ: Analytic Press.

Mahler, M. Pine, F. & Bergman, A. (1985). *The Psychological Birth of the Human Infant.* London: Maresfield Library.

Said, E. (2000). *Out of Place.* New York: Vintage.

Sennett, R. (1998). *The Corrosion of Character: The Personal Consequences of Work in the New Capitalism.* New York & London: W. W. Norton.

Swiss National Radio (2009). 'Abholzung ist der größte Klimakiller'. DRS 2, *Kontext*, 17 November, online at:
http://pod.drs.ch/mp3/kontext/kontext_200911171000_10105999.mps

UNCR Annual Report shows 412 million people uprooted, on line at:
http:77www.unhcr.org/4a2fd52412d.html

von Krockow, C. (1992). *Heimat.* Munich: DTV.

Wallulis, J. (1990). *The Hermeneutics of Life History.* Evanston, IL: Northwestern University Press.

Tuesday, 24 August 2010

Cultural Complex and the Elaboration of Trauma from Slavery

Denise G. Ramos

Brazil (SbrPA)

The idea of studying slavery from the psychological point of view occurred to me when I was giving a word-association test to a group of students in an analytical psychology workshop. To my surprise, one of the students said that he was very sad when he realized that he had associated the word 'ship' to 'black ship'.

'Black ship' was the name given to the vessels that brought Africans to Brazil to be sold as slaves. Later I found out that other students in this city had had similar reactions. I was working in the city of Salvador, the former capital of Brazil, in the state of Bahia, located in the north-east of Brazil, with a population of 80% African descendants. These students were doctors and psychologists, and it would be nearly impossible, just from their appearance, to tell which of them were of African descent.

We were in 2006, 118 years after the abolition of slavery in Brazil, so some of these students could have had relatives, grandparents or great-grandparents who had been slaves. The test revealed a conflicting and traumatic situation in the personal and collective unconsciousness. The kidnapping, breaking of family bonds, compulsory migration, the terrible journeys in the black ships, the submission and degrading situations, such as being sold, and all the mistreatment that Africans were submitted to, undoubtedly created a highly traumatic situation. According to historians, during these journeys, a third of the African slaves died; the most common disease was *Bantu*, which means to miss someone. This level of mortality in black ships was three to four times higher than among free immigrants (Eltis 2003).

Of the total of 11 million Africans that were enslaved, three million six hundred thousand are estimated to have been brought to Brazil. Today, 51% of the Brazilian population are of African origin. In the last few years a significant amount of literature has dealt with the history of these people, their rebellions and struggles to build an identity. However, from the psychological point of view much remains to be done.

One of the main questions for us today is how the descendants of these slaves are living now and how they still cope with these traumatic events.

One hundred and twenty-two years after the abolition of slavery, Brazil remains a country marked by racial inequality. Statistics show that in Brazil the majority of people who are unemployed, uneducated and poor – as well as the felons in jail – are of African descent (Henriques 2001; Kilsztajn et al. 2008). Studies show that up until the first half of the 20th century, during the process of generalization of free labour and competition, the preponderance of descendants of the old slave population lived in economic marginality (Furtado 2000; Hoffmann 2001). Brazilians themselves often attribute this to the legacy of slavery, arguing that the experience of bondage crippled Afro-Brazilians[1] so severely as a social group that they proved unable, one century after emancipation, to compete effectively against whites for jobs, education, housing, and other social goods.

Clearly, the legacy of slavery helped shape this process by producing both employers unaccustomed and unwilling to bargain with their former slaves, and a former slave population with very specific demands concerning the conditions under which they would work as free men and women. That legacy is present throughout most of Brazil, where white immigrants are clearly the 'winners' and blacks the 'losers' in the process of economic development and prosperity. Moreover, while European descendants often take pride in their ancestors' history by travelling to their family's place of origin, and taking great pleasure in the telling and retelling of how their ancestors crossed the ocean and managed to be very successful in the new land, I observed that African descendants practically never touch on this subject.

Recent studies conducted among graduate students in the cities of Salvador and São Paulo confirmed this fact (Ramos 2009). It should be remembered that São Paulo, a highly industrialized and developed city located in the South of Brazil, was essentially formed by European immigrants, mostly Italians, Spaniards and Portuguese. The majority of its population is white and the influence of European culture is significantly present in its architecture, education, and local habits and culture. The two groups' feelings about their ancestors were compared. The response to the questionnaire confirmed the significant difference that exists between the descendants of Europeans and Africans. While the former are familiar with the origin of their ancestors, what country their grandparents and great-grandparents came from, and expressed a desire to visit that place, the descendants of Africans say they do not know the origin of their family (the majority does not even mention the city/region where the grandparents lived) and left blank the question of whether they would like to know their family's

---

1 There is no such term as 'Afro-Brazilian', 'African-Brazilian' or 'African descendant' in the Brazilian society. These terms have been used here just for the purpose of differentiation. We all call ourselves, simply, 'Brazilians', which seems to indicate that a part of the social substratum that forms the national identity remains unimpaired.

origin. To the question on the influence of the colour of skin in social and work relations, all the whites answered that their appearance is a helpful factor, whereas the black residents of São Paulo considered their colour as a factor that generates feelings of inferiority and discrimination. Within this group we observe conflicting sentiments: many answered that they were proud of their origin but were ashamed of their parents and felt inferior.

Another study of this project observed and compared white and black students, aged between 12 and 18 years, in a school of the city of São Paulo. Ten hypotheses were raised to verify and compare self-esteem, whitening, racial identification, attributes of beauty, wealth, social and professional success. We used as instruments the scale of self-esteem of Rosenberg (Avanci, J. et al. 2007) and two question-naires. In one of them the students had to choose which one of the four pictures (2 whites and 2 blacks) corresponded to a quality. For example: which one of them is more beautiful?

The results show that the vast majority of black teenagers assigned to the whites greater wealth, beauty and professional success. However, the black female students believed that they could also have professional success. This is due probably to the popularity of black artists and models and great appreciation of 'black beauty' in some cultural circuits. It is interesting to note that black students see themselves as having as many friends as the white ones, revealing the same level of sociability.

Here we may reason that when a black teenager says that the blacks are uglier, poorer and with less chances of success he or she is in a dead-end street. Feeling trapped in an undesirable body, the shadow (in this case, the good qualities) is projected into the white colleagues. A natural consequence is that there was a unanimous desire to look white. In our research, most teenagers of both sexes see themselves whiter than they are and declare that they would like to be white. Similar results were found by Lima and Vala (2004). In their study they investigated the effects of perceived skin colour and of social success on the whitening and on the infra-humanization. They found out that blacks that obtain social success are perceived whiter than the blacks that fail. A mediation analysis indicated that as the blacks with success are whitened, typically at the same time the more they are attributed with superior characteristics. These surveys confirm other studies that reveal a whitening desire and the association of blackness with inferiority. Walter and Paula Boechat in their paper 'Race, racism and inter racism in Brazil: clinical and cultural perspectives' say: 'the basic, distinctive character of Brazilian racism is that it is based on the colour of skin. This turns racism into a central element in the collective shadow of Brazil' (Boechat & Boechat 2009, p. 196).

The skin colour does not allow secrets, forgiveness or easy escape.

It obliges the individual to identify with a group with whom he or she may not want to belong. There is no choice. As Kaplinsky says 'skin colour could trigger emotional reaction and is a key to the cultural complex' (Kaplinsky 2009, p. 64).

The results of these researches as of many others point to a possible psychological cause for the socio-economic distortions described above and raise the following questions:

Could it be that the self-esteem of African descendants became so low that it has made their social ascension difficult? What would be causing these symptoms? Would they be related to an underlying collective and cultural complex? Could the traumatic events of slavery be at the core of this complex? Or could slavery's traumatic situation be fixed in a cultural complex that is transmitted from generation to generation?

In this paper I will make a brief analysis of trauma and cultural complexes and how these may manifest in a segment of population of African descendants living in a specific region of Brazil. Without trying to reduce this complex phenomenon to a single psychological cause, I will explore symptoms of a possible cultural complex and a collective trauma brought on by slavery.

The historical centre of the city of Salvador, Bahia (the same city where I gave the workshop) was chosen for this study. The city of Salvador ('Saviour') is of great importance to this study for this was the place where many 'black ships' arrived and where slaves were sold. It has a very well conserved historical centre, where many 18th century houses are still preserved, as well as the sites where slaves worked and lived. Over time, after the abolition of slavery, this section of the city underwent a major transformation and was named a world cultural monument by UNESCO in 1985 (Cerqueira 1994; Miranda & Santos 2002). The name of this historical centre is very significant: 'Pelourinho', which means pillory or whipping post, a place where the slaves were sold, tortured and even killed.

The Social Psychological Research

The research was carried out between 2005 and 2009 and focused on:

A. Historical documents

B. Field observation – what happens on the streets

C. Visit to museums and art galleries in the Pillory and interviews with six painters

D. Trip to the centre of two of the most famous musical groups of the Pillory

E. Visit to black sacred places

F. Interviews with community leaders

A. *Historical Documents*

Locations of the Pillory
Originally the pillory was placed in the city's first open market, the 'Praça da Feira' which today is known as 'Praça Municipal' (Municipal Square), an open square at the top of the hill, just above the place where the 'black ships' arrived. Today, there is a modern and colourful fountain in its place.

Some time between 1602 and 1607 the pillory was moved by the governor's decree to the 'Terreiro de Jesus' (Jesus Yard), a place 'far away from the public eyes'. But Jesus Yard was the site of the Jesuit church and school, and the screams and groans interfered with church services and teaching. Today, in the same place as the pillory, stands a statue of French origin of Ceres, goddess of fertility and agriculture.

So by request of the priests, it was removed again, this time to the bottom of the 'Porta de São Bento' where 'Praça Castro Alves' (Castro Alves Square) is now located. The pillory was moved for the last time in 1807 and taken to the square which would come to bear its name. So Salvador's pillory last stood at the top of the sloping 'Largo do Pelourinho' (Pillory Square), the final stage in its journey, and it would stand there for another 28 years, until 1835 when it was destroyed. Today this is the main place for musical events to take place. The neighbouring slave-auction site was renovated and converted into a museum (Rocha 1994).

The building of water fountains, the monument to the goddess Ceres and finally a place for musical events where formerly stood the pillory may be interpreted here as an attempt to transform a spot associated with suffering and death into an area of joy and the celebration of life, even if for most of the population this is an unconscious act.

B. *Field Observation: What Happens on the Streets*

It is common to see women doing *tererê*, an African style of braiding hair, on tourists. Here there is an attitude of pride and valorization of a tradition in a culture where straight blonde hair is more appreciated. We also see women in African clothing selling traditional food and accessories made of beads and stones. African-Brazilian aesthetics have been gaining new interests through clothes, accessories, hairdos and prints.

Recently 'ethnic toys' have been appearing on the market, such as black dolls dressed as Africans. Questioned about the ugliness of the white doll, the black seller, smiling, responded to me: '*But that's the idea. See if you understand.*'

Figure 1 (Photo by the author, 2009)

Besides the ethnic dresses, there are many stores that sell African – Brazilian music as well as African musical instruments.

Scenes of people performing the *capoeira*, a mixture of dance and fight, are also a common sight in the Pillory. Many times I ran into groups of people performing this art. The *capoeira* is considered a movement of the resilience of black culture and today is taught in schools all over Brazil, as well as abroad. According to Carlos S. Paulo (personal communication, April 2008), the *capoeira* was born of the necessity to develop a physical intelligence in people whose bodies were chained and oppressed. Thus the movements express the fight and against the oppressor, but they needed to be disguised as a form of dance so as not to appear as a threat to their lords and masters.

We can see here that some African traditions are not only recollected and represented but are also recalled and imagined, through association with dance and artefacts, some of which have been arranged and designated for that purpose. Here, the 'power of telling and looking' is intimately intertwined with gestures and associated with the capacity to see and the possibility of making things visible (Hale 1998). But, which things do they want to make visible? And what's invisible in that place?

Finally, we saw some children and teenagers walk the streets begging for money and white tourists, men and women, in very open sexual behaviours with the blacks.

C. Visit to Art Galleries in the Pillory and Interviews with Six Painters

Thirty-one catalogued art galleries were visited (seventy per cent), where the most common themes among the paintings were noted and images looked for what reference they had to the local population and/or reflected slavery. The main themes found in paintings were:

- Nature: with young Indians and wild animals, especially birds and jaguars.
- Human figures: paintings of sensual, young black women, mainly just the face, always in African clothing. While the women look joyful, a possible representation of the African *anima*, the few paintings of men reveal a deep sadness and are sombre in tone. In this case, the artists were all men.

Figure 2: *The owner's daughter by Adriano Luiz Gonçalves (Salvador, 2009)*

There were only three paintings with references to African origin with just one with slaves. In the other two, the African natives had their eyes closed. What don't they want to see? The representation of human figures with eyes closed is present in great number of paintings, especially when there is a picture of a white man in the centre. However, when the frame depicts only afro-descendants the black figures keep their eyes open. Are we watching a difficulty to face the white man? Are we dealing here with conflictive feelings? What is it that is so difficult to be aware of?

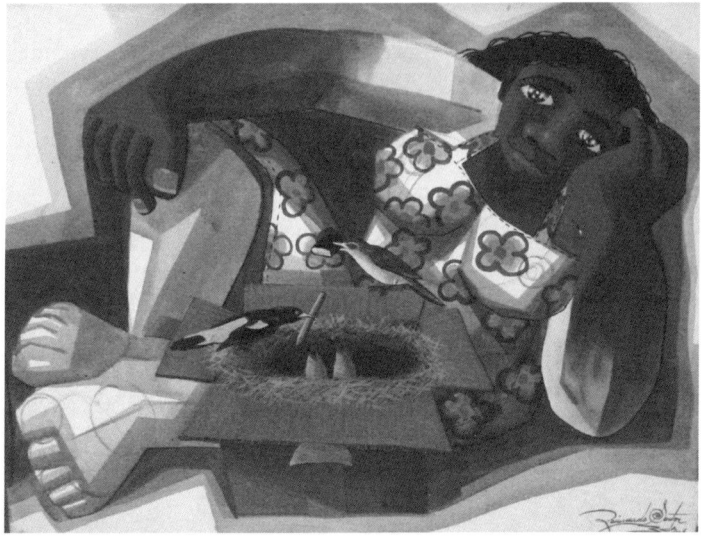

Figure 3: Food for birds by Raimundo Bastos dos Santos (Salvador, 2009)

Another very interesting painting depicts a woman with a sad look watching a bird nest. One bird carries a book and the other a pencil. In the nest there are also two pencils. According to the author, the message is that the way to freedom is through education; the people can only evolve when they know how to use pencil and paper (Raimundo Bastos dos Santos, personal communication 2009). Yet according to the same painter, another path would be football, and he pictured two children football players carrying eggs instead of balls in a nest of birds.

Figure 4: Orixá by Ricardo Miranda dos Santos (Salvador, 2009)

There were scenes from the past, portraying the activities that took place in the Pillory, probably from the end of the 19th century to the beginning of the 20th, without any reference to slavery, torture or submission. There were no figures of the present time. The reference is mostly of an imaginary peaceful, non-conflictive past. We see also scenes of people dancing the *capoeira* and playing musical instruments. However, the most common paintings are those that represent the *Orixás*, gods of the African-Brazilian religion called *Candomblé* (Figure 4). These are strong and joyful figures generally portrayed dancing and dressed in very colourful clothes and accessories. (Figure 5) Here we observe perhaps a point of pride and self-esteem for the priests of the African Brazilian religions are highly respected and consulted by politicians and prominent people in Brazil. In terms of religion, it is important to note that most Brazilian religious beliefs, besides Christianity, derive from African myths and legends, and the language used in these religions has been passed down through generations.

The mythical aspects of these beliefs have influenced the cultural development of the country.

Figure 5: São Joaquim's street fair by José Maria de Souza (Salvador, 2009)

D. Visit to the Centre of Two of the Most Famous Musical Groups of the Pillory: 'Children of Gandhi' and 'Olodum'

The group 'Children of Gandhi', with approximately 10,000 members, started as a cultural and musical (Carnival) organization whose aim was to preach peace in honour of the Indian leader Gandhi. They cultivate mystical-religious African-Brazilian traditions and their costumes are white and blue to represent the peace proposed by the Mahatma. Their songs make references to the beauty and strength of the suffering black people who, although marginalized and discriminated against, still demonstrate their art, their joy and their legacy from the land of their ancestors (old Africa).

The other group is called *Olodum* that means 'God of the gods', God creator of the universe. While most Brazilian musical groups wear yellow and green, the group *Olodum* adds red and black to their costumes. According to them, red stands for blood and black for the pride of their race. The rhythm is strong, the attitude a mix of fun and aggressiveness, and the loud sound of the drums, they say, 'keeps the ghosts away'. The songs are usually about the creation of the universe, the wonders of the creator and the origin of the slave race. In one of their most popular songs they say they were born in Egypt and are sons of the pharaoh. Here we see a fantasy of grandiosity since no slaves were sent from Egypt to Brazil.

In the quest for an identity, it is only natural that we should seek our myths of origin. In the case of African descendants, this return to the past touches on the question of the African Diaspora, since along the way, many lost their parents' background, history and place of birth. Thus the music, the dresses and accessories create an image of 'Mamma Africa', idealizing a mythical Africa in order to be able to create African-Brazilian traditions. On the other hand, some of Olodum's lyrics are famous for the joyful rhythm that expresses hope in the construction of a united country. In these songs there are no references to slavery, in fact, one of the most common themes is the black hero that shakes the country and transforms it, not with war but with an amorous attitude.

E. Visit to the Church of Our Lady of the Rosario

Former slaves built this church in the 17th century and decorated it with the gold that they could hide in their pockets while building churches for their masters. Very well hidden in the rear there is a small cemetery and a kind of glass window. An excavation revealed that the skeletons buried there were of slaves still wearing their chains, slaves that were killed in the pillory. Their bodies had to stay exposed to the public so that they would serve as an example. However, during the night the members of the community would come and bury them in a hidden place. The small glass window has two statues of the slave Anastácia, who became one of the few myths of slavery. Anastácia is the legend of a beautiful young slave. She is desired by her master, whose wife is so envious of her beauty that she has Anastacia's mouth covered so that she will die of hunger and thirst. At the bottom, this legend praises the black beauty and sex appeal as superior to the white woman's.

F. Interviews with Business People and Community Leaders

There was a strong movement of transference and countertransference while doing the interviews. Sometimes the interviewers made me wait a long time. So they made me experience, perhaps in an unconscious way, the lack of respect and humiliation that were felt in similar situations by black people. As I understood that it wasn't personal (my skin colour didn't help), I hired an African descendant as my assistant.

The main observation among shopkeepers and some community leaders is that there is a deep concern with the commercial situation of the Pillory. The main problem, according to them, is that the residents of Salvador really only go to the city's historical centre when there is a concert or event taking place, so many stores and restaurants have been forced to close their doors.

One particularly interesting interview was with Mr. Clarindo Silva, who has been living in the Pillory for 50 years and owns the oldest and most famous restaurant, the 'Cantina da Lua' (Tavern of the Moon). Mr. Silva is very proud of the Pillory and of his own history, and even showed me a suit in which he paraded in the Pillory fashion show. Undoubtedly one of the leading defenders of the preservation of this site, Mr. Silva says that the Pillory should be a place with schools and drugstores and not only a historical place or an open-air museum, meaning that they cannot just play for tourists but must go on and change their history. I think that Mr. Silva is living in the present and probably had overcome the racial problem.

Conclusions

All these observations allow us to raise several questions. The first set of questions below is similar to those raised by Eyerman (2001) in his book *Cultural Trauma: Slavery and the Formation of African American Identity* when analysing slavery in the United States:

- What pictures should African-descendants present to themselves and to the tourists and the white population?
- How has the cultural expression of African descendants evolved, changed, and revolved back to its origins over generations?

The true history of the Pillory, as we see it, is hidden in a small cemetery behind a church and in the bitter speech of the Pillory's inhabitants. There is no conscious interaction between the cultural and symbolical richness and their daily life. Although African culture is deeply ingrained in Brazil – as can be seen in music, dance, food and religious practices – it seems that its acculturation remains restricted to these activities and is not integrated with others, such as profit-making economic activities. The buildings and houses are in need of better care and many residents are burdened by financial problems. It is clear that the inhabitants of the Pillory do not use their ability to show their many qualities and creativity, that is, to make their world visible (or invisible) as a form of power and part of the social construct of their identity.

Is the Pillory just an exhibition, a kind of theatre that hides the true self of this population? Is the lack of representation of slavery a repression of the trauma or a form of resilience of this culture?

According to Singer and Kimbles' (2004, p. 19) affirmation that a traumatized group may represent a 'false self' to the world, we could say that the customs, the paintings and the dancing that we observed could be showing a 'false self', and that the more authentic and vulnerable identity is hidden from the public eye. It is possible that

> such a traumatized group with their defenses may find themselves living with a history that spans several generations, several centuries, or even millennia with repetitive, wounding experiences that fix these patterns of behavior and emotion into what analytical psychologists have come to know as complexes.
>
> (Singer & Kimbles 2004, p. 19)

The interviews with the artists and with important community figures, as well as the visit to the slave cemetery and the song's lyrics, reveal another side of suffering and trauma. Most songs refer to a fanciful and unreal past, with fantasies of power and grandiosity.

We can also note a certain depression in the interviewees for there is little perspective of the future but a sense of dismay. Is this the future of the black teenagers of our study?

The inhabitants of the Pillory expect help from the government and complain bitterly about the lack of official support. The painters don't feel recognized and valued and everyone seems worried about the possible depletion of their place. However, there is very little private initiative. We observed certain passivity and an almost childish resentment. As we know, people in whom the effects of trauma become ingrained often develop a chronic sense of helplessness and victimization, and so it is in our study. Behind the colourful paintings there is deep depression and sadness. Our data allow us to say that conflicts, suffering and aggressive energies are very seldom expressed while most of the images are soft and joyful, expressing an idealized nature or paradise.

Probably, the energy used in warding off the memory of the traumatic experience impoverished the mental life or the strength to take life in a more active and conscious way. Although the defences helped to survive at the same time there are repressing the necessary energy that could broker the racial barrier.

While this Historical Centre protects and gives a framework to its inhabitants, at same time it is a prison that forges an identity. An identity mainly based on skin colour. The African descendants may feel at home and protected in the Pillory. But this is a protection that may impede further development, a protection that does not allow any escape from this group identity. As Kaplinsky says: 'to belong implies a boundary and while a boundary provides a sense of containment, it can also be an area of intercourse, or a point to be broken through – or out of – in order to "become" and "individuate"' (Kaplinsky 2009, p. 63).

Although the trauma of kidnapping and forced subordination was not directly experienced by the subjects of this study, the memory of slavery seems to forge a collective identity even if not felt by everyone in this community. We may even wonder if the name 'pillory' somehow has an unconscious effect on the population, 'obliging' them to repeat the collective memories as a contemporary experience. As we saw it, the place where it stood for centuries has been replaced by fountains, statues and musical centres, but its name certainly lets no one forget the slavery that was practiced there and seems to be perpetuated as a cultural complex centred on a collective trauma.

We know that when trauma fails to be integrated into the totality of a person's life experience, the victim remains fixated on the trauma. Disruption or loss of social support is associated with an inability to overcome the effects of psychological trauma. Lack of support may leave enduring marks on subsequent adjustment and functioning. Freud (1893) described a compulsion to repeat the trauma as an attempt of the organism to drain this excess of energy. He thought that by redoing and repeating the trauma the victims attempted to change a passive stance to one of active coping. Wouldn't it be the case of the abandoned children on the streets? Wouldn't that explain the feeling of victimization of some inhabitants?

The ways in which the collective memory and the representation of a shared past are present in Pillory, through painting and music, do not amount to an elaboration or transformation of the trauma, but may raise two hypotheses: they could be expressing defences that might help this group's spirit to survive, or else reveal a split between the collective psyche, a trauma and a cultural complex. Perhaps both are valid.

If trauma links past to present through representations and imagination, then what we witnessed as the representation of slavery, may indicate that this trauma is acting out in the present in the form of repeated and compulsive behaviours of unconscious submission and low-esteem, which may explain the critical socio-cultural situation of African descendants in most parts of Brazil. The few historical black personages, such as the slave Anastácia and others that belong to the heroic struggle for liberty, were not incorporated in the collective consciousness and remains hidden at the back of a small cemetery, for example. Rarely mentioned, portrayed or sang by their descendants, they are not used as examples for pride or self-esteem. The cultural richness and capacity of resilience of Afro-descendants, and the contribution that their ancestors made to the development of the nation, remain unconscious. The ideas of dominion, control and power are still deposited in whites, thus provoking a defensive splitting. According to Young-Eisendrath (1987, p. 41), in this case two conditions may be present: anxiety (or fear), when the Other is experienced as powerfully evil, or envy, when the Other is experienced as powerfully good, but holds the power and 'the goodies' for itself. As she points out: 'racism is a psychological complex organized around the archetype of opposites, the splitting of experience into Good and Bad, White and Black, Self and Other.' One of the consequences of this scission is explicit in projections on the 'Negro's body' (Young-Eisendrath 1987, p. 41). Prostitution and exploitation of the body, especially the bodies of *mulatta* women sold as merchandise, and of the black male body as being strong and sensual, are based on the stereotype that blacks have better 'physical' attributes, as if they were 'closer to nature' and therefore endowed with an especially attractive sexuality and exceptional strength. This stereotype is clearly assumed by the population observed, who use their body and corporal art as the principal vehicles of their culture. We had observed the same fact in our studies with teenagers when the girls see the possibility of professional success through body exposure. Paula and Walter Boechat made a similar observation: *'the idea of the inferiority of non-white groups still remain in the cultural unconscious,* [this is] the idea that blacks may come to a social realization only in sports or in music, not though an academic profession' (Boechat & Boechat 2009, p. 112; italics in original).

On the other hand we may understand some behaviours observed in the Pillory as defensive forms of behaviour, manoeuvres to seduce and deceive the powerful, and are far from expressing the true feelings of this population. They may even be considered as a form of resilience and capacity for survival of people who still hesitate to assume their full freedom. A good example is a scene observed in a restaurant in the Pillory, with the gentle, smiling response of the (black) waitress to the aggressive (white) customer who complained about the slowness of service: 'Calm down there, *my king*, what's the hurry, your food's on its way.'

So, the more we study this phenomenon, the more complex it becomes. What is evident is that the silence and lack of studies on the matter have contributed to preserving stereotypes that are emotionally-charged beliefs based on cultural complexes that interfere with seeing people more precisely and empathically. These stereotypes probably belong to all Brazilians, which make it difficult for a large part of this population to develop, both emotionally and in socio-economic terms.

So we might say that the anthropological, historical and social studies, the epidemiological data, the black and white comparative studies allow us to affirm that there is strong evidence of a cultural complex due to slavery trauma in the observed population. (Figure 6) And we might also say that in order to have a healthier country, the new generation needs to interpret and come to terms with their collective traumatic past and their relationship to the past. And to achieve this, it is necessary to research the origins, to heal the trauma and to restore the dignity of the black heritage. It is important to notice that the question of trauma brought on by slavery has formed a complex that reaches Brazilian culture as a whole, and not just African descendants. This complex probably feeds the inferiority complex pointed out in other studies, which is considered the psychological base for the tolerance towards political corruption in the country (Ramos 2004).

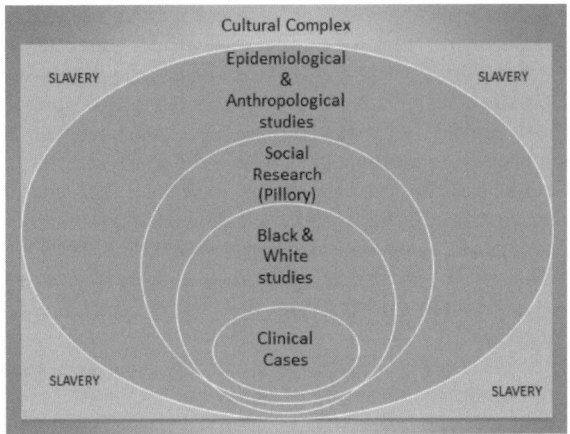

Figure 6

Once all Brazilians are in some way affected by these complexes in his or her upbringing, now identified as 'superior' and now 'inferior', the national identity and the possibility of building a healthier and fairer nation becomes endangered, perpetuating countless sinister projections independent of skin colour and disconnected from reality, but imprisoned in a shameful and tragic history. In this case we are all 'victims', and only the painful awareness of the 'nation's blackness' will be able to restore the value of the African heritage in forming a national identity.

References

Avanci, J. et al. (2007). 'Adaptação transcultural de escala de autoestima para adolescentes'. *Psicologia: Reflexão e Crítica*, 20, 3, 1-13.

Boechat, W. & Boechat, P. (2009). 'Race, racism and inter-racialism in Brazil: clinical and cultural perspectives'. In *Proceedings of the Seventeenth International Congress for Analytical Psychology*, ed. P. Bennett. Einsiedeln, Switzerland: Daimon Verlag.

Cerqueira, N. (ed.) (1994). *Pelourinho, a grandeza restaurada*, Salvador: Fundação Cultural do Estado da Bahia.

Elkins, S.M. (1968). *Slavery*. Chicago: University of Chicago Press.

Eltis, D. (2003). 'Migração e estratégia na história global'. In *Ensaios sobre a escravidão*, ed. M. Florentino & C. Machado. Belo Horizonte: Editora IFMG.

Eyerman, R. (2001). *Cultural Trauma: Slavery and the Formation of African American Identity*, Cambridge: Cambridge University Press.

Furtado, C. (2000). *Formação Econômica do Brasil*, São Paulo: Publifolha.

Freud, S. (1893). 'On the psychical mechanism of hysterical phenomena'. *International Journal of Psycho-Analysis*, 37, 1, 8-13. Translation by James Strachey, 1956.

Hale, E.G (1998). *Making Whiteness: The Culture of Segregation in the South, 1880-1940*. New York: Pantheon Books.

Henriques, R. (2001). *Desigualdade racial no Brasil: evolução das condições de vida na década de 90*. Rio de Janeiro: Ipea (texto para discussão n° 807). Retrieved from: www.ipea.gov.br.

Hoffmann, R. (2001). 'Distribuição da renda no Brasil: poucos com muito e muitos com muito pouco'. In *Economia social no Brasil*, eds. L. Dowbor & S. Kilsztajn. São Paulo: Senasc.Ibge.

Kaplinsky, C. (2009). 'Shifting shadows: shaping dynamics in the cultural unconscious'. In *Proceedings of the Seventeenth International Congress for Analytical Psychology*, ed. P. Bennett. Einsiedeln, Switzerland: Daimon Verlag.

Kilsztajn, S. et al. (2008). *Race, Equality and Income Distribution in Brazil*, retrieved from www.abep.nepo.unicamp.br, accessed on 2008, June 10.

Lima, M. E. & Vala, J. 'Social success, whitening and racism'. *Psicologia: Teoria e Pesquisa* 2004, 20, 1, 11-19.

Miranda, L. B. & Santos, M. A. (2002). *Pelourinho: desenvolvimento socioeconômico*. Salvador: Secretaria da Cultura e Turismo.

Ramos, D. G. (2004). 'Corruption. A symptom of a cultural complex in Brazil?' In *The Cultural Complex: Contemporary Jungian Perspectives on Psyche and Society*, eds. T. Singer & S. Kimbles. Hove & New York: Brunner-Routledge.

— (2009). 'The influence of ancestrally and skin color in self esteem and identity: a comparative study between graduated students from São Paulo and Salvador'. Unpublished research. PUCSP.

Ramos, D. et al. (2010). 'Identity formation and feelings of self-esteem: a comparative study between black and white students'. Unpublished research. PUCSP.

Rocha, C. (1994). *Roteiro do Pelourinho*. Salvador: Oficina do Livro.

Singer, T. & Kimbles, S. (2004). *The Cultural Complex: Contemporary Jungian Perspectives on Psyche and Society*. Hove and New York: Brunner-Routledge.

Young-Eisendrath, P. (1987). 'The absence of black Americans as Jungian analysts'. *Quadrant*, 20, 2.

Jung after *The Red Book*

Sonu Shamdasani
UK (Editor, The Red Book)

Nancy Furlotti
USA (CGJILA)

Judith Harris
Canada (AGAP, OAJA)

John Peck
USA (JPA)

The brief for this session read:

'The publication of C. G. Jung's *Red Book* raises crucial questions for the ongoing reception of his hitherto unpublished works. It heralds the possibility of a new beginning of informed discussion of the historical contextualization of the genesis of his work and its comprehensive understanding, as well the study of the actual relation of his work to his life.

However, there is a risk that this opening will be lost, through being subsumed by pre-existing templates and patterns of response to his work. What is called for is responsible and informed engagement on the part of the Jungian community and curricular reform to enable this.'

In this session, Sonu Shamdasani opened up the debate on these issues as a round table discussion, with contributions from Nancy Furlotti, John Peck and Judith Harris. The moderator was Stanton Marlan (PSJA, IRSJA).

This plenary session was not recorded as it was an audience-led discussion.

Wednesday, 25 August 2010

A Revision of Jung's Theory of Archetypes in Light of Contemporary Research: Neurosciences, Genetics and Cultural Theory – A Reformulation

Christian Roesler

Germany (DGAP)

Jung's formulation of a theory of archetypes was a seminal step in the understanding of a phenomenon which is recognized throughout different sciences and practices. However from the beginning there have been contradictions in his theory to the extent that at least four different conceptualizations of archetype can be found in his works. Additionally there was evidence, e.g., from biology, already in Jung's lifetime that some of his conceptualizations were fallacious. Jung always insisted that archetypes are a biological fact and rooted in the genetic equipment of human beings.

Since Jung's time the fields of genetics and neurobiology have developed enormously and have produced new insights in the work-ings of genes and their interactions with environmental influences. Some of these findings support Jung's speculations while in other respects some strongly contradict his basic premises. On the other hand there is evidence from different sciences that something like archetypes must exist.

So what does the term archetype refer to? Analytical psychology is at a point today where it needs a reformulation of the theory of archetypes which is informed by the new findings in the life sci-ences and which incorporates them into a comprehensive theoretical framework.

This paper revisits Jung's theory, pointing out the inconsistencies and theoretical problems inherent in it, and confronts it with new insights from the life sciences. Finally I will try to develop a reformu-lated theory of archetypes based on contemporary knowledge.

The proposed reformulation of the term archetype departs clearly from Jung's assumption that it is a biological phenomenon. Instead it has to be seen as a cultural product – with all its consequences: we cannot suppose any more that all archetypes are universal since their incorporation depends on socialization.

Jung's Concept of the Archetype

What does Jung mean when he uses the term archetype? In Jung's conceptualization the archetype is an innate pattern of perception and behaviour which influences human perception and action and shapes it into similar forms. Archetypes are unconscious factors, affectively loaded so that when we experience them they often have a numinous quality. Archetypes are autonomous from consciousness and, most importantly, Jung claims that they are universal, which means the same set of archetypes are in all human beings. When formulating this concept Jung drew on the findings of behavioural biology, namely the concept of instincts and patterns of behaviour.

Jung was not the first to speak of archetypes. Shamdasani (2003) has pointed out that the idea of archetypes was in the air in the sciences around 1900 and Jung was just the first – and brave enough – to form this idea into a psychological concept.

In the years before 1912 Jung arrived at an idea of archetypes in two different ways:

1. In his association studies where he developed the concept of the complexes he realized that over a large number of participants there were inter-individually similar complexes, for example, negative mother complexes. He assumed that there must be a prototypical pattern behind these similar complexes shared by all human beings. It is very disappointing that Jung did not continue these studies after 1912 as he would have been on the way to finding a scientific proof of inter-individually comparable psychological patterns.

2. The second way the concept of archetypes was developed was from Jung's psychiatric experience with psychotic patients and their fantasies at the Burghölzli hospital. There he found cases where psychotic patients developed fantasies which were parallel to motifs in ancient mythology. The most important case in this respect is the so-called Solar Phallus Man, a patient at Burghölzli who told Jung about a phallus coming out of the sun which produces the wind. Jung was extremely surprised by this since he had just translated an ancient Egyptian text which included exactly the same image (Bair 2003).

In 1912 Jung published his work *Symbols of Transformation* (Jung 1912/1956) where he investigated the fantasies of a young woman and for the first time described these on the basis of archetypal patterns. This was also the point where he departed clearly from Freud's psychoanalysis and started to form his own analytical psychology. We can see here how basic the concept of archetype is for analytical psychology.

Now if we look critically from a scientific viewpoint at Jung's notion of archetypes, several conceptual problems come to light. The first is that of cryptomnesia: to state that the archetype is an innate pattern

Jung also had to claim for all his cases that there had been no contact to the image or idea by the person producing the archetypal image, which of course Jung could not prove (Bair 2003).

Raya Jones (2007) also made the interesting point concerning the Solar Phallus case: if the fantasy were really archetypal, it should be found much more often than only in one psychotic case and in a single ancient text.

An even more severe problem we have today is with Jung's assumption that the archetypes are genetically transferred, to which I will come back later.

Other Jungian authors have pointed out already the inconsistencies and contradictions that can be found in Jung's works regarding the concept of archetypes (e.g., Knox 2003; Hogenson 2004; Pietikainen 1998). If we analyse Jung's writings on archetypes we can find at least four different conceptualizations or explanatory concepts which partly contradict each other[1].

1. A Biological Concept

Here Jung parallels the archetypes to instincts in animals. An archetype works in a human being in the same way as an instinct which for example makes birds build their nest in a certain way (Jung 1976, para. 1228). In the first publication where he used the term 'archetype' (Jung 1919) Jung explicitly speaks of the archetype as 'the a priori *innate* forms of intuition ...' (italics added). Jung was apparently very impressed by the works of ethologists and named his concept accordingly 'pattern of behaviour'. 'Ein vererbter Modus des psychischen Funktionierens, korrespondierend der angeborenen Weise, in der das Küken aus dem Ei schlüpft, die Vögel ihr Nest bauen, usw ... Mit anderen Worten, es ist ein pattern of behaviour. Dieser Aspekt des Archetyps, der rein biologische, ist der eigentliche Gegenstand der wissenschaftlichen Psychologie' (Jung 1976, para. 1228).

The most important protagonist of this approach in Jungian psychology today is Anthony Stevens (1983, 2003). In this conceptualization archetypes are genetically encoded and transferred and this is the explanation for their universality.

---

1 Knox (2003, pp. 24-39) has elaborated a differentiation of meanings of the term archetype in Jung's texts which focuses on the content of the concepts whereas the typology proposed here focuses on the theoretical background of the conceptualizations as well as on their development in analytical psychology up to today.

2. An Empirical, Statistical Definition

As mentioned before Jung found a number of complexes in his association studies which were inter-individually similar and he assumed
that there is a common core to these. This notion is not well known
in analytical psychology which must be regretted since this is one
of the few strong empirical findings which support that there must
be something like archetypes. This argument was taken up in 2001
by Saunders and Skar who say plainly that archetypes are those
complexes that fall into the same category.

3. A Transcendental Concept

Jung compares his concept of archetypes in several writings with
Plato's ideas. He says they are positioned in no real place but in a
transcendental sphere, a position which is strongly connected with
his idea of the *unus mundus*. The true archetype is not accessible to
consciousness but is of a transcendental nature. The archetype even
has an *a priori* knowledge of its aim which comes close to supernatural
forces (Jung 1960, para. 411; 1959, para. 68). The most important
contemporary supporter of this approach to archetypes is James
Hillman with his archetypal psychology, where he says very clearly
that archetypes have nothing to do with the physiology of the brain,
the structure of language, the organization of society or analysis of
behaviour but have their place in imagination (Hillman 1983).

4. A Cultural Approach

After 1947, when Jung reconceptualized the concept as archetypal
image on the one hand and the archetype-as-such which is content
free, he explicitly said that the content of the archetypal image is
culturally influenced. Here Jung follows in the tradition of German
philosophy from Leibniz and Kant to Ernst Cassirer (Pietikainen
1998), which has always assumed that there are a priori categories of
perception. The human mind consists of universal forms which shape
human perception and action.

Even more important in my eyes is what actually Jung did throughout most of his life: he interpreted psychologically texts, dreams and
fantasies. His practical approach to psychology was hermeneutical.
So here we find Jung in a line with a tradition of hermeneutics and
cultural theory, even though his own self understanding was different
and more that of a natural scientist.

When we look at these different approaches all together in
Jung's work it becomes obvious that they at least partly contradict
each other (see also Knox 2003): a concept that is thought to be

transcendental and having no place in this world cannot be at the same time a biological entity and part of the genetic code. Jung mixes up theories that are categorically on different levels and incompatible. There is no consistent theory of archetypes in Jung and in my view it is still missing in analytical psychology. Even more problematic is that Jung never discusses the inconsistencies and contradictions in his theory so that it must be assumed that he was not conscious of them; he insisted on the archetypes being a biological reality. His concept of the archetype-as-such is no real solution to this problem: he claims that the archetype-as-such is content free, but if we take any example, e.g., the archetype of the hero, it cannot be seen as free of content. It is difficult to imagine even a single mental concept which carries no content, as Knox (2003, p. 33) has pointed out already.

Another problem with the theory of archetypes is that in analytical psychology a huge number of things and very different concepts are called archetypal:

- Primitive modes of perception (e.g., the experience of being held)

- Objects and beings (e.g., archetype of the snake)

- Social patterns (e.g., marriage)

- Narrative patterns (e.g., myth of the hero)

- Images (e.g., the cross)

- Rituals (e.g., initiation)

- Religious ideas (e.g., sacrifice)

What I want to point out is the high necessity of formulating a consistent theory of what we mean when we say something is archetypal. The first question that has to be answered in this way is:

What do we need the concept of archetypes for in analytical psychology?

I can see two points here:

1. It is *an explanatory theory* for psychological and cultural phenomena; for example, to explain the similarity between fairy tales from different parts of the world or obviously irrational motives in collective movements.

2. The theory of archetypes has importance for the *clinical practice* of Jungian psychotherapy: there is the idea at the base of our clinical work that there are universal patterns of healthy development given to all human beings, at least as a potential, and these patterns can be activated in the process of analysis so that they guide the therapeutic process to a good end, '*deo concedente*'.

This means that a concept of *universal* archetypes is necessary for analytical psychology, since we rely on the existence of all archetypes in everyone of our clients. If we could not rely on this we could not work in the way we do.

It also means that the kind of archetypes that is interesting for analytical psychology are those of a complex and symbolic nature: archetypes that describe process patterns, transformations from a starting point to a solution, patterns which can be transferred into narrative form. The 'archetype of the stone', for example, is theoretically not really necessary for analytical psychology, neither for the explanation of cultural phenomena nor for clinical use. This aspect of archetypes as universal patterns is very important for my argumentation: in my view it is at the core of what Jung meant by the term archetype, it is at the core of analytical psychology and its clinical practice and none of the theories I will describe here has given a satisfying theoretical explanation of how this universality comes into existence up to now.

The Biological Conceptualization

To form a consistent theory of archetypes which takes into account the findings of contemporary sciences I will now discuss Jung's claim of a biological and genetical transfer of archetypes and how this is supported or contradicted by modern genetics.

First, it has to be said that the parallel Jung made between archetypes in humans and instincts in animals is not supported. Norbert Bischoff, a professor of psychology at Zürich University, has published a distinctive and sophisticated study of Jung's theory in the light of modern developmental psychology and biology (Bischoff 1997). He points out very clearly that there can be no parallel between instinctive patterns in animals on the one hand and complex symbolic structures such as mythological stories or rituals in human beings on the other. Jung mixes up two things that are on two intrinsically different levels. Unfortunately this work by Bischoff was never really received in analytical psychology as has happened with a number of important scientific findings which could have changed our views on some major concepts.

Modern Genetics

'*Looking back our assumptions about the way the human genome works were so extremely naïve that it is almost embarrassing*' (Craig Venter, Human Genome Project).

This has happened most forcibly to our understanding of genetics. As the quote from Craig Venter shows, the scientific understanding of human genetics has changed fundamentally in the last two decades.

To put it simply Jung and analytical psychology still today base the biological conception of archetypes on a view of genetics that could be called '*the blueprint model*' (Knox 2003). Jung like many people still do today thought that genes are something like a blueprint, a plan of the human being to be, which is put into reality step by step in prenatal and early life development without any influence from outside. This is parallel to a main school of thought we find in Jung, that the human being in its true nature is somehow preformatted and therefore more or less independent from societal and parental influences. This blueprint model was the base for the decade-long debate over nurture or nature. On this basis it was very easy for Jung to assume that something that is as universal as the archetypes must be genetically encoded.

This opposition of genetics versus developmental influences has become obsolete through the findings of modern genetics. There are especially two areas of research that are most interesting for our topic here: first, the findings of the Human Genome Project and, second, the new field of epigenetics.

One of the most surprising findings of the Human Genome Project was the fact that there are only 24 000 genes in the human genome (Bauer 2008). Originally it was assumed that there were more. This means that the space for information to be transferred via genes is extremely limited; genes can only encode the information for building certain proteins. The biologists are very clear about the fact that symbolic information cannot be encoded genetically. Even if it were possible, it would take an enormous space on the genome to encode something like the myth of the hero pattern. Another fact that we have to realize is that in the human infant when it is newly born there are no mental structures yet for the representation of symbolical information; these develop later in the course of the first year of life (Dornes 1993). Taken together these insights mean that archetypes that carry symbolic information cannot be transferred genetically.

We also know today that there are some innate mental patterns: research on emotions has proved that there are basic emotions that we find in every human infant which can be decoded by humans from all cultures (Ekman et al. 1987); there are innate mental systems for language acquisition (Markmann 1988), something like Chomsky's (1978) 'language acquisition device'; and there are primitive perceptional and behavioural programmes (Dornes 1993). These are important findings since they show that Jung was right and the behaviourists of his time were wrong in assuming that the human infant is a *tabula rasa*. But all these innate mental capacities are on such a primitive level that they are far from the archetypes that we are talking about here.

Epigenetics

Jung based his biological theory of archetypes on the rudimentary knowledge of genetics in his time. The field of new insights into genetics which shows how genes interact with environmental factors is called epigenetics (Bauer 2008); it describes the functioning of genes as a complex interaction of genetic information and environmental factors.

One of these mechanisms of interaction is called demethylation, another is histon-modification (Buiting 2005; Doerfler 2005). To understand this it is necessary to see how genes are built. They do not consist only of an information carrying unit, but they also have a unit which works like a switch, and this so called 'promoter' switches the gene on and off, and this happens depending on environmental cues. This means a gene is not just once activated and then it has done its job but it is switched on and off depending on the information the promoter receives from the environment of the cell and also from the environment of the organism – this is called gen-expression.

In the beginning of development the promoter of a gene can be packed into biochemical structures (methyl-groups) which inhibit the promoter to switch the gene on. Depending again on specific environmental cues the promoter of the gene can become unpacked and start to switch the gene on. A comparable structure is the so-called histon, where the DNA is wrapped around certain biochemical structures which inhibit the reading of the gene.

The most interesting finding of epigenetics for psychology is that it can also be a psychological experience in early relationships with caregivers, leading to demethylation and activation of gene promoters. A well investigated example is the modification of the reaction towards stress in early childhood (Bauer 2006). Motherly care in the first months of life leads, through several steps, to demethylation of the promoter of the glucocorticoid-receptor-gene. This activates reading of the gene and results in a permanent change of the receptor. The level of anti-stress-hormone is therefore permanently higher in humans that have received enough motherly care in the first months of life, a psychological equivalent to a buffer against stress.

To sum up the implications of these findings: of course human beings are carriers of genetic information, but this information is activated only in interaction with environmental factors, especially through experiences in relationships with primary caretakers. Experiences and relationships play a much bigger role than was assumed for a long time. The key term of modern Developmental Systems Theory is not blueprint, but interaction. The nurture-nature debate is obsolete.

These insights are in contradiction with a major line of thought we find in Jung concerning the autonomy of the individual. It is the idea that the individuality of the person, one's own true nature is somehow preformatted and independent of exterior influences. Jung made an important contribution to psychology by stressing the importance of individuality in a generally more extroverted culture, but to me his psychology became one-sided and lost sight of the importance of relationships for development. There is, however, an important exception: the 'Psychology of the transference' (Jung 1948), where he describes relationships as a necessary field for individuation.

An Interactional Theory

Several Jungians have already pointed out the implications of these new findings for archetype theory (Merchant 2006; Knox 2003; Hogenson 2004) and have formulated a new conceptual framework for the explanation of archetypes based on the emergence principle. The most outstanding author here is Jean Knox (2003), whose argumentation I will elaborate on: Newborns are equipped with rudimentary, genetically-coded programmes for perception and behaviour. Biologists of cognition (Johnson & Morton 1991) describe a gene which makes the infant fixate structures that resemble the human face for a longer time than other structures. This does not mean that the infant has a knowledge of the human face or of a person; this pattern is on a very primitive, even reflex level of functioning. But the effect of this pattern on the caretaker is enormous: the caretaker takes the fixating gaze of the infant as an initiation of communication and starts to communicate with the infant. This attracts the attention of the infant and leads to activation of neuronal structures that foster neuronal development. The caretaker is pulled into an attachment with the infant. So this very primitive genetically-fixated pattern has major implications; it starts a sequence of developments that strengthen the attachment bond and support the neuronal development of the infant. This complex development is reached by a minimum of genetic information – but (and here I am departing from Knox's argumentation) it presupposes the existence of a caretaker reacting to the gaze of the infant in the way described. So this developmental sequence depends very much on the existence of a certain environment. If the caretaker, for example, is permanently drunk and does not realize the gaze of the infant, no developmental sequence will start and the genetic information has no effect.

This has direct implications to the assumed universality of archetypes. Jung's idea was that the universality of archetypes could only be secured theoretically if the archetype was conceptualized as genetically fixated. We can see today that the fact that a person carries a certain gene does not necessarily mean that the gene will be activated, this depends very much on environmental factors. Genetical similarity is therefore not equivalent to similar qualities in people. We can say at this point:

- Complex archetypes (symbolic patterns) cannot be transferred genetically.
- Environmental factors, especially interaction with caretakers, have enormous influence on gene expression – they can influence development much more than hereditary factors.
- The similarity and universality of archetypal patterns cannot be secured by genetic encoding.

Merchant (2009, p. 355) goes as far as saying:

If contemporary neuroscience does ultimately reveal that the archetype-as-such is not innate as originally conceived, then the question arises: is the word 'archetype' itself too suffused with innatism and preformationism meanings to prevent confusion? ... for if we think, act and clinically practise as if archetypes are a priori, innate psychic structures which determine psychological life when this is not the case, then we could become irrelevant to the broader psychotherapeutic community.

I would stress even further this point: we Jungians cannot go on basing our theory of archetypes on scientific assumptions that have been proved erroneous by more recent research if we do not want to run the risk of becoming ridiculous in the scientific world. It is important that we stop arguing that archetypes are transferred genetically if we want to be taken seriously (see Knox 2003).

Evidence for the Existence of Archetypes

There is evidence that archetypes exist from different fields, namely, ethnological research and comparative mythology, experimental studies and clinical experience.

Ethnological research: Well before Jung it was widely known that a high degree of similarity prevails in mythological narratives in peoples living far away from each other in different parts of the world. It was even possible to reduce all fairy tales existing in the whole world to a set of less than 100 different types in the Aarne/Thompson-typology (Aarne & Thompson 1964). In a scientific study a randomized sample of 50 mythologies from all over the world was investigated and the incest motif was found in 39 of them (Kluckhohn 1960), which is much more than random. These high parallels in mythological motifs were a topic of heated debate in anthropology as far back as the end of the 19th century. There were two major factions: the migration theory

(Eisenstädter 1912) assumed that there was physical contact between peoples mainly through migration which could explain the parallels. An interesting outgrowth of this line of thought was the journeys made by the anthropologist Thor Heyerdahl, who reconstructed ancient boats and travelled with them across the oceans to give proof of physical contact between far away peoples. The other faction introduced the concept of elementary thoughts (Bastian 1881) according to which basic thoughts and ideas are common to all human communities and these found their way into mythological narratives. It is easy to attribute these 'elementary thoughts' to the idea of archetypes. Jung knew this debate well and took up the idea of elementary thoughts and adapted it to psychology. The interesting thing for our topic is that in anthropology the state of the art since the 1960s sees the migration theory as erroneous. It could be certified in many instances that there could have been no contact between peoples with similar mythological motifs.

Experimental research: More evidence for the existence of archetypes comes from experimental research. In the 1960s several studies with LSD were performed where subjects' phantasies under LSD were documented (Masters & Houston 1966; Grof 1978). The idea was that LSD released deeper, pre-experiential phantasies and put the brains of the participants into a comparable state. The documented phantasies were indeed very similar, the subjects projected numinous qualities on to the scientists; they saw them as gods, priests or personifications of wisdom, and moreover the motifs resembled mythological ones. But of course this research includes a high degree of interpretation.

There is even evidence from two experimental studies conducted by Jungians directly aiming at testing the archetype theory (Rosen et al. 1991; Maloney 1999). Both studies found empirical proof for the existence of archetypal structures.

Preparedness: Seligman (1972), a behavioural psychologist and certainly not a friend of analytical psychology, found a phenomenon which he called 'preparedness': it refers to the interesting fact that humans develop anxieties and especially phobias only towards animals like snakes or spiders, even though they may never have had any contact with them, but not towards birds or cows. He explains this by a biologically-based preparedness which has developed throughout evolution and serves the aim of protecting oneself against poisonous animals – otherwise it would not be possible for one to learn from a first contact experience because one does not survive it.

Attachment research: Anthony Stevens (2003), a Jungian analyst, argues that we find empirical proof of archetypes in the universality of attachment patterns. Attachment research has provided the evidence that every human infant develops an attachment relationship with a caretaker, that this follows universal patterns and that we can find the same set of four different attachment patterns all over the world.

So there is empirical evidence from different disciplines that there must be something like archetypal structures of a psychological nature. But we have also seen that these universal structures or patterns cannot be transferred genetically. So how do these patterns become universal if not by genetics?

There have been several attempts by Jungian authors and researchers to find an explanation for universal archetypes which refer to biological theories but are not grounded in an assumption of genetical transmission.

Gestalt Principle and Dynamic Systems Theory

The Berlin School of Gestalt Psychology (Metzger 1954) identified a quality of our cognitive structure to build a good 'gestalt', which means a stable configuration of perceptions. These good gestalts are therefore ubiquitous. This gestalt principle was empirically supported (Stadler & Kruse 1990). For example, in an experiment subjects were asked to complete patterns of dots again and again out of memory until a stable configuration was reached. In large series and great numbers of subjects the resulting configurations were similar. The factor that produced the similarity was called convergence. It is the same principle that makes the bodies of fish and whales so similar even though the two animals are biologically totally different. The similarities develop because these qualities are the best adaptation to the same conditions.

Gestalt psychology was later included into Dynamic Systems Theory. Saunders and Skar (2001) have adapted this theory for analytical psychology. They opine that when Jung speaks of the archetype as form without content, what he really means is not a form but a process which produces similar patterns. Psychological archetypes in this view are the products of processes of self-organization of the brain. Modern cognitive psychology also states that once the brain has developed a pattern of perception and interpretation, subsequent information is processed on the basis of these existing patterns (Anderson 1983). This explains why different information is processed into similar psychological concepts. It is just a quality of self-organizing systems. This is highly interesting for analytical psychology because it supports Jung's concept of the complexes very well but not so much his archetype theory. 'When we employ a dynamical systems view of development, we no longer need the archetype-as-such to explain the formation of complexes. In fact we could do without it altogether and still have the same basic psychological system that Jung proposed' (Skar 2004, p. 247).

Here we depart from the theory we find in Jung that every part of the archetype is preformatted. The organizational structures of the brain develop from the interaction between innate elements and experiences with the outside world, especially with relationship figures.

The Emergence Model of Archetypes

The most prominent current theory of archetypes takes up this view and sees archetypes as a product of processes of emergence (Knox 2003; Hogenson 2001; Merchant 2006). Emergence is a modern concept used in different sciences today and means that if elements interact and form a coherent system, this system can have completely new qualities which cannot be traced back to the qualities of the original elements. The interaction between basic elements leads to a qualitative jump of the whole system onto a totally different level defined by new laws. Here is an example: water consists of the chemical elements oxygen and hydrogen but has qualities which the original elements do not have, such as crystallization when freezing etc.

Modern Jungian authors use the emergence principle to explain archetypal structures; they state: universal archetypes are the emergent products of the developmental dynamics of brain, environment and socialization. The most elaborated formulation of this approach is in Jean Knox's (2003) book, *Archetype, Attachment, Analysis*. In it she sees development starting from basic schemas which are genetically-based, but these are just predispositions for development which need certain cues from the environment to unfold.

> Innate mechanisms focus the infant's attention onto features in the environment which are crucial to the infant's survival; these mechanisms are biologically based and have arisen by the process of natural selection because they improve chances of survival. Innate mechanisms are activated by environmental cues, interacting with them and organizing them, leading to the formation of primitive spatial and conceptual representations (image schemas or archetypes). These form the foundation on which later more complex representations can be built.
>
> (Knox 2001, p. 631)

Coming back to the aforementioned example of the gene that makes the infant look at faces, according to Knox the basic innate schema is the archetype-as-such, whereas the neuronal structures and the first primitive representations developing from the interaction are the content of the archetype. This complex development is reached by a minimum of genetic information – but it presupposes the presence of a caretaker which reacts to the gaze of the infant in the way described. So this developmental sequence depends very much on the existence of a certain environment.

Now the emergentists claim that the emerging archetypal structures are universal because the environmental conditions in this early stage of development are the same or, to quote Knox:

> these image schemas ... are not innate, but already reflect a considerable degree of learning. The pattern of learning is nearly identical for all children because certain key features of the environment that the child's attention is focused on remain constant across all cultures.
>
> (Knox 2003, pp. 61-62)

How can we assume the universal similarity of these processes when we look at the enormous differences in the conditions under which children grow up today? Or could it be that Knox refers to a form of archetypes that are so primitive that they are really acquired reliably by all children, e.g., 'containment' – and even this is not experienced by all children? But then there remains a huge gap between these primitive schemas and the concept Jung is talking of when, e.g., he speaks of the myth of the hero as an archetype. Either way the emergence model is no real solution to the explanation of a universality of complex symbolic archetypes. There is too much on the way of their development that could disturb the process of acquisition at least to the extent that there are major differences in the archetypes thus acquired – so they would not be universal any more. I am not the only one to criticize that. This is what John Merchant says:

> It does need to be noted at this point that it is still not clear why any one person's archetypal imagery takes the form that it does if it is not arising from innate archetypes. ... The crucial point is that such imagery would be arising out of mind brain structures which are themselves derived from early preverbal developmental experience and not from innate archetypes. The ramifications are substantial, for the very existence of archetypes as Jung conceived them is called into question.
>
> (Merchant 2009, p. 342)

As we have seen even similar genetic information does not necessarily produce similar developments. We have also seen that early developmental processes and their achievements can easily be disturbed to the extent that certain developments do not happen at all. The structure of the brain is not similar from person to person because its development is so strongly influenced by early experiences, e.g., a person with an early traumatization has a different brain than a person without this experience (Bauer 2002).

Should we therefore give up the idea of universal psychological archetypes? All these findings and new insights from modern genetics, the neurosciences and developmental research force us to reformulate our theory of archetypes.

The first and most important point is that we should give up the assumption of a genetical transmission of complex symbolic archetypes, for everything we know about genetics today speaks against it. This leads automatically to the second point: archetypes can only be understood as a cultural and social phenomenon.

I will try now to reformulate a theory of archetypes which is supported by the insights we have today.

A Reformulation

First, we have to differentiate between different levels of what we call archetypal. I can see three levels.

First Level: Innate Basic Schemas/Patterns

These are actually genetically-based but are too primitive to be compared with the complex symbolic archetypes that we talk of in analytical psychology. These very basic schemas direct the attention of the infant towards interaction with the caretaker and this starts a complex process of interaction which forms a secure relationship on the one hand and fosters neuronal development of the infant on the other. These basic schemas become templates for more complex structures in the way Knox (2003) describes it. However, this process depends very much on the psychological and social capabilities of the caretaker and is therefore easily disturbed, to the extent that when there are certain interactional qualities missing in the caretaker certain developmental processes will not start at all. So interaction plays a much more important role than Jung ever thought of in his concept of archetypes.

An interesting aspect of these innate basic schemas is that they somehow presuppose certain qualities in the environment, especially on the side of the primary caretaker. Some of the innate structures only make sense if they meet a certain activity of the caretaker in the outside world. It is as if the genetically-based equipment of the infant expects a 'good mother' outside. This could be called archetypal.

Second Level: Repeated Experiences in Relationships with Caretakers

In the early relationship with the caretaker there are certain interactions that take place regularly and are experienced by the infant as happening again and again in the same form. From infant research we know that here generalized representations of these repeated interactions are formed (Stern 1985). On the basis of these representations the infant develops expectations, which are basically what in analytical psychology we call complexes (see Kast 1990). For example, the infant experiences every time it feels uneasy and starts crying that mother will come and give care and comfort; so with time the infant will build an expectation that it can express its needs and will get a response of good enough mothering. Cognitive psychology shows that once such a cognitive pattern is established it tends to be used for subsequent experiences.

Now we have seen that the experiences of the infant in these early relationships are inter-individually different, depending on the qualities of the caretaker. On the other hand since these relationships are so basic there is not an endless number of different patterns, but a limited number of typical patterns of relationships and their development throughout mankind. Attachment research has investigated this field thoroughly and has found four typical patterns of attachment that we find in all cultures – so here we have universal patterns. Attachment patterns are just an example of the fact that human experience on this level is organized in a limited number of universal patterns. But these patterns are still on a preverbal, pre-symbolic level. What is the bridge to the complex, symbolic patterns that we call archetypes?

Third Level: Culturally-Transmitted Narrative Patterns

Narrative can build this bridge from the preverbal representations of relationship experiences to complex symbolic structures. The linguistic form in which these early experiences can be represented in the human mind is the narrative, for narratives describe action patterns including self and other, starting from a problem and leading to a solution (Gülich/Quasthoff 1985). Early representations are therefore something like preverbal precursors of narratives.

We can imagine that a child on the basis of an early experience of loneliness, at least in the emotional sense, has a certain representation of a more distant attachment figure that is not really available. Now the child gets to know the fairy tale of 'Hänsel and Gretel' and it 'recognizes' on a subliminal level a similarity between the story structure and its own experience.

The typical patterns of human experience in relationships and their development are described in symbolic form by narratives of the cultural canon (mythologies, religious stories, fairy tales etc.). They are culturally transmitted because of their typicality, because they are relevant for all men, and therefore they have become part of traditions and rituals of transmission. Individuals can recognize their own preverbal experience in the narrative patterns because they experience a similarity between story schema and their generalized representations or working models, as attachment theory would call these.

Jungian psychology has always seen the mythological narratives of fairy tales, for example, as descriptions of typical human experiences starting with a problematic situation and describing the process leading to its solution (von Beit 1952-57; von Frantz 1986). We use them for therapeutic reasons because they picture typical human experience and ways of solution.

There is a problem arising with this view: are the archetypes on this level still universal? Can we expect to find the whole canon in every individual? The transmission of the totality of the cultural narrative canon then must depend on socialization.

Ways of Subliminal Transmission

I would like to propose the thesis that there exists something like an 'acquisition device for archetypal patterns' in the sense of Chomsky's language acquisition device, a human preparedness to recognize and acquire certain information like archetypal process patterns more easily than other information. I assume that there is something about archetypal patterns or information which makes it easily accessible to the human mind either by explicit verbal transmission or by subliminal transmission.

There is evidence from different sources that there must be something as a subliminal, unconscious transmission of complex information from one generation to the other.

One source is research that was done in Israel and Germany on the transmission of traumatic experience in the context of war and the Shoa (Gampel 2009; Radebold 2009). In Israel it is a common phenomenon that the children and grandchildren of the survivors of the Holocaust suffer from symptoms and 'memories' usually connected with severe traumatization. This seems to happen especially if the first generation of the survivors did not communicate their experiences in the family. There is the general assumption that the traumatic experience was communicated unconsciously, but nevertheless in great detail.

More evidence comes from the neuroscientific research on mirror neurons (Gallese 1998; Rizzolati 2004) and the concept of the 'shared meaningful intersubjective space' (Gallese 2003). A few years ago neuroscientists discovered so-called mirror neurons which produce the same emotional state in the brain of an observer as in the brain of the person performing a certain action. This is now seen as the basis for imitation learning and empathy. There are specialized mirror neuron systems for action patterns as well as for emotions. This explains why we can get infected by others' emotions (Singer et al. 2006).

Neuroscientists now go even further and assume that through the mirror neurons human beings can develop an 'inter-individual neuronal format', a 'shared intersubjective space' (Bauer 2005, pp. 166-67; author's translation). In this space 'the spectrum of all typical human sequences of actions and experiences can be activated and communicated preverbally'. It is obvious that the development of this intersubjective space meant a major advantage in the process of evolution since the individuals do not have to make all the typical experiences by themselves but can acquire them via subliminal communication in the intersubjective space.

Neuroscientists have no intention to prove Jungian concepts, but at the same time their work seems to be a neuroscientific reformulation of our concept of the collective unconscious – they even call it 'a memory of mankind'. Of course this conceptualization is far from the idea of genetically-transferred archetypes but it stresses the importance of interaction and the socialization processes.

Are Archetypes Still Universal?

On the basis of the concept of the intersubjective space we could still argue for a certain universality of archetypes. Cultures do have specialized forms for transferring the canon of archetypal patterns from one generation to the other as with ritualistic practices, narrative traditions etc. But this depends very much on what is actually transferred in processes of interaction. So we must ask, does the transmission of archetypes depend on stable cultural structures and processes? For 'socialization into archetypes' probably certain social and cultural structures are necessary, such as in narrative traditions, religious forms etc. How can we be certain that every individual in our postmodern cultures is exposed to these processes? This has major implications for our clinical practice if we cannot count on the presence of every archetype in every one of our clients. All practising psychotherapists have experienced clients in whom the healing archetypal images cannot be activated.

Conclusion

The most important message here is that everything we know today speaks against the idea of a genetic transmission of archetypes, so we should give up this concept. The memory of mankind, the collective unconscious does not have its place in biology, but in culture and socialization. The transmission of typical patterns of experience depends much more on interaction and cultural processes than Jung ever thought of. This has already been stated by Henderson (1990) in his concept of the cultural unconscious where he says, 'much of what Jung called personal was actually culturally conditioned', and in the concept of the cultural complex by Singer where he says, 'much of what Jung called collective was cultural' (Singer & Kimbles 2004, p. 184).

There is a growing awareness in the sciences that there are processes of communication and transmission on a subliminal level, however. This gives support to Jung's concept of an unconscious interpersonal sphere. We are not born with a collective unconscious, but we grow into it. It is most important that we stay in contact with these developing theories of unconscious communication processes but that means we have to stay open to modifying our concepts.

I would like to give Jung the last word here: 'Culture is part of man's nature.'

References

Aarne, A. & Thompson, S. (1961). *The Types of the Folktale. A Classification and Bibliography.* Helsinki: Suomalainen Tiedeakat, 2nd edn.

Anderson, J.R. (1983). *The Architecture of Cognition.* Cambridge Mass., Harvard University Press.

Bair, D. (2003). *Jung. A Biography.* Boston: Little Brown.

Bastian, A. (1881). *Der Völkergedanke im Aufbau einer Wissenschaft vom Menschen.* Berlin: Dietrich Reimer.

Bauer, J. (2002). *Das Gedächtnis des Körpers. Wie Beziehungen und Lebenstile unsere Gene steuern.* Frankfurt/M.: Eichborn.

– (2006). *Prinzip Menschlichkeit. Warum wir von Natur aus kooperieren.* Hamburg: Hoffmann & Campe.

– (2008). *Das Kooperative Gen. Abschied vom Darwinismus.* Hamburg: Hoffmann & Campe.

Bischoff, N. (1997). *Das Kraftfeld der Mythen.* München: Piper.

Buiting, K. (2005). 'Epigenetische Vererbung'. Medizinische Genetik, 17, 292-95.

Chomsky, N. (1978). *Topics in the Theory of Generative Grammar.* Den Haag: Mouton.

Eisenstädter, J. (1912). *Elementargedanke und Übertragungstheorie in der Völkerkunde.* Stuttgart: Strecker & Schröder.

Ekman, P., Friesen, W., O'Sullivan, M., Chan, A. (1987). 'Universals and cultural differences in the judgment of facial expressions of emotions'. *Journal of Personality and Social Psychology,* 53, 712-17.

Doerfler, W. (2005). 'DNA-Methylierung – ein wichtiges genetisches Signal in Biologie und Pathogenese'. Medizinische Genetik, 17, 260-64.

Dornes, M. (1993). *Der kompetente Säugling.* Frankfurt/M.: Fischer.

Gallese, V. (2003). 'The roots of empathy: The shared manifold hypothesis and the neural basis of intersubjectivity'. *Psychopathology,* 36, 171-80.

Gallese V., Goldman A. (1998). 'Mirror neurons and the simulation theory of mind-reading'. *Trends in Cognitive Sciences,* 2, 493-501.

Gampel Y. (2008). *Kinder der Shoah. Die transgenerationelle Weitergabe seelischer Zerstörung.* Gießen: Psychosozial.

Grof, S. (1978). *Topographie des Unbewussten: LSD im Dienst der tiefenpsychologischen Forschung.* Stuttgart: Klett-Cotta.

Gülich, E. & Quasthoff, U. (1985). 'Narrative analysis'. In *Handbook of Discourse Analysis, Vol. II: Dimensions of Discourse,* ed. T.A. Van Dijk. London: Academic Press, 169-97.

Henderson J. (1991). 'C.G.Jung's psychology: additions and extensions'. *Journal of Analytical Psychology,* 36, 429-42.

Hillman, J. (1983). *Archetypal Psychology: A Brief Account.* Woodstock: Spring.

Hogenson, G. B. (2004). 'Archetypes: emergence and the psyche's deep structure'. In *Analytical Psychology: Contemporary Perspectives in Jungian Psychology,* eds. J. Cambray & L. Carter. Hove, New York: Brunner-Routledge.

Johnson, M.H. & Morton, J. (1991). *Biology and Cognitive Development: The Case of Face Recognition.* Oxford: Blackwell.

Jung, C.G. (1919). 'Instinct and the unconscious'. *British Journal of Psychology,* 10, 1, 15-23.

— (1912/1956). *Symbols of Transformation. CW* 5.

— (1948). 'Die Psychologie der Übertragung' ('The psychology of the transference'). *CW* 16.

— (1959). *The Archetypes and the Collective Unconscious. CW* 9i.

— (1960). *The Structure and Dynamics of the Psyche. CW* 8.

— (1976). *The Symbolic Life. CW* 18.

— (1973). *Experimental Researches. CW* 2.

Kast, V. (1990). *Die Dynamik der Symbole. Grundlagen der Jungschen Psychotherapie.* Olten, Germany: Walter.

Knox, J (2001). 'Memories, fantasies, archetypes: an exploration of some connections between cognitive science and analytical psychology'. *Journal of Analytical Psychology,* 46, 4, 613-35.

— (2003). *Archetype, Attachment, Analysis. Jungian Psychology and the Emergent Mind.* Hove: Brunner-Routledge.

Kluckhohn, C. (1960). 'Recurrent themes in myth and mythmaking'. In *Myth and Mythmaking,* ed. H.A. Murray. New York: Braziler, 46-60.

Maloney, A. (1999). 'Preference ratings of images representing archetypal themes: an empirical study of the concept of archetypes'. *Journal of Analytical Psychology,* 44, 1, 101-16.

Masters, R.E.L. & Houston, J. (1966). *The Variety of Psychedelic Experience.* New York: Dell.

Merchant, J. (2006). 'The developmental/emergent model of archetype, its implications and its application to shamanism'. *Journal of Analytical Psychology,* 51, 125-44.

— (2009). 'Reappraisal of classical archetype theory'. *Journal of Analytical Psychology,* 54, 339-58.

Metzger, W. (1954). *Psychologie. Die Entwicklung ihrer Grundannahmen seit der Einführung des Experiments.* Darmstadt: Steinkopff.

Pietikainen, P. (1998). 'Archetypes as symbolic forms'. *Journal of Analytical Psychology,* 43, 3, 325-43.

Radebold, H. et al. (2008). *Transgenerationelle Weitergabe kriegsbelasteter Kindheiten.* Weinheim: Juventa.

Rizzolati, G, Craighero, L. (2004): 'The mirror-neuron system'. *Annual Review of Neuroscience* 27, 169-92.

Rosen, D. H., Smith, S.M., Huston, H.L., Gonzalez, G. (1991). 'Empirical study of associations between symbols and their meaning: evidence of collective unconscious (archetypal) memory'. *Journal of Analytical Psychology*, 36, 211-28.

Saunders, P. & Skar, P. (2001). 'Archetypes, complexes and self-organization'. *Journal of Analytical Psychology*, 46, 2, 305-23.

Seligman, M.E., Hager, J.L. (1972). *Biological Boundaries of Learning*. Appleton: Century-Crofts.

Shamdasani, S. (2003). *Jung and the Making of Modern Psychology: The Dream of a Science*. Cambridge: Cambridge University Press.

Singer, T. & Kimbles, J. (2004). 'Emerging theory of cultural complexes'. In *Analytical Psychology: Contemporary Perspectives in Jungian Psychology*, eds. J. Cambray & L. Carter. Hove, New York, Brunner-Routledge.

Singer, T., Seymour, B., O'Doherty, J.P., Stephan, K.E., Dolan, R.J., Frith, C.D. (2006). 'Empathic neural responses are modulated by the perceived fairness of others'. *Nature*, 439, 466-69.

Skar, P. (2004). 'Chaos and self-organization: emergent patterns at critical life transitions'. *Journal of Analytical Psychology*, 49, 245-64.

Stadler, M. & Kruse, P. (1990). 'The self-organization perspective in cognition research'. In *Synergetics of Cognition*, eds. H. Haken & M. Stadler. Berlin: Springer.

Stern, D. (1985). *The Interpersonal World of the Infant: A View from Psychoanalysis and Developmental Psychology*. New York: Basic Books.

Stevens, A. (1983). *Archetype: A Natural History of the Self*. New York: William Morrow.

– (2003). *Archetype Revisited: An Updated Natural History of the Self*. Toronto: Inner City Books.

von Franz, M.-L. (1986). *Psychologische Märcheninterpretation*. München: Kösel.

von Beit, H. (1952-57). *Symbolik des Märchens*. Bern: Francke.

Emotion: The Essential Force in Nature, Psyche and Culture

Beverley Zabriskie
USA (JPA)

Emotion is a primal force. It moves us, moves in and through us, around and beyond us.

In *nature*, emotions serve survival. Alert to external conditions, they signal for action. At the effect of time and place, they provoke immediate reaction. On the spectrum of evolution, we share basic survival emotions with creatures, reptilian and mammalian.

In *culture*, emotions engage us in our surround, enabling us to adapt, calibrate, sublimate, respond, evaluate. They refract, reflect, and resonate. Acculturated emotions transmute discharge and action into expression and communication. In groups and peoples, emotions create community or cult. They also rouse – to bind and divide. They emerge in the images of art and the sounds of music.

In *psyche*, emotions announce our soul and mind states. They script our internal dialogues, landscape our dream terrains, sculpt the figures of creativity and imagination. In psyche, emotions are not bound to time, but rather collapse past, present, and future. They re-evoke, re-infuse, re-colour, re-frame, re-transcribe and re-calibrate our memories, while imprinting consciousness as 'the remembered present'. Emotions anticipate what is to come.

The emotional loops of our complexes simultaneously tell the time of our lives, but also shatter time and space as they inform the *time-less-ness* of dreams and psychic experience. In psyche, emotions leap out and up as deities on whom we call; in soma, emotions go down and within, in the pains and aches that bedevil us.

The density, complexity, and plasticity of emotions give psyche its dynamism. They influence psyche's fixity and fluidity, stability and combustibility, cohesiveness and dissociability. They infuse and display, as affect, sentiment, feeling and passion. They foment discord and allow attunement.

In this brief paper (a Jungian form of speed-dating) I hope words will carry emotion, via a phenomenon Jungians might call *coniunctio*, neuroscientists call neural coupling, or term strange-loop phenomena.

And I hope, in this large space, images of felt and reflected emotion in facial expressions, hand gestures, and body language, will create an emotional field and provide living experience of the primacy of emotion, its multiple impacts and effects.

Here and now, as 'bundles' or 'quanta' of immediate emotions and emotional memories, we are metabolizing and mutating emotions in acculturated derivatives and person-specific combinations of the basic, universal emotions: sorrow, fear, anger, joy, disgust, surprise.

Emotions *are also* images – the images we perceive in the fleeting moments of every session and in our waking and sleeping hours.

In numerous creation myths, emotion is the source of the world. The god is lonely – and creates the universe. The god laughs, cries, and from the crack between laughter and tears, humanity comes into being.

The Egyptian notions of 'thought of the heart' and 'the tongue that speaks the heart's words' prevailed for centuries, until rationalistic philosophies dualized brain and body, heart and mind. Centuries later, the alchemical notion of interconnected sympathetic correspondence was displaced by the Cartesian construct of 'I think, therefore I am.' Emotion was extracted, split from, subordinated to, and devalued by cognition.

Emotion was a *fascinosum* for Jung. Through the years, he changed his definitions of emotion, affect, and feeling, and perceived it in many guises: as numbers one and two personalities; as trance and hysteria; as personal complex and impersonal symbols; in active imagination and cultural ritual; as awe, manna and numinosity; as mythic figures and conjured gods of mantic rites; as epiphanies experienced at the margins, termed holy or religious.

Jung's passage through '*forms of dread emotions*' configured the uncanny personae of his *Red Book*. While he then called it pre-cognition, today we could also see its imagery emerging from his emotional attunement and porousness to the pre-war dread in his environment.

Emotion is assumed in Jung's complex psychology and descriptions of psyche. In various passages, he defines psyche as *a process, a self-regulating system*, a dynamic '*equilibration between all kinds of opposites*', and '*a multiplicity within a unity*'. He also terms psyche '*an un-extended intensity … gradually rising from minute extensity to infinite intensity*'.

In the various domains of psychic experience, negotiations among emotions *are* the *process* of psyche. Emotions are that which *regulates and are regulated* for the sake of equilibrium and resilience. Emotions secrete our chemistry, and form the hues, temperatures, weights and measures in the physics of psyche. Emotions configure psyche's *multiplicity and* enforce its *intensity*.

In Jung's typological scheme, right and wrong relationship to emotions determines whether ego's four functions are ordered and effective, or disordered, disoriented and dysfunctional. Emotional context determines whether we are imprinted or have choice. Right relationship to emotions allows values to be shaped, ideals to be formed. Jung quotes Goethe: 'Feeling is All.'

For Jung, emotions are the mercurial messengers between psyche and soma. Emotions are intrinsic to the surprise of dream anomalies, insights and synchronicities.

I turned to the study of emotion after years of Jungian practice. I have primarily resided in the ultraviolet realm of alchemical analogies and the mythopoeic metaphors of imaginal process. And then I read again Jung's dictum at Tavistock: '*It is even the doctor's duty to accept the emotions of the patient and to mirror them.*'

I realized that to accept and mirror patients' emotions, I must first recognize the sources, contents, dynamics and purposes of human emotions: when fear is fear, when anger is anger – or displacement of sorrow or flight from fear; when disgust serves survival; when present grief honours past fullness; when today's morbidity resists tomorrow's life; when joy invites celebration, when surprise signals entry of the emergent, the creative, the synchronistic.

My re-reading of Jung has taken me to current emotion research, and then back to Jungian psychology, as an affective, therapeutic opus, convergent with current research of emotion. In Jung, emotions *are* the link, the rainbow arc between the infrared of instinct to the ultraviolet of image,

In the Jungian corpus, and in neuroscience's literature, there is still no agreed, single meaning of emotion. Nonetheless, after centuries of dismissal, in the last two decades, emotion has been a serious subject in the sciences. Just as Jung relativised the rational ego fantasy with his theory of emotionally-toned complexes, so too the Enlightenment supremacy of a cognitive intellect is being relativised by a monistic body-mind network of 'I feel therefore I am', and 'I feel, therefore I think.'

As Jungian practitioners, we are alert to emotion. Emotion was mentioned 445 times during the programme of the 2004 Barcelona Congress; 312 times at the 2007 Cape Town Congress. Even without a consensual definition, we know emotion when we see and hear it, smell and are stirred by it.

But there are rare mentions of Jung or analytical psychology in my mountain of non-Jungian books on emotion. In *The Nature of Emotion, Fundamental Questions* (editors Ekman and Davidson), James Averill's chapter is entitled 'I Feel, Therefore I am, I think'. He writes:

> *Two types of emotion theories can be distinguished, corresponding roughly to the distinction between feelings of and feelings about. The well-known theory of William James is a good example of the former. According to James, emotions are basically feelings of bodily changes as*

they occur. Carl Jung provides an equally good illustration of the second view. According to Jung (1921) emotional feelings are essentially value judgments – feelings about. From a Jungian standpoint, if I am asked to describe my emotional feelings, I would not describe bodily sensations: instead, I would indicate how I evaluate the situation. Most contemporary theories of emotion tend to combine feelings of and feelings about.

The Encyclopaedia Britannica entry on emotion reads:

From the very beginning of scientific psychology, there were voices that spoke of the significance of emotions for human life. James believed that 'individuality is founded in feeling' and that only through feeling is it possible 'directly to perceive how events happen, and how work is actually done'. The Swiss psychiatrist Carl Gustav Jung recognized emotion as the primal force in life.

The author then quotes Jung:

emotion is the moment when steel meets flint and a spark is struck forth, for emotion is the chief source of consciousness. There is no change from darkness to light or from inertia to movement without emotion.

Referenced or not, the current neuroscience of emotions is confirming the instinctive-affective-archetypal-predisposition of the human personality, and the emotional field theory implicit in Jung's analytic mode. Cited or not, Jung and those Jungians who have studied emotion are echoed when neuroscientists write of 'theories of other minds', of attunement, mirror neurons, strange-loop exchange, emergence from complexity, neural coupling and neuronal mapping, and the emotional basis of personality.

Listen to the echoes of Jung in the following excerpts.

Le Doux writes: '*The central revelation of the scientific study of emotion is that our brain is as much if not more an emotional organ as it is a cognitive one.*' He continues: [For] '*emotional experience derives from emotional schemas not just from cognitive interpretations or physiological arousal'.* He then states: '*Many emotions are products of evolutionary wisdom, which probably has more intelligence than all human minds together.*' Another researcher notes that '*emotional memory is a particularly strong function. The current effect of prior emotional learning often is stronger than our cognitive learning or emotional process.*'

Ramachandran asserts: '*Although emotions are phylogenetically ancient and regarded as more primitive, in humans they are probably just as sophisticated as reason.*' He suggests raw emotions and automatic processes in a first brain are prepared for and delivered to a higher order, meta-representation in a second brain, and remarks: '*this implies a homunculus as either meta-representation itself, or another brain structure that emerged later in evolution for creating meta-representations*'.

Jung presented kinship emotion as the force which shapes the personality in the world. He wrote, '*without the conscious acknowledgement and acceptance of our kinship with those around us there can be no synthesis of personality ... The inner consolidation of the individual emphatically includes our fellow man.*'

Individuation is thus not a stance outside, beside, or above emotional fields, but rather in right relationship to emotion within and around us.

The neuroscientist Ramachandran makes a radical statement which confirms and furthers our views of such becoming:

> We are all merely many reflections in a hall of mirrors of a single cosmic reality ... as you grow older and memories start to fade you may have less in common with, and be less 'informationally coupled', to your own youthful self than with someone who is now your close personal friend. This is especially true if you consider the barrier-dissolving nature of mirror neurons. There is certain grandeur in this view of life, this enlarged conception of reality.

Just as miners and metallurgists once delivered materials from the innards of the earth for alchemical experiment and meditation, today neuroscience tracks the physiology of how emotions affect body and brain. The neuro-psychoanalyst Regina Pally writes:

> Neuroscience offers psychoanalysis the opportunity for a deeper understanding of how our perceptions are shaped by the past, by our emotions, and by influences of which we are unaware.

As Jungians, we in turn have data to provide neuroscience. Jung privileged emotions from the immediate therapeutic field, preferring a relativised transference within a relational model of face to face analysis. Jungian process engages the al-chemistry of emotions in the interactive fields of intrapsychic and interpersonal dynamics. We can thus illustrate how emotions affect mind, psyche, relationship in a lived life, and how these are reflected in the macro dynamics of the world.

I end with the fuller version of Jung referring to 'the fire of affects and emotions':

> Like every fire, it has two aspects, of combustion and of creating light. ... emotion is the alchemical fire whose warmth brings everything into existence and whose heat burns all superfluities to ashes ... emotion is the moment when steel meets flint and a spark is struck forth, for emotion is the chief source of consciousness. There is no change from darkness to light or from inertia to movement without emotion.

Panel
Working with Multiplicity Within –
Jung, Trauma, Neurobiology and the Healing
Process: A Clinical Perspective

Margaret Wilkinson & Ruth A. Lanius

Introduction

It was with great pleasure that I heard Ruth Lanius, Professor of Neuroscience at the University of Western Ontario, Canada, would be able to be with us at the IAAP Conference. It has been a privilege to get to know her and to learn of her cutting-edge research concerning trauma and the respect for a Jungian perspective that she brings to her work.

In our presentation we sought to explore the theme of 'Facing Multiplicity' in relation to Jung's thought, to current neuroscience, attachment theory and clinical models of dissociation. We looked at the effects of trauma and their significance concerning the development of a robust sense of self from our individual perspectives in relation to insights from neuroscience and their significance in the consulting-room.

* * *

Facing Multiplicity Within:
A Brief Exploration of the Origins and Development
of a Dissociative Defence

Margaret Wilkinson

UK (SAP)

Looking back over 30 years of practice I realize that my work with one young person early in my career was helpful to my own understanding of Jung's perspective of dissociation and of multiplicity as it is manifest within the psyches of my adult analytic patients who have suffered early relational trauma. I wish to review something of my work with this patient in the light of insights from neurobiology.

The Earliest Development of Multiplicity in the Psyche

Research has demonstrated that the baby's right hemisphere is on line from birth and readily available for the affective engagement between mother and baby that gradually builds the baby's brain-mind. The mother's feeling states directly determine the earliest feeling states of her infant, gradually building the patterns in the baby's developing mind that this new human being will use to determine future relational experience. A troubled mother will convey her sadness, anger, frustration, anxiety, fear or terror directly to her baby. Children who have become thoroughly confused and shocked by what has been offered by the mother cannot discern whether to avoid or to move closer to mother, to dread or to cling; their emotional world is filled with confusion, there is no clear path that they may follow that will take them confidently out into a world of successful relating. Schore notes that in Jung's view the self is fundamentally composed of affect experiences and observes that it 'acts as a regulating centre that brings about the maturing of the personality' (Schore 2006, p. ix). Jung explained that in adverse circumstances the dissociative response gives rise to split-off 'autonomous splinter psyches' or traumatic complexes (Jung 1934, para. 203). When the earliest foundations of the personality are flawed then the challenges that life brings are likely to overwhelm the nascent self in the way that Jung described.

Clinical Case: Rona

In thinking about children who may be experienced by their mother as a catastrophe from the beginning I was reminded of Rona, whom I have written more fully about elsewhere (Wilkinson in press, pp. 81-93). Rona was referred to me for counselling in a school-setting when she was eleven years old. I saw her on a regular basis several times a week for her first three years of secondary school and then once a week for the last two years. Rona's mother even before her birth experienced her as unknown, unwanted and feared. Rona was a first and very late child; her mother did not realize that she had become pregnant, believing that she was now past that stage of life. Recounting the arrival of her daughter it was clear that the notion had been so alien to her and so completely not wanted by her that it had seemed to her as if she had not known what was happening to her until her waters broke and then she had waited several days before enlisting medical help. This neglect must have threatened the very existence of her daughter-to-be. She recounted her experience of giving birth as being catastrophic; she went on to describe their early days together in hospital as very difficult. She felt Rona's emotional difficulties in relating were caused by the formula milk that she had been given in hospital. I understood that symbolically to be a description of the difficulties they both experienced in that earliest phase of coming to know each other.

Fonagy and colleagues note that 'affect expressions by the parent that are not contingent on the infant's affect will undermine the appropriate labeling of internal states, which may, in turn, remain confusing, experienced as unsymbolized, and hard to regulate' (Fonagy et al. 2004, p. 9). In contrast, in healthy interaction, as Carvalho comments, 'The mother's mind is the infant's mind: her orbito-frontal cortex stands proxy for his' (Carvalho 2002, p. 159).

Rona's difficult early experience was further complicated by a severe squint which must have made it difficult to 'see things as they really were'. Painful surgery for this at three years old, a hospitalization that seems to have recapitulated in a distressing way her poor early experience, reinforcing the early trauma patterns lodged in her developing mind and leading to an expectation that all new experience would feel persecutory. Rona became a lonely child; by the time we met she had developed a pretend world peopled by constantly changing characters, interaction with whom occupied most of her waking moments. In the real world of school Rona was constantly bullied by both boys and girls, despite considerable input from a skilled team of staff with very clear policies about bullying and strategies for dealing with it. The bullying and the changing states of her body as she moved into adolescence caused her acute distress.

Rona's inner world was full of what superficially seemed like rapidly changing make believe scenarios-which I understand as manifestations of alienated, dissociated aspects of her self. It is difficult in a short space to convey the fragmented, dissociated, disorientated and disorientating quality of the inner world experience that Rona came to share with me. Rona almost always began talking to me with the phrase 'in pretend' and then there would be an implicit invitation to venture together into a world that was far more real to her than what she knew to be the real world. At the beginning of our work together I felt that Rona was virtually inaccessible. It felt as if she was behind a wall of solid glass and that any attempts to interpret might shatter this and destroy her. In the first months of our work I felt that 'pretend' was a world where Rona moved freely but where I was left out and was completely at a loss. I felt as if I was in a maze and totally unable to find my way. Through my countertransference experience I felt something of her pain and just how much she was a prisoner of her inner world and the cruelty that she encountered there. In turn through the reliability, continuity of an affective relationship she gradually began to feel safe and understood. Lyons-Ruth (1998, p. 285) comments: 'Implicit knowings governing intimate interactions are not language-based and are not routinely translated into semantic form.'

Decety and Chaminade suggest that these unconscious processes 'might almost be described as *unconscious imagination, that is a generating of neural experiencing at an unconscious level of similar activities and processes in oneself*' (Decety & Chaminade 2003, p. 582; italics mine). I suggest that these insights must inevitably affect our understanding of the therapeutic process which in the past has perhaps placed undue emphasis merely on verbal communications concerning the patient's material.

Early in therapy Rona showed some awareness of the defensive nature of her pretend world: she explained that her special world had first come about when she was hiding behind the sofa watching an excerpt from 'Dr Who'. She felt as if she heard Dr. Who saying to her, 'If you are frightened come into my world and I will look after you.' Rona struggled with her sense of the utter reality of her special world and her knowledge that in fact it was hallucinatory: it only existed 'in pretend'. It may be that this capacity to distinguish between the two helped her to keep psychosis at bay. Dr. Who was for her a powerful figure who protected her in her inner fragmented world. Now as I reflect on my experience with Rona, I have the benefit of insights provided by Kalsched's work (1996) concerning trauma and the way in which unbearable experience stimulates archetypal images and often contains a powerful protector/persecutor figure within the structure of the personality who actively seeks to guard the true self from annihilation.

When I saw Rona much of the work from the world of trauma and neurobiology which currently informs our understanding of dissociated states had yet to be written. At the time Jung's notion of inner persons in the psyche, indeed in his own psyche, informed my work and I learned to understand Rona's fantasies much as dreams and each figure from within as an aspect of a fragmented self. I still work from those insights but also understand these figures as images emerging from the implicit, from the earliest memory of relational experience, lodged in the right hemisphere, unavailable to conscious mind, or explicit hippocampal memory, but emerging in the form of images which could be felt, thought and talked about.

When we returned from the first holiday break of two weeks I found that Rona's pretend world had become peopled with a cruel mother and a little Rona whose legs were broken. Interpretation in terms of her distress at her loss of me during the break brought some relief. At an unconscious level Rona often struggled with her mother's unconscious fantasies of wanting there to be no baby and her fantasies imaged damage done to her mother and to her baby self. The patterns of persecutory expectation dominating her unconscious were part of the reason why she so easily became the target for those bullies in school who reacted at an unconscious level to her inner vulnerability.

As the therapy developed, Rona's internal world became less persecu-tory, some of the cruel figures emerged less frequently and instead new, more benign material emerged. Such developments were made possible by the benign affective quality of the therapeutic attachment, which enabled encounter with previously unassimilable experiences.

The different quality of attachment, which I call 'learned secure', enabled the beginnings of the transformation of emotions previously encapsulated in the emotional brain and in the body into the feelings that were its mental representations. Material from the implicit may be difficult to work with but the analyst whose work is grounded in insights from the neurobiology of emotion and in particular the role of the right hemisphere in processing it will pay particular attention to dissociative states of mind, to the patient's own use of metaphor which through vivid, visual images will carry emotional truth from the world of the implicit. With less background noise from the past and an experience of a good attachment in the present, the patient gradually becomes more able to self-regulate affect and to move more confidently into relationships. As Bromberg points out, 'Ultimately it is on issues around attachment and affect-regulation that a person's capacity to experience a sense of self that is "simultaneously fluid and robust" depends' (Bromberg 2006, p. 32).

When Rona was sixteen it seemed important that she was given a chance to separate a little more from her parents and so plans were made for her to live with her cousin in another town for her last years of schooling and we began to work towards an ending. As our work drew to a close an important and enduring character emerged called Kemi, a very shy but very likeable girl. We came to understand 'Kemi' as the 'key to me', and this shy but likeable character as a representa-tion of just how much Rona's internal world had changed over the five years that we worked together.

I believe that the change in Rona came about not primarily through my enabling the development of her cognitive understanding of the difference between reality and pretend but rather through the affec-tive quality of the relationship that was established between us and the opportunity our time together offered for the emergence of the implicit and the chance it provided to reflect upon it together. Schore stresses that attachment communications are implicit, affective and non-verbal and that unconscious affect regulation 'expressed in rapid, non-verbal emotional communications at levels beneath conscious awareness within the dynamic intersubjective field' plays a critical psychobiological role both within patient-therapist dyads (Schore 2007, p. 762). It is these unconscious processes in analysis that lead to changes in the way a patient becomes able to relate not only to others but also to her or his own inner world.

Concluding Comment

As I look back over this work my understanding of it is immeasurably enriched by insights that I now have as a result of the recent research in attachment theory, trauma and neurobiology. Back in 1935 Jung commented, 'we ought to have a laboratory in which we could establish by objective methods how things really are when in an unconscious condition' (Jung 1935/1976: para. 12, cited in Ekstrom 2004, p. 661). Dr Lanius' work introduces us to the fulfilment of Jung's dream.

References

Bromberg, P.M. (2006). *Awakening the Dreamer, Clinical Journeys*. New York: The Analytic Press.

Carvalho, R. (2002). 'Psychic retreats revisited: binding primitive destructiveness or securing object? A matter of emphasis?' *British Journal of Psychotherapy*, 19, 2, 153-71.

Decety, J. & Chaminade, T. (2003). 'When the self represents the other: a new cognitive neuroscience view on psychological identification'. *Consciousness & Cognition*, 12, 577-96.

Ekstrom, S.R. (2004). 'Freudian, Jungian and cognitive models of the unconscious'. *Journal of Analytical Psychology*, 49, 5, 657-82.

Fonagy, P., Gergely, G., Jurist, E.L. & Target, M. (2004). *Affect Regulation, Mentalization, and the Development of the Self*. London: Karnac Books.

C.G. Jung (1934). 'A review of the complex theory'. *CW* 8.

– (1935). *The Tavistock Lectures*. *CW* 18.

Lyons-Ruth, K. & The Boston Change Process Study Group (1998). 'Implicit relational knowing, its role in development and psychoanalytic treatment'. *Infant Mental Health Journal*, 19, 282-89.

Kalsched, D. (1996). *The Inner World of Trauma. Archetypal Defenses of the Human Spirit*. London & New York: Routledge.

Schore, A.N. (2006). 'Foreword' to *Coming into Mind. The Mind-Brain Relationship: A Jungian Clinical Perspective* by M.A. Wilkinson. Hove & New York: Routledge.

– Review of *Awakening the Dreamer. Clinical Journeys* by Philip Bromberg. *Psychoanalytic Dialogues*, 17, 5, 753-67.

Wilkinson, M. (in press) 'A clinical exploration of the origin and treatment of a dissociative defence'. In *Trauma, Dissociation and Multiplicity*, ed. V. Sinason. Hove: Routledge

A Social Cognitive and Affective Neuroscience Approach to Complex PTSD

Ruth A. Lanius

Canada (Department of Psychiatry,
The University of Western Ontario)

Introduction[1]

The field of *social cognitive and affective neuroscience* (SCAN) seeks to understand how brain mechanisms mediate the complex social and emotional functions of the human mind. Topics of investigation within SCAN include the study of motivation and emotion, self-referential processing, empathy, and mentalizing (theory of mind), just to name a few.

The contemporary discipline of *affective neuroscience* originated from the landmark publications of Jaak Panksepp (1998) and Richard Davidson (2003). From the beginning, the field of affective neuroscience has been influenced by the *basic emotion* view that there might be brain systems dedicated to mediating particular types of emotional behaviour (e.g., fear versus anger), systems that might be relatively preserved across lower and higher species. Increasingly, higher-order explicitly social and meta-cognitive aspects of emotional processing and behaviour have also been studied in humans and their relationship to psychiatric disorders has been of growing interest. In contrast, *social cognitive neuroscience* from the outset concerned itself with higher-order complex social behaviours including attitudes, empathy and theory of mind. The disciplines of affective neuroscience and social cognitive neuroscience are increasingly united under the field of SCAN, although for the purposes of simplicity and clarity, I will discuss concepts that traditionally fall under the scope of affective neuroscience and social cognitive neuroscience separately.

The relevance of the SCAN paradigm for an understanding of the psychology and neurobiology of complex posttraumatic stress disorder (PTSD) and its effective treatment will be examined. For the purposes of the present paper, complex trauma will be defined as repeated interpersonal trauma occurring during crucial developmental

---

1 Fuller references for the research summarized in this paper may be found in Lanius, R.A., Bluhm, R. & Frewen, P.A. 'How understanding the neurobiology of complex PTSD can inform clinical practice: a social cognitive and affective neuroscience informed approach'. *Acta Psychiatrica Scandinavica*, in press. Permission has been granted for its republication.

periods as opposed to simple posttraumatic stress disorder which follows single incident trauma events. I will focus on emotional awareness, emotion regulation, social emotional processing, self-referential processing and the sense of self.

Affective Neuroscience

In this section, two concepts particularly relevant to understanding complex PTSD, namely deficits in *emotional awareness* and *emotion regulation*, are discussed.

Emotional / Self Awareness

Theorists have increasingly pointed out the significant role played by emotional processing in the across-species evolution of consciousness and the brain mechanisms underlying how humans become subjectively aware of their emotional feelings and behaviour is a topic of significant interest in affective neuroscience. Emotional awareness refers to the capacity to be aware of and describe emotions in oneself and others and involves the ability to reflect upon internal affective experience Since emotional awareness enables increased self-reflection and regulation of affective states, it is often considered a 'cornerstone' of emotion regulation. A history of a secure attachment with one's primary caregivers plays a key role in the development of emotional awareness.

The Neurobiology of Emotional / Self Awareness

Current theoretical models propose a superior-inferior division within the medial prefrontal cortex underlying emotional awareness and a distinction between *conceptual* and *embodied* forms of emotional awareness has been proposed. Conceptual emotional awareness refers to the ability to reflect on, interpret and make a decision about an embodied sensation or emotion. It is based on linguistic forms of expression, is usually considered to be rational, logical and explanatory, and tends to transcend the present moment. This form of awareness is thought to be partly mediated by the dorsomedial prefrontal cortex and its connections with the interoceptive and body schema networks. In contrast to conceptual awareness, embodied emotional/self awareness is based on sensing, feeling and acting, tends to be spontaneous and creative, and is usually lived in the present moment. The ventromedial prefrontal cortex has been hypothesized to be a key brain structure underlying embodied emotional awareness. It is also thought to aid in making decisions when one is in the subjective emotional present.

The Impact of Early Life Trauma on Emotional/Self Awareness

Early adverse experience can significantly interfere with the development of emotional awareness. Being trapped in a dangerous environment, such as being with a chronically physically or sexually abusive caregiver, prevents individuals from using their emotional responses to guide effective actions and behaviours. For example, if a child is in an abusive relationship with a caregiver and has the impulse to escape, he/she may quickly learn that escape is not possible. A sense of learned helplessness may ensue. Individuals with such experiences therefore learn that emotional responses to traumatic events are futile since there is no escape from the situation and hence become increasingly disconnected from their inner emotional life in an attempt to disconnect themselves from extreme emotions that are out of their control. It is therefore not surprising that individuals with PTSD often exhibit problems, being aware of their affective states, and have difficulties identifying and labelling these states. Studies have shown that these individuals have lower scores on the *Levels of Emotional Awareness Scale*, that they consistently exhibit higher levels of alexithymia (difficulties identifying and labelling emotional states and that they often show intense levels of emotional numbing, i.e., feeling like they cannot experience emotions.

The Neurocircuitry Underlying Emotional Numbing in PTSD

Emotional numbing symptoms have long been recognized as an important symptom cluster in chronic PTSD and represent negative prognostic indicators for psychological treatment. We have recently examined trait emotional numbing symptoms as a predictor of neural activation during script-driven imagery in patients with PTSD related to childhood abuse. In these studies, patients construct a narrative of their traumatic experience including as many sensory details as possible. These narratives are subsequently read to patients who are instructed to recall the traumatic memory as vividly as possible during an fMRI scan. Emotional numbing ratings are then correlated with extent of brain activation during imagery of positive (receiving others' affection-praise) and negative (rejection-criticism) scripts. In women with PTSD related to prolonged childhood abuse, increased emotional numbing symptoms predicted decreased brain activation within the dorsomedial prefrontal cortex during imagery of both positive and negative scripts, consistent with a role for the dorsomedial prefrontal cortex in higher-order reflective and meta-cognitive aspects of emotional functioning.

It is interesting to note that, within healthy women completing the same task, the more an individual exhibited the trait of 'mindful observing', referring to the intentional paying attention to one's inner and external stimuli and experiences [e.g., 'When I'm walking, I deliberately notice the sensations of my body moving'; 'I notice changes in my body, such as whether my breathing slows down or speeds up' (Baer, Smith & Allen 2004;Baer et al. 2006)], the more activation was observed within the dorsomedial prefrontal cortex (Frewen et al. 2010).

The development of the neural circuitry facilitating the human ability for conscious awareness of our emotional states, including the dorsomedial prefrontal cortex, may therefore be disturbed in PTSD, leading to the difficulties these individuals often have in reflecting on, interpreting and acting in accordance with emotion. A patient suffering from PTSD related to prolonged childhood abuse summarized feelings of emotional numbing in the following statement: 'It's like a blank, I think about my kids and I feel nothing for them. I'll be sitting there feeling confused and numb, and I wonder what I'm supposed to be feeling. It's like dead space ... and when that happens, I have trouble using words, finding my words, I can't talk.' The inability to describe feelings in words also relates to the concept of alexithymia which will be described below.

The Neurocircuitry Underlying Alexithymia in PTSD

Alexithymia refers to difficulties identifying and labelling emotional states. Researchers often assess alexithymia with the 20-item Toronto Alexithymia Scale (TAS-20) (Bagby et al. 1994), which measures difficulties (1) identifying feelings and distinguishing them from bodily sensations, and (2) describing and communicating feelings. The following quote from a traumatized client in psychotherapy with me describes the experience of alexithymia and elegantly illustrates the problems identifying and communicating feelings in words which is often so prominent in individuals with PTSD (Frewen et al. 2008): 'When I get emotions and stuff like that I don't really feel them. I can say to someone I feel sadness because tears are welling in my eyes, but I do not know what that is really. They are just physical symptoms.' This quote also exemplifies that an individual may exhibit behavioural (e.g., crying) and psychophysiological signs (e.g., tachycardia) of emotional processing without being subjectively aware of his/her emotional state. Further evidence for the latter also stems from studies that have observed lower correspondence between self-reported affective experience and objectively-coded facial affect in PTSD subjects as compared to controls in response to emotionally-provocative stimuli.

Our group has also reported that alexithymia symptoms predict brain activation during traumatic script-driven imagery in individuals with PTSD (ibid.). Associations between alexithymia and neural activation were particularly marked for regions of the embodied emotional/self awareness network. Specifically, during traumatic memory recall, increasing severity of trait alexithymia was associated with reduced activation within the ventromedial prefrontal cortex and the anterior insula. As described above, the ventromedial prefrontal cortex may be related to embodied emotional/self awareness which is based on sensing, feeling and acting and may play a role in assigning the emotional value of a stimulus during self-referential processing. In contrast, the anterior insula has been proposed to be part of the interoceptive network. Craig has postulated that the anterior insula of the right hemisphere, possibly uniquely to humans, constitutes a basis for the subjective evaluation of one's condition, that is, 'how you feel' (2002, 2010). It is therefore not surprising that higher levels of alexithymia or difficulties identifying and labelling feeling states are associated with lower brain activation of the anterior insula.

Emotion Regulation

As described above, emotional awareness has long been thought to be crucial to the regulation of affective states and is therefore often considered to be the 'cornerstone' of emotion regulation. Emerging research has clearly shown that the affective disturbances experienced by many PTSD subjects involve not just fear, but also include dysregulation of a variety of emotional states, including anger, guilt and shame This point has been acknowledged in the newly developed provisional criteria for PTSD in the DSM5 (www.dsm5.org). I am using the term 'emotion dysregulation' to collectively refer to disturbances in a variety of emotional responses and to 'the process by which we influence how much emotion we have and when we have it' as outlined by Gross (1998).

The Neural Correlates Underlying Traumatic and Non-traumatic Emotional Processing and Emotion Regulation in PTSD

Studies examining brain activation in response to trauma script-driven imagery in subjects who experienced a re-experiencing/ hyperarousal response to recalling their traumatic memory showed decreased responses in brain regions involved in emotion and arousal regulation, including the ventromedial prefrontal cortex, rostral anterior cingulate cortex, and in some cases the amygdala. In our own studies, PTSD subjects who reported re-experiencing their traumatic events in the scanner described, for example, feeling that they were 'being raped all over again. I could feel him holding down my hands.' Another subject stated: 'It felt like I was surrounded by smoke. I could smell and see it.' The latter responses were usually associated with an increase in heart rate. However, it is important to note that these brain activation patterns strikingly differ from those observed in PTSD patients who exhibited a depersonalization/derealization dissociative response to the traumatic script. For example, one subject stated, 'I was outside my body looking down at myself. It was too overwhelming to recall the traumatic memory', while she tried to recall her traumatic memory. These dissociative patients had *higher* levels of brain activation in the rostral anterior cingulate cortex and dorsal anterior cingulate cortex, medial prefrontal cortex, and areas in the superior and middle temporal cortices and usually did not exhibit a significant increase in heart rate during the traumatic memory recall.

The studies described above indicate a role for medial prefrontal/amygdala circuitry in emotion regulation in PTSD. In general, PTSD has been shown to be associated with two different types of emotion dysregulation: (1) undermodulation of affect, such as reexperiencing traumatic events, hyperarousal, and anger symptoms mediated by failure of prefrontal inhibition of limbic regions, resulting in overactivation of these regions, including the amygdala; and (2) overmodulation of affect, often associated with a feeling of subjective distance from emotional experience such as during acute depersonalization, derealization, and analgesia, thought to be mediated by midline prefrontal inhibition of the same limbic regions (Lanius et al. 2010). A recent review proposed clinical and neurobiological evidence for a dissociative subtype of PTSD in an attempt to classify PTSD patients who show significant symptoms of depersonalization, derealization, and analgesia in contrast to PTSD patients who exhibit predominantly reexperiencing and flashback-type symptoms (Lanius et al. 2010). It was suggested that individuals with a dissociative subtype of PTSD may be more likely to have experienced a history of repeated interpersonal trauma occurring during crucial developmental periods.

Social Cognitive Neuroscience

Within the scope of social cognitive neuroscience, I will discuss two concepts found to be especially important for an understanding of PTSD: disturbances in *social emotional processing* and *self-referential processing*. I also discuss the notion of a default-mode network in the brain and its relevance to self-referential processing and the sense of self.

Social Emotional Processing

Current emotion theory suggests a distinction between social and non-social *emotions*. Even though it is recognized that all emotional responses are potentially elicited by social stimuli or take place within a social framework certain emotions are considered as *necessarily* social. Social emotions (e.g., pride, guilt, shame) require metacognitive processing, specifically, consideration of the self-relevance of stimuli and the appraisal of others' thoughts and emotional states. Social emotions can be both positive and negative in valence. Positive social encounters, for example, can elicit admiration, appreciation, empathy, and pride whereas negative social encounters may provoke anger, disdain, envy, guilt or shame. In contrast, non-social positive emotions may be elicited by non-social stimuli such as taking a walk in the mountains alone. Non-social negative emotions can be evoked when an individual is confronted with threatening circumstances occurring outside a social context, for example, a fear of heights or of certain animals (e.g., spiders).

Processing of the social dimension of emotion exerts powerful effects on brain activation. The dorsomedial prefrontal cortex, the posterior cingulate/precuneus, the bilateral temporal poles, the right amygdala, and the bilateral temporoparietal junction are brain regions that have been suggested to play a role in social cognition.

Specifically, the dorsomedial prefrontal cortex and posterior cingulate cortex/precuneus are involved in self-referential processing. These areas of the brain are also implicated in, along with the temperoparietal junction and temporal poles, the task of 'mentalizing' (attending to states of mind in oneself and others) /theory of mind (the ability to attribute mental states-beliefs, intents, and desires to oneself and others and to understand that others have beliefs, desires and intentions that are different from one's own. The right amygdala has also been suggested to respond to salient emotional properties that are specifically social.

Social Emotion Processing in PTSD

In PTSD related to prolonged childhood abuse, neural activation patterns to positive standardized social (rejection-shame) and non-social (fear-anxiety) emotional imagery have been examined (Frewen et al. 2010). PTSD subjects showed altered brain responses in brain regions involved in higher-order social cognition (mentalizing and theory of mind), including the dorsomedial prefrontal cortex, temporal poles and amygdala particularly during positive social emotional imagery. These results may have important implications for key social functions in individuals with PTSD and point to important new research questions. For example, to what degree do deficits in this circuitry affect the ability to engage in psychotherapy? Can activation of the social emotional system in psychotherapy lead to a reversal of the brain activation patterns during social emotional processing in PTSD? To what extent do the neural networks underlying social emotions need to be intact in order to use available social support before, during and in the aftermath of trauma? Lastly, do deficits in the social emotion neural circuitry affect the ability to parent and thereby facilitate the intergenerational transmission of trauma, i.e., the emergence of psychopathology as a result of emotion processing/ regulation deficits in the parent(s)?

Self-Referential Processing

Individuals with PTSD often exhibit disturbances in self-referential processing. Johnson and colleagues (2002) proposed that the ability to reflect upon oneself requires a robust sense of self, which has been described as 'a collection of schemata regarding one's abilities, traits and attitudes that guides our behaviors, choices and social interactions' (ibid.). Psychological trauma can undermine the sense of an adaptive and agentive self, challenging one's sense of identity and life purpose. Foa and colleagues (1999) capture these symptoms well in the *Posttraumatic Cognitions Inventory* which includes items such as: *I feel dead inside; I will never be able to feel normal emotions again; I have permanently changed for the worse; I feel like an object, not like a person; I have no future; I don't know myself anymore;* and *My life has been destroyed by the trauma.* Disturbances in self-referential processing in PTSD are further apparent through symptoms of identity disturbance, dissociation and the related experience of a fragmented sense of self (Lanius et al. 2010). Several prominent psychoanalysts have elegantly described the fragmented nature of the sense of self. For example, Jung (cited in Wilkinson (2006, pp. 94-5) suggested:

> As a result of some psychic upheaval whole tracts of our being can plunge back into the unconscious and vanish from the surface for years and decades ... disturbances caused by affects are known technically as phenomena of dissociation, and are indicative of a psychic split.

Jung further noted:

> A traumatic complex brings about the dissociation of the psyche. The complex is not under control of the will and for this reason it possesses the quality of psychic autonomy.

Jung described such traumatic complexes as 'autonomous splinter psyches' and proposed that these complexes can suddenly return to consciousness 'pouncing upon *an individual* like an enemy or a wild animal (cited in Wilkinson 2003, p. 95).

Bromberg notes that

> this unintegratable affect ... threatens to disorganize the internal template on which one's experience of self-coherence,

self-cohesiveness, and self-continuity depends … The unprocessed 'not-me' experience held by a dissociated self-state as an affective memory without an autobiographical memory of its origin 'haunts' the self.

(ibid., p. 98)

Symptoms of shame are also representative of altered self-referential processing in PTSD (Cloitre et al. 2006). Cloitre and colleagues (ibid.) have suggested that shame can lead to the experience of the self as inferior, bad, annihilated and/or identified with the perpetrator of abuse. Furthermore, Schore has noted a shame response involves 'the self unexpectedly experiencing an affective misattunement, thereby triggering a sudden stress, shock-induced deflation' (Schore 2003, p. 155).

The Neural Correlates of Self-Referential Processing in PTSD

Neuroimaging studies suggest that self-referential processing is partly mediated via cortical midline structures, including the medial prefrontal cortex, perigenual anterior cingulate cortex, posterior cingulate cortex, as well as the temporoparietal junction and temporal poles. One model of self-referential processing proposes that the dorsal medial prefrontal cortex and the posterior cingulate cortex are involved in self-referential processing independent of whether the stimulus or task is emotionally relevant, while the ventral medial prefrontal cortex may be particularly involved in negative emotionally-relevant self-referential processing tasks.

A novel cognitive paradigm, akin to mirror viewing has been developed to investigate self-referential processing disturbances in women with PTSD predominantly related to maltreatment experienced during childhood. The paradigm involved the collection of self-descriptiveness ratings for negative- (e.g., abandoned, unlovable, despicable, broken) and positively-valenced trait words (e.g., lovable, special, adorable) and later exposing participants to pictures of themselves while such words were spoken. Results showed that PTSD patients endorsed more negative and fewer positive trait adjectives as self-descriptive, which support repeated clinical observations that individuals with PTSD, especially related to childhood trauma, often experience intense negative thoughts and even self-hatred about themselves. For example, responses from individuals with PTSD to viewing their own face paired with negative adjectives included 'I relate to the negative side'; or 'I noticed I was agreeing with all the negative words; or 'It made me feel bad about myself.' Responses from individuals with PTSD to seeing their own face paired with a positive word included 'I did not believe it'; or 'It did not mean anything'; or 'I questioned it. I did not feel the confidence.' Brain activation patterns demonstrated that healthy women showed an increased response within the perigenual anterior cingulate cortex when viewing their face and listening to positive trait adjectives whereas women with PTSD did not show this effect. The perigenual anterior cingulate cortex has been linked to self-referential processing (e.g., Kircher et al. 2000; Van Der Meer, Aleman, David 2010), and is more active during negative emotional events in healthy individuals than in individuals with PTSD.

In contrast to healthy controls, patients with PTSD exhibited an increased response within the right amygdala when viewing their face *and* responding with positive trait adjectives. Although response within the amygdala has more often been associated with negative emotional processing, particularly of threat-related visual stimuli, research also implicates the amygdala in positive emotional processing. In this study, right amygdala activation may be a sign of relatively more positive and healthy self-appraisal within women who, as a group, can be characterized by severe negative self-referential processing. It is interesting to note that the right amygdala has been suggested to be involved in social emotion processing (see earlier section), and more positive and healthy self-appraisal may be related to better social functioning.

The above findings suggest alterations in brain functioning during self-referential processing tasks in PTSD. Future studies will need to examine the relationship between the intensely disturbed sense of self and brain activation patterns in regions involved in self-referential processing in PTSD and whether psychotherapeutic interventions that are specifically designed to improve the capacity for introspection and self-awareness can restore the functional abnormalities observed in brain regions such as the medial prefrontal cortex and the posterior cingulate cortex.

The Default Mode Network

The default mode network (DMN) is one of the main intrinsic or resting state networks in the brain and has been suggested to play an important role in self-referential processing. The DMN is activated when individuals are engaged in stimulus-independent thought, and it is thought to aid in serving to consolidate, stabilize, and set the context for future information processing. A recent meta-analysis demonstrated that autobiographic memory recall, theory of mind tasks, and prospection/thinking about the future activate the DMN (Spreng et al. 2009; Spreng & Grady 2010). This may indicate that these functions bear a direct relationship to the connectivity of this network.

The DMN includes several brain regions that have been associated with self-referential processing, including the medial prefrontal cortex, posterior cingulate cortex in addition to midline parietal structures, medial and lateral temporal lobes, and lateral parietal regions.

Controls: Positive Correlation 0, -56, 20

PTSD: Positive Correlation 0, -56, 20

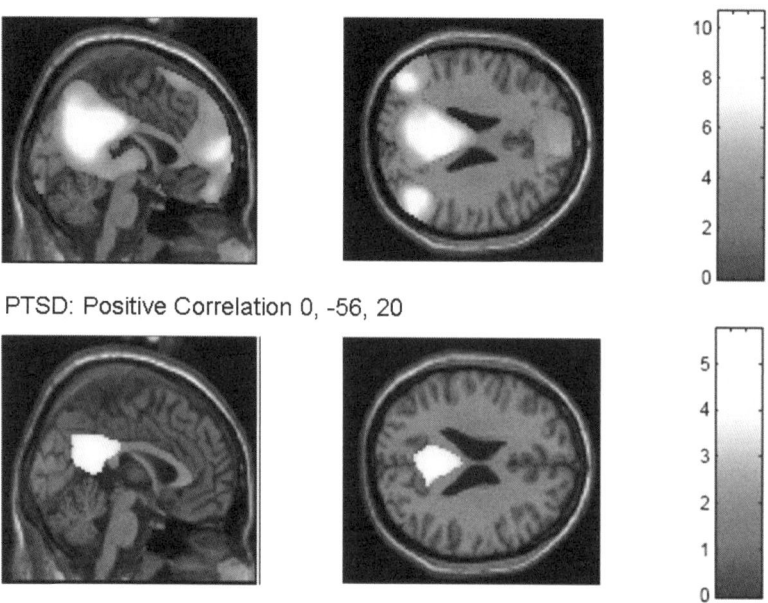

Figure 1: Default Mode Network Connectivity in Control (top panel) and PTSD Subjects (bottom panel)

Areas of correlation with posterior cingulate/precuneus in healthy comparison subjects (n=15) and in patients with PTSD (n=17), thresholded at p<0.05, corrected using False Discovery Rate Correction.
Figure published with permission in Bluhm, R.L., et al., 'Alterations in default network connectivity in posttraumatic stress disorder related to early-life trauma'. *Journal of Psychiatry and Neuroscience*, 2009, 34, 3, 187-94.

Given that PTSD has been associated with deficits in self-referential processing, as described above, and has been associated with altered activation in areas associated with the default network (e.g., medial prefrontal cortex, anterior cingulate, posterior cingulate cortex) across a variety of paradigms, our group chose to embark on a study that examined the integrity of this network in PTSD. In patients with chronic PTSD due to prolonged childhood abuse, significantly reduced resting state connectivity within the DMN was demonstrated (Bluhm et al. 2009) (see Figure 1). The PTSD group showed diminished connectivity between the posterior cingulate seed region and the medial prefrontal cortex, right superior frontal gyrus and left thalamus. Furthermore, the connectivity of the medial prefrontal seed region was strictly limited to adjacent areas in the medial prefrontal cortex. Since autobiographic memory recall has previously been shown to bear a direct relationship to the connectivity of the DMN alterations in brain activation in PTSD during autobiographic memory recall as observed during the script-driven imagery symptom provocation studies may be one underlying mechanism contributing to the altered DMN connectivity observed. Given the relationship between the DMN, autobiographical memory recall as well as prospection, altered connectivity within in the DMN in PTSD may prevent traumatic experiences to be experienced in context with the past and the future, thereby leaving the traumatic experiences unintegrated and timeless.

From a developmental perspective, it is also interesting to note that in adult patients with PTSD related to childhood abuse, DMN connectivity resembles that observed in children age 7-9, possibly indicating interference with the maturation process due to the toxic effects of stress-hormones on the myelination of the corpus callosum (Daniels et al. 2011).

SCAN-Informed Treatment Applications

As described above, a number of recent studies, falling under the scope of SCAN, suggest that patients with PTSD show problems in emotional/self awareness, emotion regulation, social emotional processing, and self-referential processing. In the following section, we consider the significance of these findings for the treatment of PTSD.

Emotional/Self Awareness

Exposure-based treatments for PTSD involve repeated imaginal and in vivo exposure to trauma-related stimuli. Although these treatments have strong empirical support, in order to be successful, it is important for patients to be able to fully engage emotionally with the traumatic material. Teaching PTSD patients with impairments in emotional awareness to identify their affective feelings early on in treatment may make exposure-based treatments more efficient because such therapies are dependent on a patient's judgment of their internal affect and as well as a reliable report of their symptom presentations. In addition, such treatments may be less effective in the early stages of treatment for patients who are unable to modulate, regulate and engage in the intense affective experiences that may be elicited by exposure-based therapies. Interoceptive awareness training to help patients become aware of and describe bodily sensations and their relationship to emotions is therefore often a crucial part of the first stage of trauma treatment. Such awareness can prevent individuals from entering severe hypo- or hyperarousal states which can prevent emotional and cognitive processing (Ogden, Minton & Pain 2006).

During this phase of treatment, patients have to develop an awareness and language that helps them identify bodily sensations and how different bodily sensations relate to different emotional experiences. For example, for one person tension in the jaw in combination with a feeling of tightness in the throat may correlate with sadness while in another individual sadness may correlate with tightness in the stomach and a feeling of heaviness in the chest. By developing emotional awareness, patients can then learn to identify precursors to extreme emotional states and learn to intervene before these states become too intense and overwhelming. Once a patient has mastered these skills, they can be applied during the exposure-based treatments, thereby preventing extreme emotional states which preclude optimal emotional engagement during exposure therapy.

Emotional/interoceptive awareness training has been incorporated into several forms of psychotherapy for PTSD. Dialectical Behaviour Therapy (DBT), skills training in affective and interpersonal regulation (STAIR), emotion focused therapy and sensorimotor psychotherapy all include a focus on increasing patients' capacity for introspection and self-awareness, particularly with regard to emotional experiences. In addition, mindfulness based approaches can be helpful to increase the capacity for emotional/self awareness. In particular, teaching patients to become aware of physical sensations through engaging in body scans at a pace that feels safe for them can help to increase their introspective ability. Yoga has also been suggested to be effective in treating PTSD, partially by increasing one's interoceptive ability.

Emotion Regulation and Social Emotions

In recognition of complex emotion dysregulation, social and self-dysfunction in patients with chronic PTSD related to childhood abuse, Cloitre and colleagues (2002) developed an empirically validated stage-oriented intervention for PTSD related to childhood abuse. STAIR is a stage-oriented treatment model that uses skills training in emotion and self regulation and interpersonal effectiveness prior to engaging in exposure-based therapy.

Early stages of STAIR teach patients how to enhance their capacity to regulate dysregulated emotional states through cognitive strategies (attention shifting, positive self-statements, positive imagery), behavioural strategies (time out, replacement behaviours, engaging in pleasurable activities), and enhancing distress tolerance skills.

Following the emotion regulation component of STAIR, patients begin interpersonal regulation training which involves understanding interpersonal schemas, changing relationship patterns through role play using appropriate assertiveness skills and an enhanced understanding of power balances in relationships. In addition, providing a corrective interpersonal experience through a therapeutic relationship that is able to provide a secure base, thereby facilitating trust and effective communication is also an important aspect of facilitating enhanced social competence (Cloitre et al. 2006).

In the later stages of STAIR treatment, exposure therapy and narrative story telling are designed to help patients reach a stage of resolution of their feelings of shame and grief. This intervention involves both telling the story of the trauma and a related meaning analysis in order to help patients understand who they have come to be as a result of what they have experienced. This understanding may decrease feelings of shame and loss, as well as related experiences of the self as inferior, bad, annihilated, fragmented and/or identified with the perpetrator (Cloitre, Cohen, Koenen 2006). The resolution of the experience of the self as an extremely negative entity will also likely result in significantly increased social functioning. It is often the experience of the self as bad and inferior that perpetuates individuals being in abusive relationships since they may feel like they deserve to be punished or treated without respect.

Self-Referential Processing

Self-referential processing is most closely related to the concept of mentalizing – attending to states of mind in oneself and others (Allen 2006), and mentalization-based treatments have been shown to be effective in individuals who have suffered from disrupted early attachments and childhood abuse. Increased self-referential processing/ mentalizing has been suggested to enhance emotion regulation skills as well as facilitate the process of exposure to traumatic memories. As Jon Allen states:

> We work clinically [using mentalization-based therapy] with patients who are prone to be swept away by emotion, carried along into impulsive action, without any felt sense of self. We encourage such patients to push a metaphorical pause button by mentalizing.
> (see Allen & Fonagy 2006, p. 11)

Moreover, Allen has stressed that the alternative to traumatic re-enactments is mentalizing, that is developing the capacity to reflect on the relationship between triggering events in the current relationship and previous traumatic experiences.

Conclusions

We have suggested that SCAN offers a novel theoretical paradigm for understanding psychological trauma and its numerous clinical outcomes, most notably problems in emotional/self awareness, emotion regulation, social emotional processing, and self-referential processing. A core set of brain regions appear to mediate these collective psychological functions, most notably the cortical midline structures, the amygdala, the insula, posterior parietal cortex, and temporal poles, suggesting that problems in one area (e.g., emotional awareness) may relate to difficulties in another (e.g., self-referential processing). We have further suggested, drawing on clinical research, that the experiences of individuals with PTSD related to chronic trauma often reflect impairments in many of these abilities. It is therefore crucial that the assessment and treatment of individuals with chronic PTSD addresses not only the traumatic memories but also takes a SCAN informed approach that focuses on the underlying deficits in emotional/self awareness, emotion regulation, social emotional processing, and self-referential processing.

References

Allen, J.G. & Fonagy, P. (Eds.) (2006). *Handbook of Mentalization-based Treatment.* Chichester, West Sussex, England: John Wiley & Sons.

Baer, R.A., Smith, G.T., Allen, K.B. (2004). 'Assessment of mindfulness by self-report: the Kentucky inventory of mindfulness skills'. *Assessment,* September, 11, 191-206.

Baer, R.A., Smith, G.T., Hopkins, J., Krietemeyer, J., Toney, L. (2006). 'Using self-report assessment methods to explore facets of mindfulness'. *Assessment,* March, 13, 27-45.

Bagby, R.M., Parker, J.D., Taylor, G.J. (1994). 'The twenty-item Toronto Alexithymia Scale I. Item selection and cross-validation of the factor structure'. *Journal of Psychosomatic Research,* January, 38, 23-32.

Bluhm, R.L., Williamson, P.C., Osuch, E.A., Frewen, P.A., Stevens, T.K., Boksman, K. et al. (2009). 'Alterations in default network connectivity in posttraumatic stress disorder related to early-life trauma'. *Journal of Psychiatry and Neuroscience,* May, 34, 187-94.

Cloitre, M., Cohen, L.R., Koenen, K.C. (2006). *Treating Survivors of Childhood Abuse: Pyschotherapy for Interrupted Life.* New York: Guilford Press.

Cloitre, M., Koenen, K.C., Cohen, L.R., Han, H. (2002). 'Skills training in affective and interpersonal regulation followed by exposure: a phase-based treatment for PTSD related to child abuse'. *Journal of Consulting and Clinical Psychology,* 70, 1067-74.

Craig, A.D. (2002). 'How do you feel? Interoception: the sense of the physiological condition of the body'. *Natture Reviews Neuroscience,* August, 3, 655-66.

– (2010). 'The sentient self'. *Brain Structure and Function,* June, 214, 563-77.

Daniels, J.K., Frewen, P., Mckinnon, M.C., Lanius, R.A. (2011). 'Default mode alterations in posttraumatic stress disorder related to early-life trauma: a developmental perspective'. *Journal of Psychiatry and Neuroscience*, January, 36, 56-9.

Davidson, R. J, Goldsmith, H.H. & Scherer, K. (Eds.) (2003). *Handbook of Affective Sciences*. New York: Oxford University Press.

Foa, E.B., Ehlers, A., Clark, D.M., Tolin, D.F. & Orsillo, S. M. (1999). 'The posttraumatic cognitions inventory (PTCI): Development and validation'. *Psychological Assessment*, 11, 303-14.

Frewen, P.A., Dozois, D.J.A., Neufeld, R.W.J., Densmore, M., Lane, R. D., Stevens, T.C., & Lanius, R. A. (2010). 'Individual differences in trait mindfulness predict dorsal medial prefrontal and amygdala response during emotional imagery: An fMRI study'. *Personality & Individual Differences*, 49, 479-84.

Frewen P.A, Dozois, D.J.A., Neufeld, R.W.J., Densmore, M., Stevens, T. & Lanius, R.A. (2010). 'Social emotions & emotional valence during imagery in women with PTSD: affective and neural correlates'. *Psychological Trauma: Theory, Research, Practice, and Policy*, 2, 145-57.

Frewen, P., Lanius, R., Dozois, D., Neufeld, R., Pain, C., Hopper, J. et al. (2008). 'Clinical and neural correlates of alexithymia in posttraumatic stress disorder'. *Journal of Abnormal Psychology*, 117, 117-81.

Gross, J.J. (1998). 'Antecedent- and response-focused emotion regulation: divergent consequences for experience, expression, and physiology'. *Journal of Personal Social Psychology*, January, 74, 224-37.

Johnson, S.C., Baxter, L.C., Wilder, L.S., Pipe, J.G., Heiserman, J.E., Prigatano, G.P. (2002). 'Neural correlates of self-reflection'. *Brain*, 125, 1808-14.

Kircher, T.T.J., Senior, C., Phillips, M.L., Benson, P.J., Bullmore, E.T., Brammer, M. et al. (2000). 'Towards a functional neuroanatomy of self processing: effects of faces and words'. *Cognitive Brain Research*, 10, 133-44.

Lanius, R.A, Vermetten, E., Loewenstein, R.J., Brand, B., Schmahl, C., Bremner, J.D. et al. (2010). 'Emotion modulation in PTSD: clinical and neurobiological evidence for a dissociative subtype'. *American Journal of Psychiatry*, June, 640-47.

Ogden, P., Minton, K., Pain, C. (2006). *Trauma and the Body*. New York: W.W. Norton.

Panksepp, J. (1998). *Affective Neuroscience: The Foundations of Human and Animal Emotions*, eds. R.J. Davidson, P. Ekman, K. Scherer. New York: Oxford University Press.

Schore, A.N. (2003). *Affect Dysregulation and the Repair of the Self*. New York: W.W. Norton.

Spreng, R.N. & Grady, C.L. (2010). 'Patterns of brain activity supporting autobiographical memory, prospection, and theory of mind, and their relationship to the default mode network'. *Journal of Cognitive Neuroscience*, June, 22, 1112-23.

Spreng, R.N., Mar, R.A., Kim, A.S. (2009). 'The common neural basis of autobiographical memory, prospection, navigation, theory of mind, and the default mode: a quantitative meta-analysis'. *Journal of Cognitive Neuroscience*, March, 21, 489-510.

Van Der Meer, C.S., Aleman, A., David, A.S. (2010). 'Self-reflection and the brain: a theoretical review and meta-analysis of neuroimaging studies with implications for schizophrenia'. Neuroscience & Biobehavioral Reviews, 34, 935-46.

Wilkinson, M. (2006). *Coming Into Mind: The Mind-Brain Relationship: A Jungian Clinical Perspective*. London & New York: Routledge.

Thursday, 26 August 2010

Cancer: Facing Multiplicity within Oneself

Guy Corneau & Marta Tibaldi

* * *

Exploring the Psycho-Spiritual Aspects of Cancer

Guy Corneau

Canada (IRSJA Inter-Regional / AGAP International)

Introduction

In April 2007, I was diagnosed with cancer. The cancer was characterized as a stage 4 lymphoma mainly located in the stomach. There were metastases in the spleen and in both lungs. A lymphoma is basically a lymph-node cancer. The white blood cells, more specifically the lymphocytes of the immune system, were affected. This was a non-Hodgkin's lymphoma of large cells.

I regained my health using three types of medicine: 1) allopathic medicine with its medications and hospital treatments such as chemotherapy, radiation therapy or operations, 2) natural medicine using herbs and plants that included phytotherapy, diet and different products or natural supplements and 3) energetic medicine which acts directly on the vitality of the body. Energetic medicine covers everything from meditation and visualization to homeopathy or acupuncture, as well as psychotherapy to balance the emotions. I view psychotherapy as a category in itself although it really belongs to the category of energy treatments *per se*.

Cancer confronted me yet again with the terrible fact that we all have an astounding number of voices inside. The voice of the Shadow resounded powerfully in me and confronted me with a very specific choice: either give up who I had been or die. In my paper, I would like to give you a taste of the various paths taken by this multiplicity through a few dreams and a few experiences that punctuated my journey through this disease.

The Rock Star of Analytical Psychology

This is the first dream I'd like to present:

I find myself on a mountain peak. I'm gazing at another peak with a little village on it. A strange atmosphere pervades the scene. The other peak is in the midst of a sandstorm that produces a heavy fog. At one moment I can see the hamlet and a moment later it disappears completely. I decide to walk towards the village. Night is falling now. I find myself in the central square of the village. There I see a bewildering spectacle. An army of teenagers – girls and boys, punks, dressed in black and covered in chains that shine in the dark, are fighting over the remains of a rock star whom they've just assassinated after his performance. They are eating him. This is obviously some kind of bloody ritual that makes me shudder in horror. I start desperately to run away to get back home but one of the youths chases me. I don't know what his intentions are, but I can't stop running and face him because I'm so afraid. I run through my house in an instant and continue my desperate flight until I wake up.

I wake up reeling. The nightmare is all around me. I try to catch my breath and calm my anxiety. At first, I can't understand a thing about my dream. Then, little by little, over the next few days fragments of meaning begin to emerge. The atmosphere of flickering reality that pervades the dream makes total sense to me. I feel exactly like that. I'm having a hard time facing my situation. I'm avoiding it, and I can't get my footing. The world is crumbling with every move I make and every step I take. The army of unleashed and bloody punks terrifies me. The scene seems to be referring to something taking place in the deepest, darkest part of myself. The square in the centre of the village indicates a central and basic element that must be questioned.

The most difficult thing to understand is the assassinated rock star that is being devoured. Is this really referring to me? Is it possible? I'm not a rock star but an analytical psychologist. Nevertheless, a memory emerges from the darkness. A cunning talk show host at a radio station in Geneva once called me the *Roch Voisine of analytical psychology,* the equivalent of which could be the *Bruce Springsteen* of analytical psychology. At the time, I played along with this comparison to a rock star and we had a great laugh on the air. It's true that with my conference tours and my television show, I kind of live like a rock star. But why did this star have to die? How did he attract the wrath of these youths? Adolescence being the age of dreams and transformations, the age where we want to change the world, I concluded that I had gone against my most vital forces. Was it possible that my career was going against my vitality and condemning a great part of me to darkness and barbarism?

Another association pointed in this direction. During the preceding summer, I thoroughly enjoyed listening to the audio book *The Dictator and the Hammock* by Daniel Pennac. In this book, the author kills off his hero, the president, the dictator and an agoraphobic in a square full of people in a little village. Was I such a dictator towards myself? In any case, there seemed to be a deadly conflict in me and this unconscious conflict had a deadly aspect. The only comforting element in this dream, even if I flee the punk who is chasing me as fast as I can, is that these youths are alive. I told myself that if one day I could hear the message of the dark aspects, I also would be able to enjoy their vitality.

Because of its bloody drunkenness, the dream overall reminds me of the Greek myth of Dionysus. Dionysus is the errant god, the eternal stranger, the god of abuses and drunkenness. His head exploded because of his delirious intoxication, only to be reborn the next morning. Due to Hera's jealousy, he was lured, dismembered and eaten by the Titans, except for the heart. Athena brought it to Zeus who swallowed it, and Dionysus was born a second time from the thigh of his father. Hence, he was named the god 'twice born'. Violent and threatening, he imposed himself upon the Greeks as a god who was indispensable for the joy of living, rebirth and eternal renewal. Representing an openness to others, he goes against 'the tendency in man and in the city to fall back on the certainties of their mastery and their native identity'[1]. Had I become the man who falls back on the certainties of his mastery and his identity?

At that time, I still did not know to what extent the disease matrix would be deeply transforming and how part of my life would be put to death in order to allow another part to be reborn. I realize today that the choice was already clear: either let go of the star, in other words the pride and the parts of myself flattered by success, or die. However, notwithstanding my protests, was there any alternative other than to bend to the force of the attack in the hope of surviving it?

What My Stomach Had to Say

On the psychotherapeutic level, I wanted to know what each of my affected organs had to say to me. I used knowledge from Chinese medicine and biological deprogramming to understand the deep meaning of my ordeal.

For example, the stomach is related to the very first food that we ingest. It is our first way of grasping the world. The child puts everything into its mouth and digests everything. Now, on the psychological level, we could say that improper food was ingested early on and that it represents the deep sources of cancer. In general, this

---

1 See the thematic file about Dionysus on the Musagora website: www.musagora.education.fr – the quote can be found in the section entitled *The Cult of Dionysus*. (Website in French only.)

food is associated with deep experiences of humiliation and loss of face that could neither be assimilated nor eliminated. The intense emotions associated with these experiences get stuck in the psyche and eventually sink into the body so that the individual can function. Now, another element can be added to this discussion. In my case, the pylorus was affected. This is the upper part of the stomach. Symbolically, it is psychologically tied to the father.

I never viewed my father as a tyrant who put us down although throughout his entire life he always wanted something different for me. When I was young, I wanted to become an actor. He was against this and threatened to cut off my support if I went to Montreal to study acting. His messages were conveyed to me through my mother who became the spokesperson for his decisions throughout my life. So much so that she's the one who looked like the shrew rather than him.

The Chinese talk about a 'wanting to live' as a way of describing the individual essence of each person and the fire of personal creation that dwells within. This fire is lodged in the kidneys and it symbolizes our vital energy. Now, if someone opposes your vital energy by wanting something *for* you and by having the power to impose it on you, your fire will weaken and your immune system will produce less immune defences. With these considerations in mind, I had the following dream. It is the most striking dream of this journey.

In the Catacombs

I am with a woman who remains enigmatic throughout the dream. We must go to the Montreal catacombs so we can see a scientific feat. Indeed, scientists were able to isolate a heart that has been beating for thirty years without technical support and without being connected to any living organ. It's virtually a miracle. I present myself with my friend at the door to the underground chamber. It's an enormous white-washed stone door. I dig into my pockets and am surprised to find the key. It has a special shape, small and square. The door opens and we find ourselves in a chamber that has not been visited in thirty years. I expect to find a heart in a jar but no. Instead I find two makeshift units placed on flimsy cardboard boxes. They are used for old-style music or film editing and have large reels. Without a doubt, they pre-date the digital era.

In contrast, the chamber in which we find ourselves is super hi-tech. It resembles a glass-walled flying saucer. I approach one of the windows. It faces a cement wharf that leads into the Saint-Laurence River. With my friend I observe the following: a woman is stretched out on the stone slab and is giving birth. She is in water up to her hips. She wants to drown her newborn child by leaving it in the river. We rush outside. I go into the water to grab the beautiful rosy child while my friend helps the

mother get up from her delivery bed. I bring her the baby and place it in
her arms. We encourage her to keep her baby and promise to help her.
As I lean towards her, I recognize to my great surprise the well-known
actress Céline Bonnier.

This dream flabbergasts me. Symbolically, it seems to be talking
about things that are buried deep in my past, in my own personal catacombs. I'm even surprised to read in the dictionary that catacombs
refer to vast underground chambers that served as burial or ossuary
sites. The dream is therefore referring to things that are dead in me,
but in my inner cemetery, an organ as vital as the heart has remained
alive. The scientific feat of 'a heart beating for 30 years without any
technical support or without the support of an organ' brings me back
to something that made my heart beat 30 years ago but that I never
supported since then. In 1977, exactly 30 years earlier (!), I entered
the Carl Gustav Jung Institute in Zürich, giving up a career in theatre
as well as my interests in music and film.

The editing units precariously installed on makeshift cardboard
boxes reminded me of my student years in Communication Arts
when, having very little money, I made do with whatever I chanced
upon and could use as a shelf or a storage unit. This space in which
I could create had remained completely intact. The whitened door
reminded me of an illustration in the Quebec catechism I was very
familiar with as a child and which represented the stone slab that
sealed Christ's tomb and that was found open after his resurrection.
It evoked renewal. It took me a long time to figure out where I could
have seen the small square key I used in the dream. I knew the key
but from where?… One day, I saw it hanging on the handle of my old
guitar case. It was used for the lock. In contrast, the 'hi-tech' and 'flying
saucer' atmosphere seemed to refer to *Star Trek* which, of course,
takes place on the *Enterprise*. No denying it, renewal was in the air!

The central action of the dream, the most moving part of it, is
without a doubt saving the child that the mother wants to leave to
drown. The infant has rosy cheeks. This too refers to renewal. But the
clock was ticking. It was headed towards certain death had I not saved
it. And for me too the clock was ticking. I had to save myself. As for
Céline Bonnier, she is an actress I admire for her talent and creativity.
I feel that she represents my theatrical *anima* and that it now wants
to give death rather than life, undoubtedly because it had long been
neglected. I saw as very auspicious the fact that my friend and I were
committed to helping the mother.

This dream represents a turning point in relation to my survival.
It seems to me that this is where everything was decided. The clock
was ticking but the child of creation had been saved. Although I have
studied my dreams for decades, I have rarely seen one as clear and

direct. Almost too clear. And too glaring. All my suspicions were confirmed. The price I paid for giving up artistic expression was my health. I have known this for thirty years but I didn't want to know this. I tried to hide it from myself. I tried to talk myself out of it. I rationalized instead of following the message in my gut.

Truly, I marvel at these discoveries. I realize with humility how writing a song, a poem or a play gives meaning to my life and thrills me. Some things in us are just not negotiable. They must be welcomed and followed because they lead us to ourselves and because they lead us to the joy of living.

What My Spleen and Lungs Were Telling Me

The spleen! I did not even know where it was located in the body. It was the occasion to learn about it. Nor did I know what its function was. It produces red and white blood cells as well as blood platelets. It also filters the blood by capturing germs and eliminating useless or degenerated blood cells. So it plays a crucial role in the immune system which, by all counts, is working very poorly in me. According to Hammer and the theory of 'biological decoding', the spleen acts as a special large lymph gland. In case of crisis, the brain turns to it for a stop-gap solution and tells it to develop, in which case it will produce an enormous pocket of blood as a reserve, 'ready to be used in case of loss, due to an accidental wound or combat for example.'[1] A spleen problem specifically symbolizes an inability to fight back as with a heavily bleeding wound – *and I have one in my stomach.*

In addition, a spleen dysfunction indicates a problem related to duties and responsibilities where weight ends up causing a loss of *joie de vivre.* Since the spleen has the function of producing blood cells, this corresponds to the notion of literally 'making bad blood', a literal translation of the French expression that means worrying oneself sick.

It's true that the accumulation of battles to wager made it so that instead of feeling any drive from my activities, I ended up mostly feeling fatigue. Instead of being light-hearted and happy while doing things I liked, I was submerged by the fear of not managing and of not being equal to the task. And I began putting myself down instead of appreciating what I was doing.

The months preceding my cancer were full of excitement and diversity but at what cost! A month of writing, then a month of filming in Montreal for my television series *Guy Corneau en atelier*[2], followed by

---

1   Sabbah, Claude & Laminne, Isabelle, *Le décodage biologique. Tome III.* Author-editor Claude Sabbah, 2002, p. 530. (Not a commercial publication)
2   3 DVD set: *Le meilleur de soi. Guy Corneau en atelier.* Thirteen one-hour episodes produced by Productions Point de mire about Guy Corneau's workshops. Edited by Point de mire, Canal Vie et Les Éditions de l'Homme, Montréal, 2008, available only in Quebec.

a month of conferences in Quebec and abroad. There was no end to the stress. I went from one activity to another with ease but with the constant fear of failing. I stayed focused without a moment to relax. I truly think that that is what finally did me in: giving everything without taking the time to replenish myself. I drew on all my reserves and, at a certain point, I was out of gas.

Chinese medicine says that worries damage the spleen. Excessive intellectual work, daily preoccupations and all kinds of negative thoughts tie our energy in knots and weaken the digestive system. Without a doubt, one of the most appropriate responses I could give to my spleen and to my immune system was to end the constant inner battle. This is what made me decide to cancel my European tour and take a sabbatical. This was another important element in my healing journey.

I turned to traditional Chinese medicine in order to try to explain what was oppressing my lungs. Chinese medicine ties the lungs to sadness. Sorrow, melancholy and regret exhaust the lungs by dissipating energy. These emotions are part of life and don't cause problems if they're accepted and recognized. But if, instead, sorrow is held back and the situation causing the problem is prolonged, energy will be lost, which can often lead to pneumonia, bronchitis or respiratory ailments such as asthma. I've had one bronchitis after another. It seems to me that relatively early on, I lost touch with the laughing child inside me. My lungs were talking to me about that.

The Dialogue with Cells

Now I'd like to talk briefly about a technique that helped me considerably on an energetic level: a dialogue with my cells. It is a kind of active imagination but with the organs and the cells taken as inner characters. First, I had to listen to each affected organ and let the degenerated cells express their message in terms of thoughts, memories, evocations, sensations and colours. Then, I had to thank the degenerated cells and give them permission to die. By doing this, I indicated to them that their job was done since I was now listening to what my body was telling me. In the third phase of the procedure, I invited my stem cells to make a whole bunch of new cells. I imagined them proliferating and dancing until I could see my organ glowing with warmth, light and health.

The degenerated cells have the function of translating the messages coming from the deeper *self* which may be having difficulty manifesting itself. By doing this, they act as the representatives of the perfection of life. The injunction that invites them to die takes on all its meaning when we consider that the problem with cancerous cells is that they refuse to die, whereas the life of a cell extends normally only up to

110 days. I practised this technique of 'dialoguing with the cells' once a day for about twenty minutes each time.

Reprogramming the Cells

Why focus on reprogramming my cells with images? Well, like other practices related to creative visualization, it helps stimulate processes of self-healing and self-conservation, and the regeneration of individual organs by offering them a new direction. Let me explain. A cancerous cell is a cell that is dysfunctional in relation to the central programme that manages its production. However, it's not simply 'crazy', even if it's lost its original direction. It's been deprogrammed in relation to the basic influx, and another programme is now managing it. It has remained intelligent. It continues to organize and to feed. It produces mass or digs into tissues. Chemotherapy helps dislodge this reprogramming which has supplanted the programme that strives for balance.

So the question is, what will 'reprogramme' these new cells? What will give them a new sense and direction? The imagination, of course! Chemotherapy is used to eradicate the deficient programme. Visualization reprogrammes the new cells for health.

Visualization works because the brain doesn't distinguish between imaginary states and real facts. We get ulcers from worrying about money whether the concern is real or imagined. Reality begins in the imagination. To the body and mind, powerful inner scenes are full-blown events just like any outer situation. In fact, everything goes through our representation of events and our interpretation of them. What is real for the brain is our inner state.

Another aspect of intensifying the movement of cells until they produce heat and light is based on the fact that, by definition, degenerated cells are slower than healthy cells. Since they are limping along so to speak, they can't follow the acceleration of movement and they disqualify themselves by simply dissolving. This is at least one way of interpreting what goes on at a cellular level and explaining how states of happiness have an effect on health.

Traumas, shocks, wounds and disillusionment deprogramme the initial imprint. Reprogramming cells requires recreating in ourselves the life drive that was behind our very birth. We have to imagine the intensity and happiness that led us to fuse with matter. It's as if our soul, our deeper *self,* or our pure basic energy cell projected itself once again into flesh in order to give shape to and programme the cells and the organic processes. This entails a marriage of three planes of existence: the plane of the soul (energy), the plane of the mind (consciousness) and the plane of matter (expression).

'We Want to Live'

From that moment on, it seemed to me that I had a pretty good idea of the psychological gist of what was going on and all I had to do after that was to keep my spirits up. *That's when I got really depressed.* The psychologist Rose-Marie Charest told me recently that 80% of cancer patients get very depressed. And yet, this is completely hidden; we only hear about the zeal to fight which means that these symptoms are neither recognized nor treated.

A friend of mine realized the state I was in and suggested guiding me and a few friends in a kind of retreat. The first evening, we were supposed to talk about our availability to life and I remember stating 'As far as I'm concerned, I don't think there's a cell in my body that wants to live!' The retreat continued for several evenings with a mixture of teachings and meditations every night.

Every exercise began with a relaxation after which we were supposed to 'listen to the message of our cells beyond our mind'. On the last night, I felt like bursting out loud. To me the suggestion was way beyond my strength. I'm not very good at going *beyond my mind*. Nevertheless, I tried the exercise like every other night, but without much hope of results this time around.

All the participants heard the message from their cells. As for me, I heard their message alright. In fact, I heard their shout:

– 'We want to live!'

And the subtext:

– 'You're blocking us!'

I understood that my depressive states were stopping the regeneration processes from taking place. At the moment I heard this shout making its way inside of me, I felt my pelvis area become completely hot. Life was boiling in my body and this boiling life had now reached my entire stomach.

Now, in my entire life, I've never felt what they call the energy centre at the base of the spine, but now I felt it perfectly. I also felt incredible joy because I wasn't trying to do anything in order to produce this magnificently comforting sensation. It spontaneously appeared and I more than welcomed it. After two weeks of exercises, my cells answered my call in a very down-to-earth way. I was inexplicably convinced that there was a wound in me and it was now disappearing. Life was pulsating from one end of my body to the other. From the crown of my head to the tip of my toes, at last things were moving!

I emerged from this retreat happy as a lark. As unbelievable as it may seem, my depression evaporated on the spot. I regained an unmitigated wish to live. In the days following this experience, buoyed by the contact that had just been established, I had more and more moments of spontaneous joy. I was exhilarated about everything and nothing. I felt light and whimsical. I became ecstatic at the mere sight of a ray of sunlight on the floor. I had felt extreme despondency, and now I was experiencing the voluptuousness of this slow-motion existence. I had been living in hell and now I was living the blessing of my state as a sick person: no responsibilities, no duties, nothing to do. I tasted life in its simplest and purest form. I savoured the present moment and it tasted like eternity.

That's when I understood that my main doctor would be whatever stimulated my taste for life. Yes, that is what was going to help me. Truly, it is joy that heals.

Conclusion

In conclusion I'd like to stress the fact that it's really important to actively participate in one's return to balance as long as we're able to. The reason is simple. Doctors and medications, therapists and techniques create environments that stimulate self-healing or self-regulating mechanisms that are already in us. The care that is given to us by people and techniques stimulates the repair mechanisms that are already part of the genetic makeup of each organism, alongside the mechanisms of self-preservation, self-organization and self-expression. We can intensify our capacity for self-healing just as well by using chemotherapy, psychology or the imagination. In short, the conscious presence and attention on our individual process is the basic factor for returning to a state of integral health that includes the body, soul and mind.

When reflecting on this episode, I realize that cancer allowed me to heal a very deep dissociation in myself. I come from a background of abuse and to survive I had cut off parts of myself, namely murderous drives asking for revenge, along with very sensitive and creative aspects that caused my parents a lot of insecurity. Cancer allowed me to do something about it. I often thought that the many cells affected talked about the many times I had said 'no' to my true self.

I will leave you with the images of a dream that I found extraordinary and that I had in 2008 at the moment I began to understand that I had got myself out of this pickle. I found myself at my home in the country. I was digging a big hole in the ground with my hands. The hole was big enough to plant a large tree in it. But I found out that I was supposed to stick my head in it. Then I saw my head planted in the ground, my face turned towards the sun and tanned. My head was surrounded by a crown of leaves as if for an African feast. I had a shining smile on my face. *I knew what I had to do to stay healthy.*

Clouds in the Sky Still Allow a Glimpse of the Moon: Cancer, Resilience, Creativity

Marta Tibaldi

Italy (AIPA)

> *Our true faces*
> *Are said to reveal*
> *Their true face*
> *When we lose clothes, food and houses*
> *At the limits of experience*
>
> Sumako Harada

> *Experience is what we got also when you didn't get*
> *what you wanted*
>
> Randy Pausch

> *I have tried to communicate what others don't see*
> *for instance the profile of a rainbow*
>
> Bruno Munari

Part I
Three Quotations

The above quotations sum up what I want to point out: 1. that severe trauma in general and cancer trauma in particular represents a breakdown of the Ego, in consequence of which the Self dynamics can reveal themselves clearly; 2. that when cancer patients become testimonies of their traumatic experiences they show others the healing power inside their body-mind and how it is possible to deal with a difficult illness such as cancer in a resilient way; 3. that it is possible to look at oncologic disease in a new, unusual and unconventional way.

Speaking about Cancer Is an Exercise of Resilience and Self-healing

There is no doubt, in the experience of cancer, as in severe trauma, that speaking about it, telling and sharing our stories represent an exercise of resilience and self-healing, which sustain and stimulate self-recovery processes, towards a new, even if different, *restitutio ad integrum* (coming back to a full recovery). It is important to speak about cancer and to know its characteristics before we meet it personally or vicariously in order to mentalize and to master it in advance ('psychological prevention of cancer trauma' [Tibaldi 2010]).

Speaking about It in a Light and Creative Way

In order to transform cancer stories from mere individual confessions to creative and social resources, patients should develop the ability to communicate their experience in a light and creative way, with a modality which might prove good to the teller as well as to the listener. I am referring to a way of telling our stories of trauma which, even if it exposes us to the fear of cancer, is done with a positive attitude and in the right measure, stimulating our internal resources more than depressing them and transforming the negative statement 'I am powerless' to the positive 'I can manage it'; in particular, doing it in a way that pushes creatively our personalities beyond trauma and reveals the mighty and radical renewal appeal which belongs to the disease itself.

Some General Data

According to M. Giannantonio, *Psicotraumatologia e psicologia dell'emergenza* (2005, p. 59) the percentage of the population that will face one or more traumatic events varies from 40% to 75%; an even larger part of the whole population will have a traumatic experience, probably without any tool to overcome it. This is one of the reasons why it is important to speak of trauma and to know its characteristics before we encounter it. As for cancer trauma, in 2008 the Italian newspaper *La Repubblica* asked a representative sample of people about the disease they feared most; 84,2 % of the interviewed persons declared that cancer occupies the first place among their worst fears, followed by heart attack, Alzheimer, stroke, multiple sclerosis, AIDS, depression, Parkinson, diabetes etc.

Epidemiological Data

In Italy in 2005, 202 cases of cancer out of 10,000 men (2%) and 256 out of 10,000 women (2.5%) were diagnosed; therefore in 2005 550,000 men and 720,000 women had or have had cancer; currently 250,000 new cancer patients are anticipated annually. In Italy the survival rate within 5 years of diagnosis is on average around 46%; this rate is higher for women because of the different types of cancer: more lethal in men, less severe in women (these data are from the Italian Superior Institute of Health).

Cancer Is a Severe and Complex Traumatic Event

The experience of cancer is a severe and complex trauma, acute and chronic at the same time. It is a traumatic event which affects either the individual or the relational and social existence and may lead to the most diverse outcomes; the more we face the deep dark side of cancer, pushing it to its maximum extent and letting the experience go, the more we can live the creative side of it, discovering that the living processes unfold themselves through the cycle of birth, death and renewal; this means that the experience of 'death' belongs to life as do birth and renewal.

Cancer, Resilience, Creativity

Diagnosis, surgical operation/operations, oncologic treatment, uncertainty related to one's own survival etc. request from the patient their maximum effort of resiliency; but it is also important to be aware that the worsening of our physic health state mobilizes per se (in itself) our inner resources and our body-mind's self-healing system. This means that we can meet our living good energies through meaningful images, coming from our self-healing inner system which opens up our consciousness to new and unexpected perspectives; the experience of cancer if lived to its extreme gives to our life a new and deeper value.

Jungian Analytical Tools and Complementary Therapies

In Jungian practice dreams, spontaneous images, active imaginations, deep writing, together with the possibility of telling and sharing our story in the analytic space and beyond are the elective tools we can use to sail through the difficult and committing experience of cancer; useful complementary therapies to relieve and calm down patients' body-mind pain and suffering and to activate images are mindful exercises such as slow and deep breathing, progressive voluntary relaxation (isometric exercises), EMDR (Eye Movements Desensitization and Reprocessing).

Towards a 'Path of Sense'

Regarding the experience of illness and the importance to give it words, Bianchi e Manicardi in *Accanto al malato* (2006, p. 11; my translation) writes:

It is essential to dare to say a word on this reality [of disease], which belongs to every single human life: it is the word which specifies human beings, it is in the act of speaking that we could invent paths of sense. [...] Human beings humanize themselves by asking about themselves on themselves, and the question and reflection on disease and, more in general, on suffering, is inherent to this task of becoming human beings. [...] Between the impotence of dumbness and the arrogant presumptousness of definite and final words, we are asked to dare a word, a humble word arising from silence which lives again in itself the Easter dynamism of death-resurrection.

Part 2
My Story of Illness

In order to describe the deep meaning that can arise from practical confrontation with cancer, using Jungian analytic tools, I will briefly recall my own experience of cancer. I will report here only a short part of the story in order to stress in particular what may arise from the active confrontation with the 'dark night of the body' (for the extended version cfr. M. Tibaldi 2007, pp. 53-69 & 2010).

Prior Events

Without any suspicion about my health state, in the months before my diagnosis of cancer, various dreams warned me about the need to overcome some ordeals. Consequently I wrote these notes down:

I keep on dreaming that unexpectedly I have to cross some water, dirty water. I do not want to do it. I try to escape from this ordeal, I want to find a path on the solid ground; crossing water gives me the sensation of coldness, it is uncomfortable, I do not want to get wet.

Then just before the diagnosis of cancer two dreams in particular warned me about a problem of life and death.

First dream. The first dream tells me that in order to reach the 'destination' – a white house where a master dressed in white is waiting for me – I have to cross on foot a stretch of water, in which I am very reluctant to enter; I have my bag with me and I am afraid of losing it; the master informs me that this will be my 'last ordeal'.

Second dream. In the second dream I am observing the Earth globe from the atmosphere, seeing existence from far away: If we could look at our life objectively in this way from this distance – I am saying to myself inside the dream – we would be able to decide what kind of voyage we want our life to be and where we would like to go ...

Turning to the Imaginal Master

Shortly after these two dreams I was diagnosed with breast cancer
– for which I was immediately operated – requiring very strong
chemotherapy. After my first chemotherapy, in a moment of great
physical and psychic difficulty, I decided to turn myself to the master I
saw in the first dream, using the Jungian method of active imagination;
in the imaginal dialogue which emerged from it, the master spoke to
me through these words, which I quote here briefly.

'Throw your bag away, free yourself and proceed lightly forward.
Leave the past, what you build is inside yourself. Leave all that weighs
you down.'; 'Live in the present moment, the only true moment to
which you have to give an answer'; 'I will be with you if you look for
me inside your heart'; 'Follow your intuition, dare the hidden path,
fruits are ripening'; 'I am your master A., the one who will be along
with you in this voyage towards light'; 'Your old way of being will die';
'Afterwards belongs to afterwards'; 'Meditate, remain in silence, refer
to yourself, go into your heart'; 'Let it go, stay calm, concentrate on
the present moment, do not let yourself be shaken by the waves of the
sea which are moving on the surface. Do not let yourself be distracted
from what is happening at that level. This is the extraordinary time
of initiation, do not waste it, you will not have another one so fruitful
and lucky. This is your great opportunity, live it fully'; 'Look for my
name'; 'I am your master.'

Practical Aspects

Curious about the dialogue, I decide to look for the master's name
on the web; to my greatest surprise, I find out that the master's name
refers to a community in the Italian Umbrian hills where 'body and
spirit healing' are actively searched for; the 'universal and practical'
teachings offered by the community are based on Self-realization
principles; the master's name refers also to a meditation centre in my
town, only a hundred metres away from my home. But surprises did
not finish there: I discovered that the master, who the community and
the meditation centre are based on, is also the author of a book, given
to me many years before by a Jungian Swiss analyst, in a very unusual
way, after my first interview before beginning my analytical training. In
her dedication the analyst wrote:

Here it is the book I promise you, which contains, according to me,
the best image of an analyst!

After the greatest effort of resilience in treatment, I start reading
the book given to me by the Swiss analyst and I decide to get in touch
with the community and the meditation centre; the encounter is
good, they teach me to meditate; meditation gives me new energy and

calms down my emotions; my uneasiness changes into an unexpected well-being; I am amazed and surprised; I would never have found the way to meditation without the imaginal master's indications.

Cancer from a Deep Point of View and the Journey to Recovery

According to my experience, active confrontation with unconscious images coming from illness offers the possibility of giving shapes and words to traumatic emotions, to bodily pain, to self-healing processes, sustaining life in its self-renewal; if experienced consciously and to its worst point, cancer can represent an initiation to the mystery of life and its transformation.

On this point Thomas Moore writes (2004, p. 270):

Illness is always an initiation of sorts. It invites new thoughts and daydreams. It takes you to a special *plateau* on which you exist in a way different from all that you have known. You have to cope and come to a new understanding of yourself. Your illness fills you with wonder, and perhaps fear. You have to find new resources within yourself and in your world.

About the journey to recovery, he notes as well (p. 280):

You have to let your darkness shape your journey to the place of healing. You have to go deeper than your mood, far beneath your emotion, and down into the underworld of the very meaning of your life. You don't have to manufacture any of this. Your illness will shake you up and provide you with the necessary anxieties and hopelessness. You have to own up to these and let them be. You have to speak for them and about them. You have to track their roots in your dreams and in your history. You have to talk to your loved ones about them and learn as much as you can. You have to gather your depths, and in the resulting darkness penetrate through the skin of meaning that has kept you healthy so far. Now you have to transcend yourself in a downward direction and have a glimpse of your fate.

Part 3
Ancient Stories for Cancer Patients

Although in present times cancer patients live and suffer their disease above all as a private pathology, confined in the space of subjectivity, as a matter of fact it contains much wider horizons; if we begin to consider cancer trauma not only as a subjective and personal event, but also an objective and collective one, if we go in search of old stories treating the same theme from a broader and more universal perspective, then it will be possible to catch the archetypal renewal potential hidden inside cancer. Two stories going in this direction are: Jacob fighting with God's angel and Philoctetes and the bow.

Jacob Fighting with God's Angel

It is a story that shows the 'dark night of the body' as the place in which the human being meets the divine – the encounter of the Ego with the dark (and then the bright) aspects of the Self through the experience of physical disease – it is that of Jacob fighting with God's angel. The biblical story is in *Genesis* 32, 24-31:

> And Jacob was left alone; and there wrestled a man with him until the breaking of the day. / And when he saw that he prevailed not against him, he touched the hollow of his thigh; and the hollow of Jacob's thigh was out of joint, as he wrestled with him. / And he said unto him: What is thy name? And he said: Jacob. / And he said: Thy name shall be called no more Jacob, but Israel: for as a prince hast thou power with God and with men, and hast prevailed. / And Jacob asked him, and said: Tell me, I pray thee, thy name. / And he said: Wherefore is it that thou dost ask after my name? And he blessed him there. / And Jacob called the name of the place Penuel: for I have seen God face to face, and my life is preserved. / And as he passed over Penuel the sun rose upon him, and he halted upon his thigh.

Why Jacob?

We know that when someone is hit by cancer their relationship with life, with God etc. seems more of an endless fight and an experience of damnation than a blessing; the patient curses at God, at the events, at destiny and do not accept that their identity and their body have to be tested in such a hard way; the patient forgets (or discovers to have never known) that all the nights, also the darkest ones, contain the promise of dawn. As happened to Jacob, patients who became aware of the 'divine' (archetypal) dimension of their illness, know that the Self 'dark' power can change into a blessing when it has been recognized for what it is: this means that when patients can place their disease into a broader horizon than the egoic one – within the living process which winds itself through the cycle of life, death and renewal – they can get in touch with an absolute truth: destruction is a form of existence, which always recreates itself also through death.

Blessing, Being Blessed

It is important to get consciously in touch with the possibility to bless and to be blessed because blessing is an effective act which focalizes our mind on vital energies and puts us in active and conscious relationship with the creative aspects of the Self; blessing offers to our creative energy a channel through which it can flow freely and improves our deep trust in life; blessing creates a virtuous cycle between the one who blesses and the one who is blessed with a positive effect also on the blessing person.

Another Story from Ancient Time: Philoctetes' Myth

A famous bowman, Philoctetes was Heracles' good friend; Heracles gave him his bow and arrows as a present, thanking him for having set fire to Eta's pyre. During the Trojan war, Philoctetes led seven ships and fifty bowmen, but his ship never reached its destination; during a port of call in Tenedo, perhaps during a sacrifice, Philoctetes had a foot bitten by a snake; his wound soon became purulent and Odysseus convinced the Greek leaders to leave Philoctetes on Lemnos island.

Philoctetes According to Sophocles' Tragedy

Sophocles' tragedy shows Philoctetes has been living for ten years in complete isolation on Lemnos island; meanwhile the Oracle informs the Greeks that in order to win Troy's war they have to get Philoctetes' bow that he keeps on the island; the Greeks decide to send Odysseus and Neoptolemus to Lemnos in order to subtract treacherously the bow from Philoctetes. After several events, Philoctetes, deceived by them, gives his bow to his false friend Neoptolemus; the latter, repenting of his behaviour, reveals to Philoctetes that he has deceived him and gives him back the bow. Neoptolemus' decision makes Odysseus furious. Heracles appears, *deus ex machina*, smoothes over the disagreements between Odysseus and Neoptolemus, and Philoctetes is convinced to go on board towards Troy; once in Troy, Machaon heals Philoctetes' wound and the latter kills with his own bow Paris, the cause of Troy's war, bringing back justice and order.

Why Philoctetes?

Philoctetes is a symbol of the traumatized human being, shunned and dismissed by the community, who nevertheless is essential for it to win Ego's *hubris* and its war against Self.

The social problems that the disease creates among both cancer patients and healthy people describe well what may happen to a patient who, without having done any crime, is burdened with all the weight of the disease and is emotionally dismissed by the community; but Philoctetes's story teaches us that, although wounded, he owns the bow necessary to restore the order between humans and the divine.

Symbolically What Does It Mean Owning Philoctetes' Bow for Cancer Patients?

The patient who has been tested by physic trauma can discover inside themselves, and be testimony then to others, that the body has a self-healing and recovering natural power, resilience and creativity, a living spirit that they did not know before. Becoming aware of this inner power is fundamental individually and for the collectivity in order to face the traumas of life with positive, well-balanced and creative attitudes, transforming the story of trauma into one of resilience and the story of destruction and death into one of renewal and rebirth; cancer patients who have become aware of the resilient, creative and renewal dimension inside their experience of illness, 'who have torn away from misfortune [as Walter Benjamin states] all the possibilities it implies', become living testimonies that passing through death can mean the chance to gain renewal; cancer is an experience of renewal which happens through the 'dark night of the body' and the confrontation with death.

Cancer Patients Own Philoctetes' Bow

As Richard F. Mollica writes (2006, p. 240):

Violence [of illness] can lead us on an unexpected journey into a strange land where, like Philoctetes, we have committed no crime, but have been abandoned and ostracized by society. Even our professional healers are capable of exploiting and abusing us. But we know that located within our bodies and mind is a powerful force, bursting to find expression, that is capable of healing any injury. The invisible wounds of violence are no longer invisible, and the invisible process of self-healing is now evident. As new scientific discoveries are made, they will continue to show the tremendous power to heal that has been built into human beings over time. If society learns to use this empirical knowledge, no longer relying on social fictions and half-truths, the modern age can be an exciting one, where the effects of violence need no longer be feared, and we can welcome back into our communities those who have had to sojourn alone in the land of violence.

In Conclusion

It is no more about asking how we can avoid our physical mortality – task anyhow impossible – but how we can live in a resilient and creative way with illness and death, which are after all a life experience and belong to existence itself; every patient who has fulfilled their voyage into the abyss of illness agrees in saying that it has transformed them into a better person. In my experience, cancer has thrown away from me the dimension of the future (tomorrow I could be ill again) and that of health (this illness cannot be healed permanently, at least not now) but as a result, cancer has grounded me strongly in the present moment; the life that I am living now is more intense, calmer, wiser, more full of joy and benevolence, more full of the only thing that has consistency towards death: completely developing our capacity to live and love.

Cancer Patients are an Individual and a Social Resource

For everything that disease has taught me and teaches cancer patients, for the voyage we did together, for the 'power of the bow' which comes to us from archetypal levels of existence, I will conclude this paper by addressing an invitation to healthy people: take oncologic patients into account, expert patients of clouds which still allow a glimpse of the moon, they are a resource, they could be masters.

References

Bianchi, E., Manicardi, L. (2006). *Accanto al malato*. Mangano (BI): Edizioni QiQajon – Comunità di Bose.
Giannantonio, M. (Ed.) (2005). *Psicotraumatologia e psicologia dell'emergenza*. Salerno: Ecomind.
Holy Scripture, King James Version, *Genesis*.
Moore, T. (2004). *Dark Nights of the Soul*. UK: Piatkus Books.
Mollica, R.F. (2006). *Healing Invisible Wounds. Paths to Hope and Recovery in a Violent World*. US: Hartcourt Books.
Tibaldi, M. (2007). 'L'intero universo è un'unica perla brillante. Un approccio junghiano alla scrittura autobiografica del profondo nell'esperienza oncologica'. In *Scrittura e terapia*, *Adultità* 27, eds. D. Demetrio, C. Borgonovi. Milan: Guerini, 53-69.
– (2010). *Oltre il cancro. Trasformare* creativamente *la malattia che temiamo di più*. Bergamo: Moretti & Vitali.
Wilson, E. (1940). *The Wound and the Bow. Seven Studies in Literature*. Ohio: Ohio University Press (Ital. tr. *La ferita e l'arco*. Milan: Garzanti, 1991).

Panel:
What Could Be Jungian about
Human Rights Work?

Astrid Berg, Tawfiq Salman & Tristan Troudart

Abstract: The question of whether Jungian analysts should move beyond the consulting room to engage with mental health issues that pertain to the collective is the focus of this panel[1]. Two narratives are presented: one from the view point of a psychiatrist in Occupied Palestine, the other from the conflicted situation which faces an Israeli analyst.

Despite the strong ambivalence that is experienced on both sides, there is a willingness to meet and to take a standpoint without necessarily coming to a resolution. A third position is offered by describing experiences from the South African perspective. The African notion of *Ubuntu* is offered as a moral entry point that states that community goes beyond one's own; from this point of view, Jungian analysts can do no other than to act.

***

Astrid Berg
South Africa (SAAJA)

Introduction

Although our starting point will be the conflict between the two peoples of the 'Holy Land', the aim is to go further than that. The question that forms the backdrop to this plenary is: Can and should we, as Jungian analysts, move beyond the individual in the consulting room and open ourselves to encounters across the 'divide' – whatever that 'divide' might constitute? As a group of analysts it is our task to think about moving with modern times where we no longer can afford to live in isolation; to think about where we as psychotherapists position ourselves. There are circumstances all over the world, circumstances that affect the mental health of people immediately and directly on a large scale and we could do well to consider our roles in our own societies.

All too easily we hide behind our profession, behind the work

---

1 The papers in this panel were first published in the April 2011 edition of the *Journal of Analytical Psychology*.

with the individual and his or her 'Self'; however in today's age we no longer have the luxury of doing only that – there are too many people we know about who are in distress and once we know, we have an obligation. We have to use the knowledge and insight which our theories offer, so that these may guide us into considered and constructive action. We need to be nudged into stretching ourselves in the direction of doing something for the collective in whatever part of the globe we live.

Tawfiq and Tristan will share with us their stories, memories and recollections of the meetings and interactions between themselves and their groups and talk about some thoughts regarding Jungian psychology and human rights. I will conclude by attempting to answer three questions and will also bring in some parallels from my own South African experience.

***

Tawfiq Salman

Palestine (SOS Children's Village, Bethlehem)

What follows is a personal story of mental health co-workers' reactions and emotions in a time of conflict.

I work for SOS Children's Villages International in a mobile psychosocial clinic, around the West Bank (part of the Occupied Territories of Palestine since 1967), trying to heal traumatized children who lost their parents or who are facing emotional problems because of the violence of the Occupation.

A Palestinian from present day Israel who is a coordinator with Physicians for Human Rights Israel (PHR), called me about a group of Israeli mental health co-workers who wanted to work in cooperation with Palestinian mental health co-workers. My first reaction was one of rejection: The same Israelis, who kill and destroy, now want to help? The main feeling was a negative one: What's the reason to meet? It's not useful.

When thinking about the Israelis, I immediately remembered bad and good experiences. The bad ones: When I was 7 years old in my small village, I walked with my friend close to Israeli soldiers; when we got near, the soldiers shot at us with their guns, not hurting us, but threatening to kill us if we didn't leave. Following this incident, I reacted with fear, insomnia, and irritability. A second instance occurred when I was an adolescent at the beginning of the 1st Intifada (popular resistance) when the Israelis gathered males older than 16 years into open spaces; then, especially during cold and rainy weather, they sat us down with our hands around our heads thus putting us into a frightening and uncomfortable situation.

I can list all too many bad experiences. On the other hand, I can report a good memory: in 1998, during a trip to the seashore in Israel with the Bethlehem medical team, a group of Palestinian nurses nearly drowned, and Israeli lifeguards saved them. The doctors were also very welcoming, treated us well and invited me to visit the hospital.

So, the Israeli offer in 2003 put me in conflict with intense ambivalent feelings. At that time, it was very difficult to acknowledge that there are good and willing Israelis. We Palestinians saw them as occupiers who pushed us in the direction of not wanting to see, hear or meet with them. However, something inside was pressing me: Why not? Let's see what they need, see what we can do with these meetings.

I decided to give it a try, so I called the PHR coordinator and I accepted the Israeli invitation. Nevertheless, before the first meeting, I was worried and asked myself: What am I doing? Will it be accepted by my community? I asked other colleagues who noted that in Israel there are intelligent people who have been against the settlements and the Occupation, that it might change something in our own community if Palestinians could see that there are good Israelis. We believed that such meetings would reveal Palestinian reality to the Israelis and that this would promote the will to live in peace and mutual acceptance. Even with conscious intention to trust, we felt something opposing deep inside.

Our meetings began with a specific focus on professional issues; we accepted each other as colleagues exchanging experiences in psycho-trauma work and techniques. The atmosphere was acceptable with limited personal relations during coffee breaks. One-to-one interactions were easier than those in the group as a whole. Over time we developed our own experience of being together and consequently our discussions in general opened up and became more active.

When the Israelis came to Bethlehem we were afraid for them, and our thought was that we had to do our best to protect them. I felt conflicted as I was committed to protecting our Israeli colleagues at the height of actions by the Palestinian Intifada resistance fighters to kill Israelis; we felt that with the killing, there was some basic justice being done even if there were some unwitting victims. As a result of the Israeli Occupation too many Palestinians civilians lost their lives with relatively few losses on the other side.

On another occasion when we met at a restaurant in East Jerusalem, a psychologist on our team was angry; I was angry as well, due to the location of the meeting. We had no other option than to travel there with a special Israeli permit. Our group felt it absurd that the Israelis would invite us to *our* Jerusalem. We asked ourselves: Who here has the right to invite the other? Of course I felt I have the right. *They took our city and they are inviting us to our city.* I felt awful, but it even gave me a reason to meet again and again …

Maybe we can all work together to change attitudes and to work for a nonviolent solution. Yes, we the Palestinians are the victims of this Occupation, but we don't like the status of being victims because something from our deeper level is telling us that victims are weak and helpless.

Our staff members at SOS continued to be suspicious and asked me: Do you trust these people? What do they come here for? How can they help our community? We wondered if perhaps our Israeli visitors didn't feel free to express their feelings in their own community; further we wondered if they were coming here as a way of stating that they were against the Occupation and the killings and that they supported Palestinian rights.

On the other hand, we were suspicious and were curious as to whether or not they wanted to show the Israeli community that we didn't have any problems, that we were liars or just aggressive and violent people. Or maybe they were coming to see our weak points, so that they could take advantage of them. Furthermore, they might later go to the international media and show that the Israelis are peace loving people who were helping the Palestinians. Additionally, they could show that the Palestinians were acting violently in response to Israeli good will. This would parallel the pattern of the official media in Israel which explains all of their military violence as acts of self defence. After a few meetings, we continued to believe that there was no divide between good and bad Israelis; there were no good Israelis at all.

At one point, we met after a terrible event in which many Palestinian civilians were killed by the Israeli Air Force. The members of the Palestinian staff felt sadness, anger and resentment. They said that it may be that our Israeli visitors were good people but they are members of their larger community which includes an army that is violent toward the Palestinians.

Our feelings at that time centred on the uselessness of meeting with the Israeli group, even if they were good people, because the aggression was persistent and their small group, could not possibly influence the larger home community to make any change. We were also worried that if the relatives of the Palestinian victims were to know of the joint meetings, we would be seen as collaborators.

During another meeting, the Israelis presented the case of a fighter pilot's son who suffered from severe anxiety symptoms. It was presented as a clinical case, but it aroused strong emotions on both sides. My thoughts were as follows:

1. The case was presented without any hidden intention, as any clinical case.

2. The presenter intentionally wanted to show the power of the Israeli army and at the same time to project an image of being victims.

3. I felt that the Israelis should not have presented the case of the son of a combat pilot, who shot helpless Palestinian civilians.

Again, we thought as we did at the beginning that Israelis are all the same, selfish and not caring about our feelings.

Our meetings took place during a most difficult period when the Israeli army was invading and reoccupying Palestinian towns and villages; so it was like a nightmare or a surreal experience to be meeting them at that disorienting moment. Despite these feelings and circumstances, we continued to participate, believing that our gatherings might bring some change to the situation. However, with every meeting we had the same bad feelings.

We continued to wonder how much either side could do to stop the Occupation which was the cause of so much violence. We asked ourselves: How can we build bridges of trust and peace? How can we destroy the hate in these difficult times?

I struggled with who the real victim was. They killed thousands of Palestinians, they wounded tens of thousands, and they also arrested tens of thousands. The Palestinians from time to time killed a small number of Israelis by bombings here and there. But they wanted us to recognize them as equal victims. We have always thought that we are the real and direct victims and that they are indirect victims, both of which have been caused by their bad leaders' policy of Occupation and settlements. How can they find it acceptable to occupy another people?

We wished that they would come together as a group to give voice to both the direct and indirect victims and influence their own bad leaders to sign a peace agreement, so that we could begin to heal one another's wounds.

Also we have observed just a few of the Israeli groups who have been working for peace by doing something practical on the ground; for example, some groups have worked to prevent house demolitions and to open check points. For our part, these gestures have been too little and we remain pessimistic as the Occupation continues to exist.

But personally I felt optimistic with Tristan and his colleagues to go on with these meetings in order to have more influence for justice and peace in the 'Holy land'.

With passing of time, our meetings became less frequent and we did not experience a positive process taking place in the group; so the end of our gatherings came as a relief for those of us on the Palestinian side. But I keep in mind our Israeli colleagues and others on both sides who still try to change the situation at ground level with the hope that it will benefit future generations for all.

Now, with this last sentence, I'm thinking of Tristan and his colleagues.

I am glad to meet them again – Israelis of good will whom I know. 'Where love rules, there is no will to power, and where power predominates, there love is lacking. The one is the shadow of the other' (C.G. Jung 1953/1966, para. 78).

***

Tristan Troudart
Israel (IIJP)

This is the story of an encounter of people who belong to two communities in tragic confrontation. It is quite a surreal tale of professional lectures and clinical meetings being held against a complex background of monstrous violence with both communities severely shaken by death and destruction. Our intention was to use our psychological skills to fill professional needs and also to open a constructive and supportive dialogue with Palestinians. We expressed our solidarity with their struggle for freedom, as Israelis who support peace, human rights and non-violence. We, a group of Israeli mental health professionals, backed by Physicians for Human Rights-Israel, held meetings with a bigger and younger group of Palestinian colleagues from SOS-Bethlehem, whose arrival was frequently delayed because of the military checkpoints. We conducted joint intensive meetings, lectures and group discussions on clinical cases with psychological trauma of children and adolescents as the central issue. We believed that trauma destroys people emotionally, but learning together how to treat it could unite us in an atmosphere for healing. We did not talk openly about politics although dialogue and socializing developed during the sessions and the coffee breaks.

In the course of the meetings we asked ourselves what is the real, deep reason that drives us to meet with Palestinians? At the conscious level our intention was to link our professional, therapeutic skills to socio-political action. We live a drama of collective traumatic situations, resulting from the constant bloodshed between both communities. At a deeper level, I felt that the real common emotional ground that drove our group was the wound that we carry from our collective traumatic past, the Second World War Nazi genocide of the Jews. If we add the displacement of the Palestinians from their land by the Israelis in 1948, we have two peoples afflicted by collective trauma, who, since then, blame each other for constant death and re-traumatization. Both communities keep trying to weaken, undermine or even destroy the other, and this reinforces unipolar archetypal projections. These tragedies are recent; many of us are descendants of Holocaust survivors and the Palestinians' parents were uprooted from their land. These are cultural complexes that affect our peoples, which, if left untreated, can lead to archetypal Evil.

The real motivation for contacting the Palestinian SOS group could have been the healing of the Other's wound, provoked by a sense of guilt, of feeling that our people could inflict so much pain on others, especially after what we went through in the most extreme racist crime in recent history. We were conscious that they were also causing much pain to us, and had to deal with our anger and suspicion. As 'good Israelis' we played a Mercurial role of middlemen, or tricksters, and thus got the dubious role of absorbing shadow projections from both sides: we were looked on with suspicion by the Palestinians as representatives of the Israeli aggressors, like in our case presentation of the anxious son of a pilot; simultaneously, we were seen almost as traitors by some of our own people.

In the encounter between the two groups there was a basic asymmetry and duality such as Palestinian/Israeli, Moslem/Jew, young/old, less experienced/more experienced, oppressed/oppressor which made fertile ground for shadow projections. The asymmetry and the military power gap between Israelis and Palestinians are strategically very clear. At the psychological collective level, the aggressor/victim archetype is central. The feeling of victimization is common to both peoples while the aggressor pole is projected onto the other. Palestinians are the victims of the Occupation, with its intrinsic violence and abuses. We Israelis, while sometimes being really attacked, tend to feel constantly vulnerable without any relation to our enormous military strength.

The other question we asked that leads to the third motivating factor is as follows: Can professionals who belong to the oppressor develop a teaching and therapeutic relationship with the oppressed? Formally, we showed that it was possible. In archetypal terms and, assuming I feel close to the archetype of the Wounded Healer, I can ask if Israelis can be healers of the collective psychological wound of Palestinians who feel hurt and are being really hurt by us. Being conscious of our internal wound and of the Paternalistic Doctor shadow that can so easily appear in a colonial situation, we tried to develop an empathic, egalitarian relationship. As a result we could advance, mainly in healing our own wound, by allowing an atonement of guilt feelings.

From the Palestinian side it seems that the real, concrete need that we were expected to fulfil in an omnipotent way was to put an end to the Occupation. On the other hand, the emphasis on the common language of therapy and the personal relations created trust and 'humanization of the archetype' (Papadopoulos 2009). Some reparation could be achieved by the attitude of plain human good-will and respect towards the other side by those who were perceived as their aggressors. During a Jungian workshop a Palestinian psychologist cried emotionally, while admitting that for the first time in her life, she had met Israelis in a position of equality. My impression from the meetings was that no real healing could be achieved, only 'moments of reprieve' in Primo Levi's words, those brief moments that can humanize the other (Levi 1987).

So, what could be Jungian in embracing human rights as the main issue?

During the meetings I wondered what I was doing. I often felt that I should become the political activist I had always dreamed of becoming and stop just talking. But politics may be seen as the art of transforming into slogans the complexities of the psychology of the collective. On second thought, talking therapeutically has a very political meaning. This raised the need to use my Jungian skills that were usually confined to my private practice.

Our ideological position, despite rationalizations, appears to be based mostly on emotional, moral and ethical factors, all rooted in a deep archetypal level of collective myths. Erich Neumann in his book *Depth Psychology and a New Ethic* written in 1949 with the Holocaust and the Second World War in mind (Neumann 1990), gave analytical psychology a moral, ethical dimension; he described the 'old ethic' based on suppression and repression of the shadow, and agreement with the values of the collective. Only the Inner Voice, the individual expression of psychic truth, the voice of the revolutionaries, can stand against the conscience of his time. He proposed a 'new ethic', based on acceptance and integration of the shadow, of his 'own evil', on fuller insight and wholeness thus permitting 'reconciliation with the dark brother of the whole human race' and 'solidarity with others, with the whole human species and its history' (pp. 95-96). Acceptance of my own dark shadow can lead me to solidarity with the most rejected in our society, mainly the Palestinians. Who inhabits our shadow? Neumann says symbols, archetypal ideas, and primitive behaviour patterns. In my case, it may be the shadow of Power, which developed over the wound of the Holocaust.

I am tempted to say that human rights concepts contribute to Jungian practice more than Jungian ideas do to help the understanding and practice of human rights. These rights are meant to be basic and universal. Questioning them ideologically could open the gate for their weakening. Let us not see only shadows. Focusing on the shadow might prevent us from seeing that sometimes Evil is Evil and there are not two sides to it. The new ethic can give us a clue on how to be a psychological militant who defines Good and Evil in a non-fanatic way.

It can be done by opening our ears and our hearts to the Other and listening to the Inner Voice that comes from the Self and not from collective values denying its own dark side. Admitting the tension of opposites in our inner world does not mean that we must avoid taking sides in the outside world.

Let us use empathy and subjectivity on a socio-political level. We should not be ashamed to try to be more generous and compassionate, and shout loud and clear that something is Evil. Above all, the brutal manifestations and dumb bureaucracy of the military Occupation are Evil and totally strange to the humanistic, subtle, humorous, warm and trickster tradition of the Jewish Diaspora. Also suicide bombings can be explained ideologically as violence of the Intifada, the uprising, but cannot be accepted in terms of human rights.

Our Jungian psychological knowledge can help in our encounters with the Other by a creative and intuitive use of the countertransference (Samuels 1993). At times, during our project, paternalistic and angry feelings came forward in me when the Palestinians did not 'behave' according to expectations, when they reacted passive-aggressively. They were frequently dissatisfied with our contribution, failed to arrive to scheduled meetings, to read papers, or to prepare clinical presentations. Understanding my 'colonialist shadow' can give me a clue to how strongly Palestinians harbour feelings of victimization, of rejection, and how much they seek respect and dignity.

At the peak of writing this paper, I had a dream:

I am in a classroom, an officer with a military unit dressed in civilian clothes. We have to leave for a battle with a far more numerous Roman military legion. I can visualize the battle, with our unit being massacred like in the battle of Thermopylae. I see myself fighting heroically, and staying alive by faking death among the corpses. Back in the classroom I flirt with some young girls and accept to drink herbal tea instead of coffee so I will fall asleep after the battle. My boss convinces me to drink coffee. Suddenly we decide spontaneously to escape and avoid battle. We sneak out into the darkness of the streets of Tel Aviv. I feel very relieved.

I need to guard against heroic inflation and the inevitable destruction it brings with it, like it happened in the suicidal rebellion of the Jews against the Romans. Instead of the shadow of the patriarchal hero, I chose the feminine side of Eros and connectedness while being a trickster and keeping my consciousness awake. I believe this may be the way of therapy and peacemaking.

***

Astrid Berg

In Conclusion

These narratives are painful to hear and to think about – they are expressive and convey powerful feelings that are palpable and moving. The openness and non-defensiveness of both colleagues, of both groups, are signs of courage and strength. In the midst of a 'surreal' situation they are willing to take a standpoint, to take action while at the same time holding the tension of opposites within.

The ambivalence about reaching out to the other ran deep for both sides. On top of this was the stigma both groups would carry for having gone against their respective collectives. The motivation to take this risk was complex – it had to do with the traumas that their peoples had suffered, it had to do with wanting to heal the others' wounds, but ultimately it had to do with the healing of their own wounds. It was also linked to a sense of hope, a wish to show the other who one really was, a wish to trust and be trusted.

In order to focus our minds, here are some questions which can be thought about:

- What kind of role do mental health professionals have to play in situations of political and social conflict?
- Do they stay on their respective sides, work with their people – that is, do they remain 'self' orientated and leave the rest to the political powers that be?
- Politics may be seen as the art of transforming into slogans the complexities of the psychology of the collective … talking therapeutically [on the other hand] … has a very political meaning.

Given the 'truth' of this statement, is it not an ethical obligation for us as mental health professionals to engage with the other, particularly if this 'other' forms part of our lives, but happens to be on the other side? My fifteen year South African experience of providing a psychotherapeutic space for mothers and infants who do not have the privileges of the middle classes, and who form part of the black, indigent community, previously so discriminated against, is such that I would say it is not only do-able, but vital, and, if sustained, becomes highly significant (Berg 2003). But it requires a conviction and a preparedness to follow a not so easy path. The work done in such circumstances often goes much deeper and has more meaning than in more 'self' orientated therapies with one's own kind.

Can analytical psychology help us in thinking about meeting with the other?

Jungian psychology's particular contribution is that of the objective psyche with embedded complexes. The 'shadow' is a real thing, one we all carry; it has roots that reach deep within our collective unconscious; and, most importantly, it can initially only be seen in the other. If we take this seriously, then we as Jungian analysts are even more obliged, ethically and morally, to engage with the 'enemy'; how can we not at least attempt to open ourselves to the challenge of facing an other who has been cast in a particular way by the powers that be? How can we collude with collective projections?

We in South Africa have had that experience for over 50 years, and coming out of it has caused enormous pain and turmoil for some people, and for others it has led to the firming up of defensive denial, and continued splitting and projection of the shadow. However, these defences are being challenged at all levels, and we, as the collectively guilty white generation, cannot get away with it any more – it is an ongoing confrontation, which, while painful and frustrating, is necessary in order for working through to be possible. We do not enjoy it, we become angry and defensive, but we allow it to surface – we have no choice. In the end it is healthy as it results in a robustness and resilience that have become quite particular to our national psyche.

What would be the actual ingredients of a constructive engagement, of being able to build a bridge across a very deep divide? Tristan talks about a 'creative and intuitive use of the countertransference': it implies an openness to see and to acknowledge one's subjectivity, the positive and negative sides in the self and in the other; not to foreclose, but to leave the door open for new possibilities of transformation – even if outer reality seems to make this impossible.

It is this containment of the different perspectives which was strongly present in both narratives. 'On the one hand ... on the other hand' is literally being lived and experienced all the time. There is an ability to hold the tension between the opposites, an ability to move from one point of view to the other – and be able to look at the situation through both lenses.

This very human attribute, this ability to empathically connect with the other, generally gets lost in the larger group which functions at a less differentiated level where splitting is more prominent; it becomes about 'for or against', with nothing in-between. There is no 'good other' – there are only groups of bad perpetrators and good victims; complexity is minimized and the humanizing of each other cannot take place. Meeting with the other is thus a sine qua non; my experience with the xenophobic attacks which occurred in South Africa on a large scale in May 2008 brought this home to me; once I had visited an actual refugee camp and had interacted with the people there and listened to their stories, I could no longer be a passive bystander, but became an activist within my very academic department (Berg et al. 2009).

In situations of human rights abuses, such as what we had in South

Africa, and periodically still have, there are no clear answers as what exactly to do and how to do it – we each have to find our own way; but what we have to acknowledge is that as Jungian analysts there is an imperative to face that, and to face those whom we want to evade, fellow human beings who have been categorized as belonging to an inferior grouping. Our moral imagination has to extend to include the other, and avoidance has to give way to active witnessing and engagement. Connecting with the other restores not only their humanity but our own. At a recent Cape Town conference on reconciliation Archbishop Tutu said in his inimitable way: 'It is blasphemous to make a child of God doubt that he/she is a child of God.'

I want to conclude by very briefly touching on an African concept (Berg 2004). There is a proverb which describes the African philosophical, spiritual notion of *Ubuntu* and it states: *Umntu ngumntu ngabantu*, translated as, 'A person is a person because of persons.' There are many layers, many nuances to this seemingly simple idea. If we were to unpack these and think about them more intensely, we might see that this concept could provide us with a new *collective ethic*. South African writer Antje Krog1 regards *Ubuntu* as a radically new way coming from an indigenous world view which could serve as a new moral entry point for the world. The sense that 'community' goes beyond one's own could provide all of humanity with a fundamentally new way of resolving complex matters.

Modern analytical psychology and modern Jungian analysts could do well to heed the call of *Ubuntu* and to truly embrace it, not only in theory, but in action. Perhaps we have to try to move out of our private consulting rooms and reach out to the other side.

I leave you with a question posed by Jung himself and which is an injunction to us all:

> But what if I should discover that the least among them all, the poorest of all beggars, the most impudent of all offenders, yea the very fiend himself – that these are within me, that I myself am the enemy who must be loved – what then?
>
> (C.G. Jung 1958/1969, para. 5)

References

Berg, A. (2003). 'Beyond the dyad: parent-infant psychotherapy in a multicultural society: reflections from a South African perspective'. *Infant Mental Health Journal*, 24, 265-77.

– (2004). '*Ubuntu*; a contribution to the "civilization of the universal"'. In *The Cultural Complex. Contemporary Jungian Perspectives on Psyche and Society*, eds. T. Singer & S. Kimbles. Hove, East Sussex: Routledge.

Berg. A. et al. (2009). ' "Linking the breaks": containing the psychotherapists responding to the 2008 xenophobic crisis'. *Psycho-analytic Psychotherapy in South Africa*, 17, 1-19.

Jung, C. G. (1953/1966). *Two Essays on Analytical Psychology. CW 7*

– (1958/1969). *Psychology and Religion: West and East. CW 11.*

Levi, P. (1987). *Moments of Reprieve.* London: Sphere Books.

Neumann, E. (1949/1990). *Depth Psychology and a New Ethic.* Boston & Shaftesbury: Shambhala.

Papadopoulos, R. (2009). 'Extending Jungian psychology: working with survivors of political upheavals'. In *Sacral Revolutions*, ed. Gottfried Heuer. London: Routledge.

Samuels, A. (1993). *The Political Psyche.* London: Routledge.

Friday, 27 August 2010

Like Lao Zi's Streams of Water:
Implications for Therapeutic Attitudes

Bou-Yong Rhi

Korea (KAJA)

Abstract

In this article I introduce essential thoughts in Lao Zi's *Dao De Jing* and C.G. Jung's comments on the Dao of Lao Zi in connection with the Jungian therapeutic attitude. Emphasis is laid on the nature of Dao as the unfathomable deepest secret and also as the union of the opposites.

C.G. Jung recognized in the Dao of Lao Zi the meaning toward psychic totality. To rest in Tao was understood as the fulfilment of the whole personality, the self in Jung's terms. I call Jungians' attention to keep in mind the self in Jung's terms, the objective psyche as the numinous, ego-transcendent autonomous nature of the psyche, in their encounters with analysands. Lao Zi's deep insight into the dual aspects of the universe and life expressed in many chapters of *Dao De Jing* is demonstrated in comparisons with C.G. Jung's comments on these chapters.

Several important images of Dao such as uncarved block, infant, water and valley are presented and amplified to elucidate the eastern ways of approaching the symbol of the self. Jung paid more attention to the aspects of dynamic streams of water and the fullness of the valley with spirits in *Dao De Jing* than the downward streams of water and the emptiness of the valley that were emphasized by Lao Zi.

I see in Wu-wei, Not-Doing, the central concept of Lao Zi, the therapeutic attitude of self-centredness: that is, actively giving up the ego-centric attitude, the attitude of 'religio', a sincere careful observation of the numinous nature of psyche.

I further mention thoughts of Lao Zi on ethical values parallel to Jung's notion of 'Ethos', *Vox Dei*, primordial conscience which should be distinguished from morality as the collective behavioural codex. The 'absolute good' (*sang seon*) was meant by Lao Zi to rest in Dao, the psychic totality.

In my closing remarks I present Lao Zi's Chapter 20 in which the solitude of Lao Zi is reflected and I introduce Jung's emotional sharing with it. C.G. Jung was enthusiastic about Lao Zi and Taoist philosophy for he discovered there the parallel concepts of his psychology. Though inclined to extremes of introversion and the possibilities of misunderstanding mobocracy or quietism in several chapters, Lao Zi's *Dao De Jing* can serve through its symbolical understanding as good advice to Jungian analysts to widen and deepen our insight and attitude in psychotherapy.

*　*　*

In Jungian psychotherapy and in the training of Jungian psycho-therapists, the most important thing is the basic attitude of the therapist towards the individual person who is suffering. No methods, no therapeutic techniques are more important than the therapist's attitude, which is how to see the individual analysand. What is the best attitude for Jungian therapists? I think able to see the wholeness of oneself and of the person who comes for help (Jung 1954a, paras. 3, 6-7; Jaffé 1965, p. 131).

Schools of psychotherapy other than Jungian also claim the importance of seeing and making the whole person. In the analytical psychology of C.G. Jung, however, the scope of the 'whole person', the self, is enormously profound, for it is ultimately beyond the conscious estimation.

C.G. Jung mentioned the Dao of Lao Zi, whenever he was dealing with psychic totality, as the far eastern parallel to the symbol of self and the self archetype. 'Living in Dao' meant 'Living in psychic totality'.

In the following Lao Zi's Dao De Jing[1] is introduced as well as C.G. Jung's comments on the Dao of Lao Zi in connection with the Jungian therapeutic attitude. We will begin first with the question: 'What is the Dao by Lao Zi?' In Chapter 1, is one of the answers:

1. What is the Dao?

1) Dao as the unfathomable

Chapter 1

> The Dao that can be expressed
> is not the unvarying Dao.
> The name that can be named
> is not the unvarying name.
> 'Non-Existence' I call the beginning of Heaven and Earth.
> 'Existence' I call the mother of ten thousand creatures.
>
> Therefore does the direction towards Non-Existence

---

1 The main reference was the text of Wang Bi's Commentary of Lao Zi. For the English translation I referred to the work of A. Waley, H.G. Ostwald (R. Wilhelm) and R.C. Hendricks.

lead to the sight of the miraculous essence
the direction towards Existence
to the sight of spatial limitations.

Both are one in origin
and different only in name.
In its unity it is called the Secret.
The secret's still deeper secret
is the gateway through which all miracles emerge.

Chapter one says to us: If you speak of Dao as a way of life and demand people to follow it, it is no unvarying eternal Dao. You can put names to Dao like the Confucian ethical codes of human relations; it does not represent an unvarying eternal name. Dao is very old in origin and is called Non-Existence. From heaven and earth all creatures emerge; this is called Yu(Yŏu), the Existence. Mu(wu), Non-Existence, the invisible, formless, nameless one becomes Yu, the Existence, the visible one in the phenomenal world. Non-Existence and Existence are rooted equally in the one Dao and only differ in name; we call this Hyeon(Xuan), a deep secret.

Through the unvarying Non-Existence, Sang-mu(chang-wu), you will see the secret essence (myo) of Dao, and through the unvarying Existence, Sang-yu(chang yŏu), you can see individual differentiation or outcome, Yo(Yao).

This strophe was translated differently, for example, A. Waley: 'Only he that rids himself forever of desire can see the Secret Essence, and he that has never rid himself of desire can see only the Outcome' suggesting the importance and the superiority of Non-desire. However, in the philosophy of Lao Zi there is no discrimination between the superior and the inferior. The important thing, however is to know the unfathomable depth of Dao, the gate of Secret Essence, expressed in the word Hyeon (玄).

The Chinese character Hyeon(Xuan) (玄) according to the Chinese etymological dictionary means a red tinged black colour, or the colour of heaven, the profound, the deep, the serene, the ineffable, the mystic and the female. Accordingly, Hyeon is regarded as the dark, yet comprises everything like the sea. It was thought of as the sum total of all colours. The whole process of transformation is going on within the dark and deep mystery, which is called Hyeon. Chapter 1 is intended to convey to us this mystery of Dao, the gate of all mysterious subtlety, 'Chung-myo-ji-mun' (zhóng miao zhi mén) as the source of Dao.

Dao is something beyond perceptive human capacity: one cannot see it, cannot hear it, and cannot sense it, but there it exists, things intermingled to form One as stated in Chapter 14.

And in Chapter 21 it was stated:

The substance of the great Life
Completely follows Dao.

Dao brings about all things
so chaotically, so darkly.
Chaotic and dark
are its images.
Unfathomable and obscure in it
is the seed.

Jung put this Chapter 21 at the top of his article the Empirical Study of the Individuation Process without any interpretation.

In psychological terms, we should recall Jung: consciousness comes from the unconscious. In the beginning, there was the unconscious, which comprises the seeds of consciousness, and the potentialities of all future development of the personality. Therefore, we agree with Jung when he claims: 'Personality (*Persönlichkeit*) is Tao', in his lecture on the 'Development of the Personality' with the following comment:

> The undiscovered vein within us is a living part of the psyche. Classical Chinese philosophy named this interior way 'Tao' and likened it to a flow of water that moves irresistibly towards its goal. To rest in Tao means fulfillment, wholeness, one's destination reached, one's mission done; the beginning, end, and perfect realization of the meaning of existence innate in all things. Personality is Tao.
>
> (Jung 1954b, para. 323)

C.G. Jung has praised R. Wilhelm's translation of *Dao* as *Sinn* (Meaning) (Jung 1960, para. 917). For me it was not immediately convincing, but when I recognized the common meaning in *Sinn* and the Korean word 'ddutt', I could understand his enthusiasm. The Korean word 'ddutt' has various meanings: intention, will, spirit, significance, value and meaning. From these I imagine Dao having an intention, its own purposeful meaning and value: the substance and the seed. Jung apparently meant by *Sinn*, a 'purpose' – the hidden, invisible organizer that was also called Nothing, Mu(wu) by Lao Zi. His following comment in reference to Chapters 25 and 14 in his article on synchronicity confirms it: 'Nothing is evidently "meaning" or "purpose", and it is only called Nothing because it does not appear in the world of the senses, but is only its organizer' (Jung 1960, para. 920). And with the concept of *Sinn* he could relate Dao to his acausal principle of synchronicity phenomena (ibid., paras. 916-924). Jung said: 'Where meaning prevails, order results' (ibid., para. 920).

For the Jungian therapist to see his or her client as an individual who is pregnant with immense creative potential of objective psyche is not the simplest thing, particularly when we remember Jung's notion on the self:

> The self as an archetype represents a numinous wholeness, which can be expressed only by symbols, e.g., mandala, tree, etc. As a collective image it reaches beyond the individual in time and space and is therefore not subjected to the corruptibility of the body: the realization of the self is nearly always connected with the feeling of timelessness, 'eternity', or immortality. We do not know what an archetype is, since the nature of the psyche is inaccessible to us, but we know that archetypes exist and work.
>
> (Jung 1976, para. 1567)

Today, the use of the term self is somewhat confusing since several schools apply the same term with quite different connotations to Jung's concept of the self. The fundamental difference from other schools in the concept of the self according to Jung lies in its numinous nature, its ego-transcendent depth and its autonomy.

Lao Zi awakened his rationalistic contemporaries to see the existence beyond the conscious, cognizable world and therefore to an unknown, indescribable, numinous entity or nature; he paved the way to approach that transcendent world.

2) Dao as the Union of Opposites

C.G. Jung tried to define Dao psychologically as the 'conscious way' by which to unite what is separated (Jung 1967, para. 30) and he saw in Dao the idea of a middle way between the opposites. He mentioned in *Psychological Types*: 'Dao is an irrational union of opposites, symbol of what is and is not' (Jung 1971, para. 362)

The term 'opposites' or 'Gegensätze' is, strictly speaking, not a successful expression of Lao Zi's concept of the primordial polarity: yin and yang in Tae-guk(daiji), the great pole or primary beginning. Yin and Yang are not opposite elements from the beginning. They are two poles of one entity and may become antagonistic when one ignores totality and takes one pole, suppressing the other. We don't need a third one to reconcile the two opposing elements as Jung suggested as the counterweight to two mutually antagonistic tendencies (Jung 1971, para. 369), because the two poles dwell in one, the Dao in harmony. I use the term 'opposites' only for convenience sake.

It was obvious, however, that C.G. Jung apparently knew these subtle differences in the Eastern thought of polarity as we see in the following remark in his notions of the *Tibetan Book of the Great Liberation* about Chinese cosmic principles: 'It is characteristic of Our Western mentality that we should separate the two aspects into antagonistic personifications: God and the Devil' (Jung 1958, para. 791).

That there is since the emergence of heaven and earth two poles in the universe and in the human mind is the self-evident condition of all phenomena. To know this prevents us from unnecessary tension between the two poles. Thus, Chapter 2 points out that the collective judgement of beauty or goodness inevitably calls upon the opposites.

Chapter 2

If all on earth acknowledge the beautiful as beautiful
the ugly is thereby already posited.
If all on earth acknowledge the good as good
then thereby is the non-good already posited.
For existence and non-existence generate each other.

Heavy and light complete each other.
Long and short shape each other.
High and deep convert each other.
Before and after follow each other.

The Dao as union of opposites mysteriously mitigates the extremes of opposites and solves the conflict in life as stated in Chapters 4 and 56.

Dao is like an empty vessel.
Yet, when you use it, you never need fill it again. (Chap. 4)
It files down sharp edges;
unties the tangles;
softens the glare;
settles the dust. (Chap. 4, 56)
                    (Im, H.G (2005)/ Henricks, RC (1989) p. 43,
                                      Im, C.Y. (2004) 155-160)

'Softens the glare' inevitably calls up an interesting concept of Mimyeong(weiming), 'dim light' mentioned in Chapter 36, as concern with a strategy based upon alternating interactions between opposites. Thus, in Chapter 36, it was said:

What you want to compress
you must first allow truly to expand.

What you want to destroy
you must first allow truly to flourish.
From whomever you want to take away to him,

You must first truly give.

This is called Mimyeong, 'Being clear about the invisible.'
(Wilhelm 1989, pp. 42-43)

Mimyeong 'dim light' was interpreted here an achievement of definite effect by knowing subtle principles or 'concealing of brightness'. I am inclined to see the word simply as 'dimming one's light' as A. Waley (Waley 1958, p. 187) and Kim Hyeong Hyo (Kim 2004, pp. 294-95) have suggested, and as the expression equivalent to what was mentioned in Chapter 4, 'Softens the glare, settles the dust.'

Lao Zi disliked the revelation of one's cleverness, brightness and the glare of social or personal fame. Lao Zi would certainly recommend in critical moments of life the attitude of the dimming of the light, the state of gray, dawn or evening dust, the in-between night and day, black and white, or yes and no. In the *Book of Chuang Zi* there is a beautiful story about a poor man who wished to get rid of his shadow and ran away to his death. Were he to have hidden under the shade he wouldn't have died.

The achievement of the middle path beyond the psychic opposites is more clearly illustrated in Chapter 77 using the symbols of a bow and shooting an arrow.

Chapter 77

Dao of Heaven how it resembles the archer!
He presses down what is high and raises that which is low.
Whatever has too much he reduces,
Whatever does not have enough he completes.

It is the Dao of Heaven
to reduce what has too much and to complete
what does not have enough.
Man's Dao is not so.
He reduces what does not have enough
in order to offer it to what has too much.

The action of bending the bow and shooting an arrow into the centre of a target represents one's utmost concentration into the centre of total psyche (mandala) by symbolizing the middle position between the psychic opposites. It is the symbol of the whole-making process.

Therefore, archery has been since ancient times a special sport, a means of spiritual integration and self-cultivation and therefore called Gung-do(Gông-Dao), Dao of the Bow.

This illustrates psychologically the way of integrating the inferior function in analytical psychology.

2. Symbols Representing the Effects of Dao

In Chapter 28, we get a wonderful picture of wholeness where the dual components of life are harmoniously brought together, and also of the central symbols of Dao favoured by Lao Zi: the valley, the infant and the uncarved block.

Chapter 28

He who knows the male, yet cleaves to what is female
becomes like a ravine, receiving all things under heaven.
And being such a ravine
the constant virtue will never leave.
This is returning to the state of infancy.
He who knows brightness, and yet cleaves to the darkness
becomes the standard by which all things are tested.
Being such a standard:
the constant virtue (Life) does not leave him.
He returns to the Limitless.

He who knows glory, yet cleaves to ignominy
becomes like a valley that receives into it all things under heaven,
And being such a valley
His constant virtue is complete
he returns to the state of the Uncarved Block (Simplicity).

Now when a block is sawed up it is made into implements,[1]
but when the Sage uses it, it becomes Chief of all Ministers.
Truly, the greatest carver does the least cutting.

Sage uses the sawed up blocks and integrates all of them into one organization. He never discriminates between people.

The Uncarved Block

Chapter 32

Dao is eternal, but has no fame (name);
The Uncarved Block, though seemingly of small account
is greater than anything that is under heaven.

---

1 a subordinate, an instrument of government

The uncarved block is nature itself without any artificial processing, the symbol of simplicity, the Dao. The simplicity is beyond fame, a state without glory, without private desire and without one-sided discrimination. Simplicity is a state of Non-doing, the most essential nature of Dao.

Noteworthy is the last sentence in Chapter 28: 'Truly, the greatest carver does the least cutting' (Waley 1958, p. 178).

A psychotherapist is in a sense an artist and a carver, who intrudes into the soul of his or her clients and helps them to become whole persons. Chapter 28 attracts our attention, telling us not to interfere in the client's individuality with a rationalistic approach, but rather to focus on the psychic centre of the self within the mind of the client and of oneself.

Infant

Chap. 55

Whosoever holds fast to Life's completeness
is like a newborn infant.

(Wilhelm 1989. p. 51)

Chapter 55 mentions inviolability, the highest energy and harmony of an infant, a state before the knowledge of competition. Jungians may be surprised to discover the resemblance of the symbolic meanings of the child to the state of being one with Dao that was stated in Chapter 10, for we know Jung's view of the divine child as a symbol of self (Jung 1959, paras. 290-300).

Chap. 10

Can you keep the unquiet physical soul from straying,
hold fast to the Unity, and never quit it?
Can you, when concentrating your breath, make it soft
like that of a little child?

(Waley 1958. p. 153)

Lao Zi was a great advocate of the small, the weak and the soft, and pointed out their strength. Firm and rigid are the dead, and the soft and weak are companions of life (Chap. 76). Therefore the softest can overcome the hard and strong:

The soft wins victory over the hard.
The weak wins victory over the strong (Chap. 36)

Water, Valley

Chap. 78

Nothing under heaven is softer or more yielding than water,
but when it attacks things hard and resistant
there is not one of them that can prevail.

The softest one is water, but it flows endlessly and changes the
shape of the hardest things whatever they are. Jung mentioned: 'Man
becomes one with Tao, with the unending durée-créatrice … for Tao
is also the stream of time' (Jung 1971, para. 362). Lao Zi states in chap.
34: 'The Great Dao is overflowing: it can be to the left and to the
right.' Dao flows all over the earth.

Has water a distinct form? Certainly, but it changes its form freely,
without struggling because such is its nature. Hence, it acquires soothing and has a redeeming effect upon people. Water is yielding, but
nourishes and changes all creatures on earth. Therefore it deserves
to be the symbol of life and transformation. The implications of the
image of water may be different from individual to individual, but the
image has a common healing effect upon everyone for it evokes the
archetypal precondition of the unconscious.

Chapter 8

The highest good is like water;
Water is good at benefiting ten thousand things and yet
it does not compete.
It dwells in places the masses of people detest.
Therefore it is close to the Dao.

Jung was particularly interested in the essential quality of Dao
represented in the image of water. Citing this Chapter 8, Jung was
surprised that the idea of a potential (*Gefälle*, fall) could not be better
expressed (Jung 1971, para. 360).

In *Mysterium Coniunctionis* Jung mentioned *aqua permanens* or spiritual water as a medium of conjunction, marriage maker, and pointed
out that a common synonym for water was the 'sea' as the place where
the chemical marriage was celebrated. Citing from alchemical text
Jung said: 'The marvels of this sea are that it mitigates and unites the
opposites' (Jung 1963, para. 658).

Lao Zi mentions further in Chapter 66:

The reason why rivers and oceans are able to be
the kings of one hundred valleys
is that they are good at being below them.

Thus also is the Man of Calling:

if he wants to stand above his people he puts himself below them
in speaking.

Because he does not quarrel,
no one in the world can quarrel with him.

'No quarrelling', non-competiveness, femaleness, stillness and the
below are interconnected in the symbolic meaning of the image of
water in *Dao De Jing*.

Chapter 61

By keeping itself downstream
a great realm becomes the unification of the world.
It is the female in the world.
The female always wins over the male by its stillness.
By its stillness it keeps below.

'The great realm' means literally a big nation but can be interpreted
psychologically as the realm of the unconscious and may even be
compared with the self as 'the unification of the world' and Dao is
the source of everything, and therefore the female, the mother of ten
thousand things.

Why does Lao Zi so persistently insist that the image of flowing
water into the lower place (downward stream) is close to the Dao?
Dao De Jing mentioned this in connection with governing people, but
psychologically we understand it as an ego's accepting attitude toward
the unconscious inferior personality. 'Downward' or 'below' expresses
not only physical potential but also the meanings of 'disdained' and
'disliked' by people. It seemed also difficult for the people of the time
of Lao Zi to follow his words, therefore Chapter 43.

The softest thing on earth
overtakes the hardest thing on earth.
The non-existent overtakes even that
which has no interstices.
From this one recognizes the value of non-action;
teaching without words, the value of non-action
is attained by but few on earth.

'Wordless teaching' and 'actionless activity' was the way of the
sage.
'The below' and 'the water', 'the female', are combined with the
image of the valley, the symbol of Dao. The valley is characterized

by its emptiness and the below like an empty vessel, from which we always can take energy without cessation.

Chapter 6

> The Valley Spirit never dies.
> It is named the Mysterious Female.
>
> And the Doorway of the Mysterious Female
> is the base from which Heaven and Earth sprang.
> Is there within us all the while;
> Draw upon it as you will, it never runs dry.

Man in Dao is the valley of the world, and the eternal Life does not leave him as stated in Chapter 28 (Wilhelm1989, p. 39). Man in Dao therefore had the look of the valley so deep that one cannot know, broad (empty) like the valley and impenetrable as it was turbid. Lao Zi asks in Chapter 15 finally:

> Who can clear up the turbidity, little by little,
> through stillness.
>
> (Wilhelm1989, p. 32)

Like flowing water Man in Dao doesn't fight against the evil. He dwells with dust or in turbid water and changes it slowly with the way of stillness, that is, Non-doing. I see here an attitude of 'religio' in Jung's term, the sincere and careful observation, the giving up of the ego's haughtiness, providing for the natural flow of the unconscious which is capable of creative transformation.

In one of his articles on archetypes, Jung uses the symbol of water in relation to the dreams of valleys and lakes of a Protestant theologian.

> Water is the commonest symbol for the unconscious. The lake in the valley is the unconscious, which lies, as it were, underneath consciousness − Water is the valley spirit, the water dragon of Dao, whose nature resembles water − a yang embraced in the yin. Psychologically, therefore, water means spirit (Geist) that has become unconscious.
>
> (Jung 1959, para. 40)

This interpretation of valley, lake and water should be understood in the context of the specific dream of a theologian. But it is interesting to note that Jung saw the valley spirit and the water dragon of Dao in the image of the lake water of the dream, instead of in the emptiness below and stillness of Dao. Jung also saw in reference to the water the potential and dynamic stream towards Dao, while Lao Zi likened it to the emptiness of the valley and stillness of the sage.

3. Mu-wui (Wu-wei) Non-doing

Wu-wei (Mu-wui) Non-Doing is the central concept of Lao Zi. It is the basic nature of Dao as well as the attitude of the sage. C.G. Jung understood Wu-wei not as Doing-Nothing but as Not-Doing in a rationalistic way comparable with the art of letting things happen as in Meister Eckhart and Jung's own techniques of active imagination (Jung 1971, para. 369). Wu-wei is an attitude of active giving up of ego-centricity and the process of decreasing non-essential components from oneself as chapter 48 confirms:

Whosoever practices Dao decreases daily.
He decreases and decreases until at last he arrives at non-action.

Noteworthy is the point that the Non-Doing of Dao is responsible for the desire to act among creatures because it takes shape under the influence of Dao. Then, the restraining of desire with the name-less simplicity becomes necessary in order to establish the state of tranquillity.

Chapter 32

Once the block (Uncarved) is carved, there will be names,
and so soon as there are names,
know that it is time to stop.
Only by knowing when it is time to stop can danger be avoided.
(Waley 1958, p. 183)

Dao itself has no name, i.e., it is not objectively definable, but once it begins to manifest its action in the world it obtains names – taking shape as systems, methods and rules. The systems begin to interfere with natural simplicity. Therefore, one should know when to stop.

Whenever we rely on ourselves in psychotherapy, mainly on our conscious knowledge and intentions, theories and techniques in order to enhance the adaptation of the analysands to external reality, we are easily captured by the details of the external reality, by symptoms, concerns with outward success and failure of therapy etc. These are all right, as long as the therapists are able to watch the intention of the self within themselves and within the unconscious of the clients. In extreme cases, however, therapists can lose their connection to self, to the whole person. Therefore, they should know when they need to stop the one-sided extraverted approach and return to the original holistic attitude.

Non-Doing and Doing and all the dualities in connection with Non-Existence and Existence seem to belong to one entity, the Dao. Dao embraces all those things together not only as an origin but also as a purpose. This circumstance illuminates the last strophe of Chapter 32:

> To Dao all under heaven will come
> as streams and torrents flow into a great river or sea.
>
> (Waley 1958, p. 183)

4. Morality and 'Ethos'

If the highest good, Sang Seon(Sháng Sháng)(上善) means 'the absolute good' beyond the collective value judgement of the good against that of evil, it corresponds psychologically to 'Ethos', not Morality, in Jung's terms. C.G. Jung distinguished 'Ethos' (the ethical aspect of conscience) from Morality. Morality is the collective norms of behaviour, a moral codex recognized by the society. 'Ethos' is like the voice of God (*Vox Dei*) within the unconscious of individual persons, primarily unknown, but emerging when the individual is seriously confronted with moral conflicts. The voice of God does not always suit the collective conscious value of the society. It comes from the ego-transcending objective-psyche within us, the primordial regulator; the totality of psyche, which we call self (Jung 1964, paras. 855-57).

The 'absolute good' is seen from the analytical psychology of Jung as behaviour in accord with psychic totality. We don't know the scope of 'psychic totality' just as we don't know the ultimate nature of Dao because they are unconscious. Through the process of self-knowledge we gradually approach the whole personality. Therefore, we must be careful in our judgements as to whether others are good or evil. In this respect, ego's alienation from the total psyche can be regarded as alienation from the absolute good. If the self-alienation becomes increasingly accelerated and threatens the people with neurotic dissociation, the same neurotic defence is increasingly reinforced and aimed at the superficial, immediate symptom's elimination. Lao Zi points out this fact in Chapter 18 as follows:

> If the great Dao perishes
> there will be morality and duty.
> When cleverness and knowledge arise
> great lies will flourish.
> When relatives fall out with one another
> there will be filial duty and love.
> When states are in confusion
> There will be faithful servants.

In the matters of good and evil, Jung's analytical psychology shares a common attitude with Lao Zi's *Dao De Jing*. This not because Jung and Lao Zi are generous toward 'inferior' people and 'inferior' deeds, but because the judgement of good and bad actually depends on the entity beyond the ego and personal or collective conscious values. It depends upon the Dao of Heaven in *Dao De Jing* and the objective-psyche in analytical psychology.

It was stated in Chapter 27 that the Man of Calling does not solely reject the non-good:

The Man of Calling always knows to rescue men
therefore for him there are no abject things.

Thus good men are the teachers of the non-good,
and non-good men are the subject-matter ('pupil material')
of the good.
(Wilhelm 1989, pp. 38, 127)

Because as stated in Chap. 62

Dao is the homeland of all things,
the treasure of good men,
the protection of non-good men.

One may shine before others
with honorable conduct.
But the non-good among men – why should one throw them away?

Lao Zi declares in Chapter 73: "Heaven's net is wide; coarse are its meshes, yet nothing slips through" (Waley 1958, p. 233) and in chapter 74 he mentions that the ultimate one who decides the death and life of men is not man but Dao as a great carpenter (Wilhelm 1989, p. 61).

Epilogue – Dao's Solitude

Chapter 20

Banish learning, and there will be no more grieving.
(Waley 1958, p. 168)

Between *wei* (yes, polite form) and *á* (Yeah, impolite way of expression):
what difference is there?
Between 'good' and 'evil'?
What difference is there?

What men honor, one must honor.

O loneliness, how long will you last?
All men are so shining-bright
as if they were going to the great sacrificial feast,
as if they were climbing up the towers in spring.
Only I am so reluctant, I have not yet been given a sign:
like an infant, yet unable to laugh;
unquiet, roving as if I had no home.

All men have abundance,
only I am as if forgotten.
I have the heart of a fool: so confused, so dark.
Men of the world are shining, alas, so shining-bright;
only I am as if turbid.
Men of the world are so clever, alas so clever;
only I am as if locked into myself,
unquiet, alas like the sea,
turbulent, alas unceasingly.

All men have their purpose,
only I am futile like a beggar.
I alone am different from all men:
But I consider it worthy
to seek nourishment from the Mother.

(Wilhelm 1989, pp. 34-35)

In *Memories, Dreams, Reflections* by C.G. Jung (Jaffé, p. 359) Jung in advanced age mentioned this chapter of Lao Zi and said:

> When Lao Zi says: 'All are clear, I alone am clouded', he is express-
> ing what I now feel in advanced old age. Lao Zi was the example of
> a man with superior insight who has seen and experienced worth
> and worthlessness, and who at end of his life desires to return to
> his own being, to the eternal unknowable meaning.

A man who enters the path no one's ever stepped on, who sees things nobody's ever seen, does what nobody has ever done and knows the things nobody ever knew; here the solitude of such pioneers in history was expressed.

Chapter 20 is actually a shocking confession of Lao Zi. How could it be possible that such a great man like Lao Zi is falling into depressive self-depreciation? Curious people immediately wish to diagnose the state of Lao Zi with psychopathologic terminology and psychoanalytic theories. But, such people are too naïve to realize that Lao Zi is sad exactly because of such naïvety. Seen from another chapter of *Dao De*

Jing, the solitude of Lao Zi or solitude of Dao itself is a predestined condition of Dao, the absolute one, as the self in Jung's term.

The following verses confirm this:

Chapter 41

> If a sage of the lower order hears about Dao
> he laughs loudly about it.
>
> If he does not laugh loudly
> then it was not yet the true Dao.

Again in Chapter 25 Dao as the absolute one and consequent solitude is depicted.

> There is one thing that is invariably complete.
> Before Heaven and Earth were, it was already there:
> So still, so lonely.
> Alone it stands and does not endanger itself.

The words of Lao Zi indicate the wholeness – the wholeness and its centre. Today people are preoccupied with concrete reality and are not capable of seeing the whole of life and its deep seated roots. But, who knows, there stands amongst the masses in the streets of modern time illuminated by wonderful technological decorations, a man or woman in rags, who appears not very clever but who carries treasure in his or her bosom. Such a person can be found certainly not among high intellectuals but among those who are suffering and lonesome, 'inefficient'.

Jung apparently was enthusiastic about Lao Zi's philosophy, but as a modern European he was more active in conveying his thoughts and feelings. He neither showed himself off, nor hid himself in rags. He took solitude as the indispensable condition for the creative activity, as a dynamic force to explore the nature of the psyche.

C.G. Jung rarely made any critical comments on Lao Zi's *Dao De Jing* although he seems to have intervened in debates in the Dream Seminars in the 1930s about the quietism and extreme introversion, and issues of the inefficiency of Non-Doing of Taoistic thoughts (Jung 1984, pp. 621-23). But he turned the subjects to their own problems in their Western tradition. His main concern was to discover the parallel ideas that he had obtained through his experiences in Western culture.

Dao De Jing has certain sections that can elicit suspicion of stoicism, mobocracy. By close observation and psychological explorations of its symbolical meanings we obtain the real meanings of the thoughts of Lao Zi. Sometimes one asks why Lao Zi illustrates only the soothing and benevolent aspects of nature and rarely its destructive aspects – the harsh confrontations of men with them and the process of overcoming destructive powers within and without? Sometimes, I get almost the same feeling as Jung expressed concerning the goal of Indian meditation.

I want to be freed neither from human beings, nor from myself, nor from nature; for all these appear to me the greatest of miracles. To me there is no liberation à tout prix. I cannot be liberated from anything that I do not possess, have not done or experienced. Real liberation becomes possible for me only when I have done all that I was able to do, when I have completely devoted myself to a thing and participated in it to the utmost. A man who has not passed through the inferno of his passions has never overcome them.

(Jaffé 1965, p. 276)

I think I can understand why Lao Zi rarely mentioned the destructive aspects of nature. The reason lies in the fact that *Dao De Jing* was the last prescription by Lao Zi for those who have suffered enough as he himself did from the conflicts and all kinds of pain in the time of the warriors in ancient China. The Book was for the uprooted, namely the self-alienated.

Lao Zi's *Dao De Jing* may serve as a good instructor or adviser to us when we become bold enough in our therapy and excessively ambitious for the achievement of immediate complete healing; when we rely on our one-sided rationalistic ways of treatment while ignoring the irrational spiritual aspects of the personality of the client; and when our sight becomes narrow and unable to see deeply into the soul of the client.

References

Henricks, R.C. (1989). *Lao-Tzu Te-Tao Ching.* Cited in Im, H.G. (1987). *Interpretation of Lao Zi Dao De Jing* (Korean). Seoul: Cheolhak-gwa-Hyeonsil-sa.

Im, C.W. (Trans.)(2005). *Wang Bi's Commentaries of Lao Zi* (Korean). Seoul: Hangilsa.

Jaffé, A. (Ed.) (1965). *Memories, Dreams, Reflections by C.G. Jung.* New York: Vintage Books.

Jung, C.G. (1954a). *The Practice of Psychotherapy. CW* 16.

– (1954b). 'The Development of the Personality'. *CW* 17.

– (1958). *Psychology and Religion: West and East. CW* 11.

– (1959). *The Archetypes and the Collective Unconscious. CW* 9i.

– (1960). *The Structure and Dynamics of the Psyche. CW* 8.

– (1963). *Mysterium Coniunctionis. CW* 14.

– (1964).Civilization in Transition. *CW* 10.

– (1967). *Alchemical Studies. CW* 13.

– (1971). *Psychological Types. CW* 6.

– (1976). *The Symbolic Life. CW* 18.

– (1984). *Dream Analysis*. Princeton, MA: Princeton University Press.

Jung, C.G., Wilhelm, R. (1965). *Das Geheimnis der goldenen Blüte*. Zürich, Stuttgart: Rascher Verlag.

Kim, C.Y. (2004). *Lectures on Lao Zi*. Seoul: Yemun-Seowon. (Korean)

Kim, H.H. (2004). *Philosophy of Dao De Jing*. Seoul: Sonamu. (Korean)

Waley, A. (1958). *The Way and Its Power – A Study of Tao Tê Ching*. New York: Grove Weidenfeld.

Wilhelm, R. (1957). *Laotse Tao Te King*. Düsseldorf-Köln: Eugen Diederichs.

– (1989). *Tao Te Ching. The Book of Meaning and Life*. Trans. H.G. Ostwald. ARKANA: Penguin Books.

Panel: The Alchemy of Attachment Trauma, Fragmentation and Transformation in the Analytic Relationship

Linda Carter, Jean Knox,
Joseph McFadden & Marcus West

Abstract: This panel[1] emerged from shared clinical concerns when working with adult patients whose presentation style was reminiscent of a disorganized (Type D) infant attachment pattern. Psychotherapeutic work with such patients poses complicated transference and countertransference dilemmas which are addressed by all four panellists via theory and clinical vignettes. In common is an interest in contemporary attachment, neuroscience and trauma theories and their relationship to analytical psychology. Intergenerational trauma seems to be a salient factor in the evolution of fragmented and fragmenting interactions that lead to failures in self-coherence and healthy interpersonal relationships. Such early relational trauma is compounded by further episodes of abuse and neglect leading to failure in a core sense of self. These clinicians share how they have integrated theory and practice in order to help dissociated and disorganized patients to transform their dark and extraordinary suffering through implicit and explicit experiences with the analyst into new, life-giving patterns of relationship with self and others. The alchemy of transformation, both positive and negative, is evident in the case material presented.

---

1 The papers in this panel were first published in the *Journal of Analytical Psychology* in its April 2011 edition, Vol 56, 2. Permission for their republication has been granted.

A Jungian Contribution to a Dynamic Systems Understanding of Disorganized Attachment

Linda Carter

USA (JPA / NESJA)

Experienced clinicians know all too well – dynamically, explicitly and implicitly – the ambivalent back-and-forth movement of analysands who have suffered early relational trauma. Threads of connection can be woven together into a co-created fabric only to be unravelled and left in tatters by the next session. Disruptions can become sequences of explosions and repair not experienced in early relationships or held in current memory – a novel and unexpected experience. The dyad is at the edge between order and chaos where the analysand is surprised by repair and the clinician is surprised that the repair can seem to dissolve between sessions almost without a trace.

Jungian psychology places high value on notions such as *integration, teleology, wholeness, synthesis and the transcendent function.* Of course, this has consistently been juxtaposed to Freud's reductive method with its emphasis on causality and early history. Beginning with Bowlby, however, the world of psychoanalysis has been profoundly affected by the burgeoning work in studies of communication, attachment and trauma. The observational and clinical work of researchers and writers such as Beebe and Lachmann (2002), Stern (2004), Tronick (2007) and Sander (2008) have profoundly altered theory development and clinical practice. Undergirding these new ideas is dynamic systems theory which explores the emergence of ever more complex networks forming spontaneously through self organization. This way of thinking moves beyond simply causal models and necessarily into the realm of multiplicity, so well described through Jung's theories of complexes and archetypes. The work of Cambray (2004), Hogenson (2004) and Knox (2004) suggests that we need to move beyond ideas of incarnation of pre-existing forms into understanding that archetypal patterns are emergent properties. As the neuroscientists have taught us, there is an inclination to repeat interaction patterns that have become instantiated in the brain but these patterns themselves can be altered when something new is introduced into the relational system which leads to reorganization of brain in conjunction with interactive tendencies. At the emergent edge between order and chaos, the clinician is alert to indications of the presence of the transcendent function – not necessarily bringing together the tension of opposites in content – but in the process of being together. The focus on process is central to the clinical dilemma that I will present. Through attention to process can come cohesion in the moment, coherency of self over time and, potentially, an 'earned secure attachment' (Hesse 2008, pp. 586-88).

In a recent JAP article (2010), I have discussed the case of Alan and I will turn to a specific moment in that analysis for discussion here as I think it highlights the significance of process in the work with patients whose interaction patterns remind me of those described by infant researchers as disorganized attachment. I would like to make clear that it is impossible to diagnose adults with this particular pattern as there is no way to draw a direct *causal* line between early interaction and adult behaviour. Further, disorganized attachment is not a diagnosis of pathology, it is descriptive of a particular style and is used as a research classification that may *correlate* with adult dissociative symptoms. Therefore, it may predict with a probability greater than chance alone that an adult may show dissociative symptoms but it does not *cause* them. I see development not in linear steps but as emergent with multiple variables contributing to the emergence of the self. As we have learned from the Boston Change Process Group (Stern et al. 1998), interpretation tends to be related to the transference grounded in early history while a moment of meeting or, in Jungian parlance, the transcendent function tends to emerge from new, co-creative aspects of the current analytic dyad. Such relational encounters can lead to the emergence of new archetypal patterning that, with repetition, becomes instantiated in brain functioning. The clinical moment that I will present helps to consider both the success and also the failure to achieve the dyadic consciousness of the transcendent function. With the following case, I consider the pattern of disorganized attachment as a kind of amplification for my experiences with the patient. I believe that the manifest affects of anger and aggression were employed to protect against deeper feelings of shame with the consequence of preventing the attachment system from moving toward greater cohesion, coherence and complexity.

Alan was ambivalent. Ambivalent about everything – especially about analysis. After several years of four times a week treatment, he told me about his internal turmoil in the waiting room: He simultaneously wished to run toward me and to run away. In my mind, I imagined him saying, 'To and fro, to and fro. Should I come or should I go.' This back and forth movement that characterized his silent contradictory struggle at the moment of greeting was kept secret for several years. Prior to that time, I had only known what I could observe or implicitly sense: each session began with Alan's stony and silent hostility. He would glare at me as if I had made some grievous error even though the end of the previous session may have gone quite well. This repeated pattern never ceased to amaze me and I would find myself in a state of acute hyperarousal requiring deep breathing in order to self regulate. There was something aggressive and hateful about his presence, his body posture and what felt like disdain. Moving through my own distress, I would embark on a quest to find him, or more specifically the part of him that I remembered from the previous session as related and engaging. I guessed, I commented, I imagined until finally I would hit on something that would open the door. There was not a particular topic but this messy process of hide and seek seemed to work. This was not necessarily a playful process as the stakes were high. I continually felt that I might lose him and that he might lose himself.

Verbal acknowledgement of the 'to and fro' behaviour heralded a change in the analysis. Alan was reflecting on his behaviour which opened a discussion between us. This did not unfold easily and it was only with time that I began to appreciate that the intensity of his aggression was related to the depth of shame that he felt over his longing for a secure attachment and a home base. He had an almost phobic resistance to coming close to me as if I were his hostile, intrusive and abusive mother who herself had suffered early relational trauma. This style of interaction reminded me of a disorganized attachment pattern that is thought by some researchers to be intergenerational (Liotti 2004, p. 11). Hesse and Main (2000, p. 1117) quote Carlson (1998) who states that '[i]n late adolescence, early disorganized attachment status has been linked to disruptive/aggressive disorders, and to increased vulnerability to dissociation'. Sroufe and colleagues (Ogawa, Sroufe et al. 1997) have concluded that early more so than later trauma has a greater impact on the development of dissociation (Schore 2003, p. 199). Studies by Ogawa & Sroufe (1997), Liotti (2004), Lyons-Ruth (2006) have found a positive *correlation* between disorganized attachment and dissociation.

Attachment is, of course, central to survival and is dependent on proximity to the caregiver for comfort, safety and support. With Disorganized or Type D infants, the mother tends to be frightened or frightening. Main and Solomon (1990) reported that unclassifiable [or disorganized] infants exhibited a diverse array of inexplicable, odd, disorganized, disoriented, or overtly conflicted behaviours in the parent's presence (Hesse & Main 2000, p. 1098). What characterized these infants was the theme of disorganization, or an observed contradiction in movement pattern. This contradiction could be sequential or simultaneous (Hesse & Main 2000).

Alan's intense longings for closeness terrified and shamed him, triggering a wish to run. When I met him in the waiting room, he was in a state of rageful hyperarousal with the fight/flight mechanisms of the autonomic nervous system in gear. I eventually came to learn that, once seated in the consulting room, he would feel angry and then go blank, falling into dissociation. He later let me know that any closeness that he may have felt in the previous session was something that he both wanted to replicate and simultaneously wanted to destroy. The overwhelming nature of his shame set off hateful and destructive feelings that manifested in aggressive behaviour toward me and toward the analysis.

In this case, it took me some time to realize that shame was an emergent property of the constellated attachment system. Overseeing the co-creation of the analytic dyad was the presence of a many headed hydra threatening every positive interaction. Shame over longings for closeness, shame over his history of abuse, shame over tyrannical behaviour toward me and even shame over shame secretly stood between us. Due to his concealment, I couldn't fully appreciate that, consumed by shame Alan was oppressed by anxieties over abandonment, expulsion or emotional starvation which may have endangered coherence and threatened his psyche with disintegration (Hultberg 1988, p. 116). Hultberg (ibid.) notes that shame threatens the individual with psychic death which he sees as equivalent to extinction – 'destruction of the personality without any possibility of resurrection'. Indeed, Alan came into analysis with a limited repertoire of relational skills. That disruptions and mismatches could be repaired and that our dyadic system could come back to a regulated state was surprising to him. There was most certainly an asymmetry to this process as I 'pedalled hard' to find words and sometimes images to match what I imagined his state to be. However, being accurate and finding him sometimes caused further shame as my ability to 'see' him exposed what made Alan feel vulnerable and small. A barrage of hate would often ensue. I, would then, in turn, feel belittled and shamed by the intensity of my anger toward him. We both were frequently surrounded by an atmosphere of anger and shame. The pull to withdrawal was great. I could feel in me an intense yearning to split and blame the patient rather than see our dilemma as co-constructed. I wanted to quit. I wished that he would quit. I had lost my grounding and felt powerless. Shame as an aspect of the shadow had emerged between us. As Judith Herman (2007, p. 13) notes, shame is a contagious emotion.

What helped me to persist was honest and full expression of my dark emotions in the context of consultation. Open discussion of my anger and shame with an empathic other allowed me to take a more empathic position toward myself and therefore use shadow material as a lens for understanding the patient. I could use my own experiences of humiliation to appreciate Alan's affective states. Further, remembering that our current dilemma reflected Alan's early pattern that could be compared to disorganized attachment helped me to regain my bearing. Exploration of this pattern in my imagination created breathing room. Eventually, internal repair and forgiveness led to the possibility of reengagement with Alan. I hoped that we could develop a new pattern other than one where parents of disorganized infants induce fright without solution (Liotti 2004, p. 13). The consultant functioned as a mediating and transcendent third facilitating a move from the constriction of symbiosis to a more separate and differentiated position, thus allowing me to access reflective functions more flexibly.

In her 2007 John Bowlby Memorial Lecture, Judith Lewis Herman noted that we see disorganized attachment where the primary attachment figure is a source of fear. She argued that we also see disorganized attachment where the primary figure is a source of unremitting shame. In this case the child is torn between the need for emotional attunement and fear of rejection or ridicule. Herman says that the child forms an internal working model of relationship in which his/her basic needs are inherently shameful (p. 3). Further, Schore states that '[e]arly experiences of being with a psychobiologically dysregulating other who initiates but poorly repairs shame-associated misattunement are also incorporated in long-term memory as an interactive representation, a working model of the self-misattuned-with-a-dysregualting-other' (Schore 2003, p. 31). The child comes to experience him/herself as unworthy of help and comfort (ibid.). This internal working model of shame is necessarily triggered in the close proximity of the therapeutic relationship but exerts its presence covertly as it is by nature hidden. Shame resides in the shadow as the underside of narcissism as has been pointed out by Andrew Morrison (1989). Further, an internal working model of shame with disorganized attachment emerges in the first years of life when non-verbal communication predominates in the nonconscious system of the implicit domain which is outside conscious awareness. Like the Titans, this emotion is primitive, imageless, formless and overpowering when set in motion. Its searing nature is hot and manifests in the redness of blushing which results from a rapid shift in the autonomic nervous system.

Shame as both an affect and a defence (Morrison 1989) is fundamentally isolating. It results from a failure of the attachment system to emerge and become more complex, cohesive or coherent; instead the mother and baby function in a state or mutual withdrawal and the system dissipates. For development to proceed in the therapeutic dyad or in the mother-infant relationship, dyadic expansion of consciousness is required whereby the interaction between two partners contains more information and is more complex than either partner's state of consciousness alone (Tronick 2007). This model of emergence resonates with Jung's notion of the transcendent function which is a lynchpin of a prospective model for the unfolding of the self in the individuation process. Shame constricts forward movement into the future which can be witnessed in the compulsion to get small and even disappear.

Rage and dissociation are evident as defensive manoeuvres to protect the integrity of the self. Morrison (1989, p. 103) notes that narcissistic rage reflects 'an attempt to rid the self of the experience of searing shame'. Alan's revelation was a movement away from rageful defence and a movement away from paralytic withdrawal. Indeed, he was self reflectively engaging in the process of mutual collaboration in a new kind of interactive exchange with the potential for expansion rather than dissipation of self and relationship. A new paradigm was emerging alongside the limiting pattern of disorganized, disoriented attachment. His ability to think through and observe the contradictory wish to run toward me and to run away marked a turn toward cohesion, coherence and complexity of the self within relationship. The transcendent function was constellated within each of us and within the relationship. Micro-processing of significant analytic moments with an empathic consultant allowed me to metabolize my own anger and shame and to use my self understanding as a means to help move the system toward expansion rather than dissipation. Constellation of shame in the mutually constructed therapeutic relationship threatened to constrict or even sever the work but full expression of shame and rage within the mediating third of clinical consultation renewed energy and mobilized empathy thus allowing for a difficult but ongoing and ultimately creative process.

References

Beebe, B. & Lachmann. (2002). *Infant Research and Adult Treatment.* Hillsdale, NJ: The Analytic Press.
Cambray, J. (2004). 'Synchronicity as emergence'. In *Analytical Psychology: Contemporary Perspectives in Jungian Analysis*, eds. J. Cambray & L. Carter. London & New York: Brunner-Routledge.
Carlson, E. (1998). 'A prospective longitudinal study of attachment disorganization/disorientation'. *Child Development*, 69, 1107-28.
Carter, L. (2010). 'The transcendent function, moments of meeting and dyadic consciousness: constructive and destructive co-creation in the analytic dyad'. *Journal of Analytical Psychology*, 55, 2.
Herman, J. (2007). 'Shattered shame states and their repair'. The John Bowlby Memorial Lecture.
Hesse, E. (2008). 'The Adult Attachment Interview: protocol, method of analysis, and empirical studies'. In *Handbook of Attachment: Theory, Research, and Clinical Applications*, eds. J. Cassidy & P. Shaver. New York & London: The Guilford Press.

Hesse, E.&Main, M. (2000). 'Disorganized infant, child, and adult attachment', *JAPA*, 48, 1097-127.

Hogenson, G. (2004). 'Archetypes: emergence and the psyche's deep structures'. In *Analytical Psychology: Contemporary Perspectives in Jungian Analysis*, eds. J. Cambray & L. Carter. London & New York: Brunner-Routledge.

Hultberg, P. (1988). 'Shame: a hidden emotion'. *Journal of Analytical Psychology*, 33, 109.

Knox, J. (2004). 'Developmental aspects of analytical psychology: new perspectives from cognitive neuroscience and attachment theory'. In *Analytical Psychology: Contemporary Perspectives in Jungian Analysis*, eds. J. Cambray & L. Carter. London & New York: Brunner-Routledge.

Liotti, G. (2004). 'Trauma, dissociation, disorganized attachment: three strands of a single braid'. *Psychotherapy: Theory, Research, Practice, Training*, 41.

Lyons-Ruth, K. et al. (2006). 'From infant attachment disorganization to dissociation: Relational adaptations of traumatic experiences'. *Psychiatric Clinics of North America*, 29.

Main, M. & Solomon, J. (1990). 'Procedures for identifying infants as disorganized/disoriented during the Ainsworth Strange Situation'. *In Attachment in the Preschool Years: Theory, Research, and Intervention*, eds. M. Greenberg, D. Cichetti & E. M. Cummings. Chicago: University of Chicago Press.

Morrison, A. (1989). *Shame: The Underside of Narcissism*. Hillsdale, NJ: The Analytic Press.

Ogawa, J., Sroufe, L. et al. (1997). 'Development of the fragmented self: Longitudinal study of dissociative symptomatology in a non-clinical sample'. *Development and Psychopathology*, 9, 855-79.

Sander, L. (2008). *Living Systems, Evolving Consciousness, and the Emerging Person*. New York: The Analytic Press.

Schore, A. (2003). *Affect Dysregulation*. New York: W. W. Norton.

Stern, D. (2004). *The Present Moment in Psychotherapy and Everyday Life*. NewYork: W. W. Norton.

Stern, D. et al. (1998). 'Non-interpretive mechanisms in psychoanalytic psychotherapy: the "something more" than interpretation'. *International Journal of Psychoanalysis*, 79.

Tronick, E. (2007). The *Neurobehavioral and Social-Emotional Development of Infants and Children*. New York: W. W. Norton.

Dissociation and Shame:
Shadow Aspects of Multiplicity

Jean Knox

UK (SAP)

In this paper I shall explore a shadow side to multiplicity, namely when multiple and distorted viewpoints cannot be integrated into any meaningful whole, but exist as dissociated fragments inside the psyche. A baby's sense of identity comes from the meaning attributed by themother to his or her actions, which, when positive, provide the foundation for the healthy development of self-agency in early infancy. But the infant's dependence on key attachment figures to give meaning to his/her actions makes him or her uniquely vulnerable to negative attributions from parents who interpret their infant's healthy appetite as greed, or see normal aggression as evil. This kind of parental rejection, which often takes the form of a mere facial expression of disapproval or even disgust, is often fleeting and usually entirely unconscious.

These negative attributions are internalized to become a core part of the sense of self, with devastating consequences – a kind of antithesis of 'moments of meeting'. The child becomes literally 'ashamed of himself', of his or her self-agency and libido in the sense Jung used. Echoing Jung's insights (1920), Alicia Lieberman says that the child may become 'the carrier of the parents' unconscious fears, impulses and other repressed or disowned parts of themselves' and that 'these negative attributions become an integral part of the child's sense of self' (Lieberman 1999, p. 737). I have suggested (Knox 2007) that this is the basis for the 'fear of love' – a kind of autistic defence against relationship in those who have experienced such colonization by the disowned parts of the parental psyche.

Very recent research provides striking evidence of the powerful and enduring effects of such negative parental attributions to their babies. Broussard and Cassidy (2010, p. 165) found that even something as apparently innocuous as a mother's mild sense of disappointment that her baby is not a 'better than the average' baby correlates with a higher risk of psychosocial problems in later childhood and that this negative effect continues right into adult life, making them 18 times more likely to have insecure attachment patterns than adults whose mothers had perceived them positively.

A key question is how the baby detects such negative attributions. A one-month old baby cannot mentalize about his mother's state of mind, cannot think 'oh, she doesn't think I'm good enough'. What the baby does see is the caregiver's reactions to his or her agency in the turn-taking that forms the core of human communication. A caregiver's negative attitudes show themselves in avoidant, aversive or conflictual responses to the baby's agency so that, in the words of the Boston Change Process Study Group (BCPSG), the baby learns 'what forms of affective relatedness can be expressed openly in the relationship and what forms need to be expressed only in "defensive" ways, that is, in distorted or displaced forms' (BCPSG 2007, p. 851).

A number of research studies highlight how crucial are the caregiver's reactions to the baby's agency:

1) Ed Tronick (2007) emphasizes that mother and infant collaborate to communicate and coordinate the timing of their respective contributions, with rules governing their interactions that allow each to predict the response of the other. Tronick suggests that in general, when the caregiver does not follow the rules of reciprocity, a helplessness is learned by the infant – he or she gives up trying to elicit a normal response. When a depressed parent responds to the child's positive displays with negative reactions of withdrawal, anger or despair, the child comes to experience his or her own agency as the cause of these negative reactions and may well conclude that any expression of agency is destructive (ibid., p. 217). Tronick concludes that 'in such withdrawal a denial of the child's self is produced' (ibid., p. 261).

2) Beatrice Beebe and colleagues have found that many 4-month old infants who later show disorganized attachment have mothers who are preoccupied with their own unresolved abuse or trauma and cannot bear to engage with their infants' distress. Essentially, the mother is unable to regulate her own distress when faced with her infant's distress and so cannot regulate that of her baby. These mothers are unable to allow themselves to be emotionally affected by their infants' distress; they 'shut down' emotionally, closing their faces, looking away from the infant's face and failing to coordinate with the infant's emotional state, a self-protective dissociation, as though they are afraid of the facial and visual intimacy that would come from more 'joining' the infant's distressed moments. These mothers are showing disrupted and contradictory forms of affective communication, especially around the infant's need for comfort when distressed (Beebe et al. 2010, p. 99). It is as though these mothers might feel:

'I can't bear to know about your distress. Don't be like that. Come on, no fussing. I just need you to love me. You should be very happy.'
'Your distress frightens me. I feel that I am a bad mother when you

cry' ... 'Your distress threatens me. I resent it. I just have to shut down.'

(Beebe et al. 2010, p. 100)

These 4-month infants, who are later classified as having disorganized attachment at one year learn to expect that their mothers are happy, surprised, or 'closed' when they are distressed (ibid., p. 100). For the infant, this kind of discordance between his or her own emotional distress and the non-contingent, aversive response from the parent that follows is a profound assault on his or her experience of agency in the relationship. Under these conditions, splitting and dissociation become the mechanisms for creating multiple selves, each reflecting different aspects of self-agency of which the individual has come to feel ashamed as a consequence of the rejecting response of the parent (Slade 1999, p. 802; Bretherton 1995; Fonagy et al. 2002, p. 239). In its extreme form, in dissociative identity disorder, self-agency may be distributed to one or more alternative dissociated personalities. This is the shadow aspect of multiplicity, the failure of integrative processes, such as the transcendent function and the deintegration-reintegration cycle.

3) Now the briefest of words about possible neuroscientific mechanisms that contribute to the findings such as those of the BCPSG, Tronick and Beebe. fMRI scans show that observing disgust on another's face activates the same parts of the insula as the participants' direct experience of disgusting smells, suggesting that mirror-neuron activity occurs in the insula. But the insula may also be a critical relay from the mirror-neuron system to the cortical and sub-cortical midline systems that underpin the core-SELF experience described by Panksepp (1998).

These pathways may provide the route by which the negative expressions on a mother's face in response to her infant can therefore directly impact on her baby's core-SELF experience. The infant's joyful agentive communications are met by an expression of disgust or fear on the mother's face. The infant's mirror-neuron system activates the corresponding networks in the baby's brain so that he or she also experiences disgust or fear at his or her core-SELF positive or negative emotional states.

Analytic approaches and the effect on the patient's sense of self

Just as a parent's responses of her infant's intentions can profoundly damage the child's developing sense of self-agency, the same can also be true in a psychotherapy relationship if the therapist's approach also denies the patient an opportunity to express his or her agency in the relationship between them.

But this denial of the patient's need to experience agency in the therapeutic relationship can be the unintended consequence of psychotherapy theories and practice which focus primarily on innate or objective aspects of the unconscious. The most obvious example of this is the psychoanalytic view of unconscious phantasy as an expression of the death instinct. A therapist's constant focus on unconscious 'destructiveness' may be experienced by the patient as a denial or pathologizing of the patient's relational needs. For example, one therapist described a case vignette about a patient who one day took a present of a loaf of bread she had made to give to the therapist. The therapist did not take the bread but simply let it drop on the floor between them, treating the gift as a manipulative seduction. Such a therapist focuses on interpreting the negative transference and sees no need to co-construct a dialogue and a relationship with the patient that will create a safe framework within which painful material can be explored. It is a toxic combination of a failure of turn-taking with a negative perception of the person's intentionality. Such an approach is deeply alienating, especially for those who have suffered from the early relational trauma and negative parental attribution in childhood that has already made them feel like a 'bad' person. It takes no account of the need for the therapist to facilitate a process of disruption and repair (Beebe & Lachman 2002) in which the patient has an opportunity to correct the therapist's misattunements (Benjamin 2009).

A brief vignette from a transcript of an analytic session demonstrates the destructiveness of this kind of impasse. This session powerfully illustrates the patient's frustration that there was no room for him to assert his self-agency in the relationship with the analyst. I have the patient's permission to use the transcript.

> *Analyst:* 'I wish to interpret not how you think you are or claim that you are, but how you actually are behaving, by the way that you're communicating to me.'

> *Patient:* 'You can talk about how I actually am behaving and communicating to you today but I would like you to answer the question: how can we be remotely confident that tells us anything very much about how I was five hours ago or how I've been in the last twenty-four hours since I last saw you?'

> *Analyst:* 'That's not a question that interests me.'

> *Patient:* 'But it is the question I'm addressing.'

After continuing in this vein for the rest of the session, towards the end the patient neatly summarizes the problem:

Patient: 'Your basic premise is that I'm here to help you find out what's in my unconscious.'

Analyst: 'Yes.'

Patient: 'And I say that is not how I perceive your role and I do not want to employ a psychoanalyst to do that. I want to employ a psychoanalyst to help *me* to find out what is in *my* unconscious.'

The analyst's refusal to consider that the patient's conscious perception of himself has any relevance for the analytic work is experienced by the patient as so destructive of his subjectivity and agency that the work quickly reaches a stalemate. This patient had an enduring belief that he was, in essence, a 'bad' person, an experience partly rooted in his early childhood experience of a depressed, disorganized mother who could scarcely hold herself together at times, retreating to bed where she would curl up in a foetal position with one arm under the pillow and the other over her head, as though she was afraid of being hit. At such times the patient was told that 'Mummy must not be disturbed' and he somehow knew that she was feeling suicidal. He came to feel that any emotional demand was too much for her and caused her distress and that he was a bad person for wanting his emotional needs to be met. This belief, that any expression of his self-agency in terms of a need for emotional engagement and relationship was bad, meant that the analytic experience described above was simply disastrous for him, re-inforcing his belief that his need for relationship and dialogue produced catastrophic defensiveness and withdrawal from his analyst.

In contrast to the previous illustration, Frieda Fordham described 50 years ago how she modified her clinical approach in the light of her intuitive understanding of the patient's need to have a real emotional impact on her. This patient clearly suffered from an extremely traumatizing childhood and in fact one of her comments had been, 'My mother had to die so that I could live.' As a baby, she said, her mother had got to hate the sight, or perhaps the sound, of her. There had been feeding difficulties which meant that she had cried perpetually.

Fordham then goes on to make the point that

> Up to this point an ordinary technique had been used in as much as I had remained passive and interpreted the material when I could, but now I found that for a long time I had to adapt myself to my patient as though she were in fact a hungry wailing baby, and I had to evolve a method of dealing with it. Her needs became absolute and I had to adapt myself to them.... Though she consciously tried to be otherwise, she was in fact quite ruthless in her demands on my time. The session had to be at a certain hour, which could not be changed. I did not accept this at first but found the distress caused

by a change and the hindrance to analytic work so great as not to be worthwhile. Nor could she be kept waiting without sinking into despair and feeling utterly rejected. Any change in the room caused agitation, as did real or fancied changes in my appearance. There was nearly always a threat as to whether she would leave or not at the end of the hour, and though this was never actually carried into effect on some occasions it was a near thing.

(Fordham 1958)

Fordham recognized that her patient needed to experience and express her own self-agency in the therapy. She needed to discover that to have such a powerful effect on the analyst did not drive her away, the effect it seems to have had on her mother. The hardest part of our work as analysts and therapists is to hold this balance between allowing the patient to 'get inside' us without having our own sense of identity annihilated and so becoming ourselves victims of the very colonization process for which they seek our help, an issue that Marcus West explores in his paper (see further on).

Conclusions

Research evidence is rapidly accumulating that

- the unconscious is inextricably rooted in intersubjective turn-taking;
- what makes effective clinical practice is the co-construction of meaning between therapist and patient, rather than the meaning being determined by the therapist's interpretations.

Georgia Lepper (2009) uses the method of conversation analysis (CA) to identify more precisely the fine details of the therapist-patient turn-taking, in a way that parallels the second-by-second study of videos of mothers with their infants. Both methods highlight the turn-by-turn interactions of each partner in the dyad, which in adult therapy take the form of the conversational responses of patient and therapist to each other, as they try to achieve a shared understanding.

In the study of conversations, it is the response of the hearer to the previous turn, and the production of the next turn in the conversation, rather than the interpretations of the investigator, which provide the evidence for what meaningfulness is.

(Lepper 2009, p. 1078)

This is a cooperative meaning-making effort on the part of therapist and patient that is far removed from the patient as a passive recipient of the analyst's interpretation of his or her unconscious, a model in which the patient's own views are seen as irrelevant. In contrast, an intersubjective, relational approach in which the patient's experience of self-agency plays a vital role is in keeping with the studies that demonstrate the central role of the relational processes that contribute to healthy psychological and emotional development in childhood and also in psychotherapy.

References

BCPSG (2007). 'The foundational level of psychodynamic meaning: implicit process in relation to conflict, defence and the dynamic unconscious. *International Journal of Psychoanalysis*, 88, 843-60.

Beebe, B., Lachmann, F. (2002). *Infant Research and Adult Treatment: Co-constructing Interactions*. Hillsdale, NJ & London: The Analytic Press.

Beebe, B., Jaffe, J., Markese, S., Buck, K., Chen, H., Cohen, P., Bahrick, L., Andrews, H. & Feldstein, S. (2010). 'The origins of 12-month attachment: a microanalysis of 4-month mother-infant interaction'. *Attachment and Human Development*, 12, 1-135.

Benjamin, J. (2009). 'A relational psychoanalysis perspective on the necessity of acknowledging failure in order to restore the facilitating and containing features of the intersubjective relationship (the shared third)'. *International Journal of Psychoanalysis*, 90, 3, 441-50.

Bretherton, I. (1995). 'The origins of attachment theory'. In *Attachment Theory: Social Developmental and Clinical Perspectives*. Hillsdale, NJ & London: The Analytic Press.

Broussard, E., Cassidy, J. (2010). 'Maternal perception of newborns predicts attachment organization in middle adulthood'. *Attachment and Human Development*, 12, 1-2, 159-72.

Fonagy, P., Gergely, G., Jurist, E., Target, M. (2002). *Affect Regulation, Mentalization and the Development of the Self*. New York: Other Press.

Fordham, F. (1958). 'Ruthless greed'. Paper given to the Clinical Group, Society of Analytical Psychology, 2nd Feb.

Jung, C.G. (1920). 'Foreword to Evans "The problem of the nervous child"'. *CW* 18.

Knox, J. (2007). 'The fear of love'. *Journal of Analytical Psychology*, 52, 5, 543-64.

Lepper, G. (2009a). 'The pragmatics of therapeutic interaction: an empirical study'. *International Journal of Psychoanalysis*, 90, 5, 1075-94.

Lieberman, A. (1999). 'Negative maternal attributions: effects on toddlers' sense of self'. *Psychoanalytic Inquiry*, 19, 5, 737-54.

Panksepp, J. (1998). *Affective Neuroscience: The Foundations of Human and Animal Emotion*. New York: Oxford University Press.

Slade, A. (1999). 'Representation, symbolization and affect regulation in the concomitant treatment of a mother and child: attachment theory and child psychotherapy'. *Psychoanalytic Inquiry*, 19, 5, 797-830.

Tronick, E. (2007). *The Neurobiological and Social-Emotional Development of Children*. New York London: W.W. Norton.

The Role of Disorganized Attachment and Insecure Environment in the Development of Pathological Dissociation and Multiple Identities

Joseph McFadden

USA (IRSJA)

Dissociation is a splitting or separating of different aspects of experience and its representation, whether that experience arises from an internal or external source, environment or the psyche-soma. Normal dissociation is a useful process that occurs and is used by all humans. Pathological types of dissociation result from the experience of trauma greater than that which can be processed by the psyche. It is the premise of this paper that dysfunctional or pathological dissociation has its roots in very early developmental, relational dysfunction between the infant and mother or primary caregiver, resulting in the failure of a good-enough secure or protecting environment and leading to acute or chronic trauma. Pathological dissociation ensues in both the sense of identity (vertical splitting), and in the representation of experience (horizontal splitting of experience and its compartmentalization or layering). Both are the results of trauma and become defensive processes against trauma. Furthermore, trauma produces a sensory and emotional overload in the infant that cannot be transformed into symbolic form to be known or thought because it exceeds the mother-infant unit's capacity to metabolize and integrate it (Bion 1967; Stern 2003). It is this last aspect, described by Bion as an impairment or deficit in alpha function that leads to an accretion of un-metabolized sensory experience, experienced in dreams as ideograms, or somewhat similarly described by Winnicott as the 'cataloguing' of mental functioning which 'acts like a foreign body if it is associated with environmental adaptive failure that is beyond understanding or prediction' (Winnicott 1954, p. 248).

Winnicott first presented his ideas of the relationship of the mind to the psyche-soma in 1949. He describes the psyche-indwelling-in-the-soma as the successful outcome of the process of 'personalization' that occurs as a result of the mother's 'handling' of her infant during the holding phase. This is the time of absolute dependence, when the (healthy) mother is in a state of primary maternal preoccupation[1]. He recognized the critical infantile need of a secure and protected

---

[1] Winnicott's use of the word 'psyche' is described by Abram as the 'imaginative elaboration of somatic parts, feelings, and functions' (Abram 1996, p. 263).

experience for the development of what he termed the 'true' self. In health the singular *infant-mother* unit, the initial perfect environment, is provided through maternal preoccupation and attachment. Rapidly this becomes the 'good enough' environment through graduated, manageable and expectable maternal failures or impingements on the psyche-soma. Mind and thought develops as compensation for these gradual failures and traumas and the gap in containment or security. Whether through acute, repetitive or chronic trauma or failure of protection from excessive or conflicting stimulation – what Winnicott describes as the 'tantalizing' and inconsistent mother – there occur not only the splitting of identity nuclei, but also the establishment of mind as an entity isolated and separate from the psyche-soma. Goldberg (1995) has further elaborated on this process as a defensive relationship between mind and the sensorium – the various types of cognitive-sensory input that become a sensory cocoon, separating mind from true connection to psyche-soma. Left in its wake is a sense of numbness, deadness, disconnection, amnesia, fugue states etc. – a lack of any linkage to needed sources of aliveness or vitality. Dissociation occurs between behaviour, affect/feeling, sensation, and cognition, preventing their integration into a unified personality.

In 1969 John Bowlby, in presenting his theories about the attachment system, emphasized the innate property of the infant to seek protective proximity to an attachment figure whenever exposed to any fearful or traumatic event. Bowlby also introduced his concept of internal working models as a basic mental representation of encounters with objects, experience and their effects. Knox (1999) has described the similarities and differences between Jung's complex theory, internal objects, and internal working models. Bowlby recognized that the original internal working models of the early attachment relationships influence all subsequent searches for the protection a secure attachment provides and, under some circumstances, even inhibit it. He attributed the development of these models to implicit memories of the patterns of attachment in caregiving interactions that would normally become gradually integrated with the parallel-developing semantic knowledge system. It has been postulated that *secure attachment* constitutes a protective factor against the development of acute or chronic PTSD following trauma (Liotti 1999). In *disorganized attachment*, however, the most impairing of the insecure types of attachment where there has been gross impingement and inconsistency, unusual vulnerabilities to trauma result. Due to their expectation of additional fright and pain, children with these types of attachment relationships experience inescapable and paradoxical feelings of ever-increasing fear accompanying their need for closeness. This becomes a major risk factor for reacting to trauma with dissociation.

Liotti (1999) cites evidence that disorganized infants and children are unable to synthesize their overall experience with their caregivers into a cohesive memory structure. Memories in such children appear to be composed of multiple separate meaning structures that cannot be reciprocally integrated. They are developed by the synthesis of repetitive, implicit, *contradictory* memories of the infant-caregiver interactions, complicated by excessive and disorganizing sensory stimulation. With time, these differing implicit memories of attachment relations become generalized and developed into multiple semantic memories that can be expressed verbally.

Internal working models of secure attachment and their associated semantic memory meanings carry an expectation of receiving appropriate care and comfort. With this goes a positive appraisal of one's feelings and emotions. In children with disorganized attachment, based on frightened and/or frightening parental reactions, the internal working models contain the experience of fear in the child and the memory of negative parental reactions. There result mental structures that are split between these implicit memories of fear and aggression and those involving comfort. It is not surprising to find that, as well as the ambiguous and multiple perceived behaviours of the attachment figures, the sense of self is also correspondingly split. Each structure also carries its own divergent or oppositional expectations. From this, Liotti posits that where there have been adequate, secure and consistent infantile attachments to the caregiver, later stresses and traumas will not produce multiple identities.

In the clinical case that I will now discuss, dual aspects of pathological dissociation were seen with splitting both of identity as well as aspects of sensory and cognitive experience.

Anna and her Alters

Anna (a pseudonym), a 55-year-old mother of two adult children, in her second marriage of over 20 years when we met, has given me permission to discuss her case. She had been a lifelong healthcare worker. Following a job-related back injury she had undergone several failed surgeries and extensive rehabilitation efforts. She continued to have severe disabling pain, marked limitation in strength and activities of daily living, and significant depression.

Anna was found to suffer from Dissociative Identity Disorder and to have an array of alter personalities, each with its own different experiences, and emotional and physical sequelae. There emerged a history beginning at the age of three or four of physical, sexual and mental abuse and overt torture at the hands of a maternal uncle and grandmother – her caretakers in the absence of a father and a mother working in another city. Anna had no memory of her mother being aware of or trying to stop the abuse that had continued well into adolescence. Neither was there any memory or feelings of closeness between Anna and her mother. Anna had completed college and had a lifetime history of successful work and a relatively functional family life in her second marriage, although not in her first. Her physical condition clearly had worsened considerably from her initial denial of her injury, with increasing pain symptoms and physical limitations. During the third year of her twice weekly therapy, just before a holiday, an alter personality informed me that hospitalization was needed so that Anna could tolerate the memory that was about to emerge. In an inpatient setting, a child-alter told of the holiday visit of an aunt and young cousin, Ella, to be with Anna and her family – both girls were six or seven at the time. Living in a distant city, Ella had not been subject to the extensive torture and conditioning to block crying or reacting to sexual abuse that Anna had suffered. During the holiday, both Anna and her cousin were molested by the uncle. The young cousin became hysterical and continued screaming in spite of threats from him. Anna watched as he murdered Ella. She was then forced to help him dig a grave and bury the body. Her uncle manufactured a fictional story to explain Ella's disappearance, saying she had wandered off and that no one knew her whereabouts. Following the emergence of this dissociated trauma-history these many years later, Anna informed her family. Ella's remains were recovered and given a proper burial. This was only one example of the extreme abuse and torture experienced by this woman.

By the sixth year of Anna's therapy, her mother had developed severe Alzheimer's and was living in a dementia facility. She knew and recognized no one, including Anna. As we worked, a child-alter manifested, that might be designated as carrying the 'personal spirit' (Kalsched 1996) or true-self representation (Winnicott 1960). This alter was persistently troubled by her inability to adjust to 'present time', and her lingering questions over what had happened to her mother, whom she had loved.

Anna was, by this time, able volitionally to switch to the child-alter state. With considerable advance planning, she induced such a change while visiting and alone with her demented mother. At first, the child-alter could not accept that this woman could possibly be her mother. After a period of time, and a number of such encounters, a startling event occurred. In the presence of the child-alter, her mother had a period of considerable lucidity. She recognized her daughter in the child-alter state. In repeated episodes over the next several months, Anna's mother sang songs which she had sung to her as a little girl, and expressed her love and care for her. When asked by the child-alter why she had not protected her when the abuse began, her mother told of her own childhood abuse by Anna's uncle with the consent of her own mother. She had been told by her brother that if she interfered or reported anything, he would kill her and her daughter. Now having this knowledge and experience, the child-alter was able to move in to present time and circumstances. Within the next several months Anna's mother died. Over the years of our work, there had been a diminution of Anna's dissociative self-numbing and distracting defences with a greater connection to her psyche-soma and true self. Concomitantly there was a diminution of her residual physical pain, amelioration of her depression, and a marked increase on her part to be able to recognize and experience impingement, trauma or boundary violation. With this there was significant integration of her sense of self and cessation of any overt identity switching.

Discussion

Liotti has suggested that disturbance in the earliest attachment relationship to the primary caregiver is a basic feature of the development of multiple identities. Where this relationship has been reasonably secure, he posits that pathological dissociation does not occur. Without speaking directly to the issue of multiple personality, Winnicott laid a groundwork for understanding of this phenomenon with his concepts of the development of the true and false selves. Smith (1989) has expanded Winnicott's original thinking about the true and false selves in relation to multiple personality. He suggests that rather than there being multiple selves, there is one true self – often the most hidden and regressed child-alter, even if only a potential self. Following Winnicott's thinking, he believes there is also one principal compliant or adaptive false self, with any number of layered false-self derivatives. Each of these has catalogued some further unacceptable, un-metabolized impingement or trauma, and has its own way of adaptation or compliance which further distances the trauma from the true self. Kalsched (1996) has described a similar process in which the archetypal defences of the self-care system develop to protect what he designates as the 'personal spirit', akin to Winnicott's true self. In addressing the development of multiple personality, Smith (1989, p. 143) writes,

> it is not sufficient merely to withdraw cathexis from the body and experience the self as localized in the mind. A more drastic, but significantly more effective solution is to develop another false self to experience the physical sensations as they occur and to catalogue them (in Winnicott's terms). Thus, the bodily sensations are neither experienced nor lost. They remain potentially available for future integration.

It is not often that we have a glimpse into the mental state of a caregiver in such situations. Nonetheless, it was a dramatic interaction between a victim of child abuse and her mother, herself a similar victim. There were clear indications that for Anna there had been some appreciable degree of maternal reverie, containment and development of a true self, separated and isolated as it had been. This history may well explain the degree to which Anna was better able to function on a higher level than many other similarly abused patients. There was a massive traumatic impact from the loss of this early relationship. This, with the later overwhelming intrusive hyper-stimulation and abuse led to additional conflicting internal working models or complexes. Thus Anna, with the occurrence of additional adult trauma and sensory hyper-stimulation, responded with dissociation of both identity and of sensory experience and processing and interpretation.

An early positive attachment with environmental security, even with some deficits, when predominantly positive and coupled with an ability to develop coping defences – dissociative and otherwise – did facilitate better adaptation for Anna. Excessive stresses and trauma broke through her adaptation, with repeated emergence of maladaptive responses. The dissociative process recognized and described by Jung (1934) thus continues to have major implications for understanding, experiencing and working analytically with individuals lacking in early appropriate attachment relationships in whom retraumatization frequently occurs.

References

Abram, J. (1996). *The Language of Winnicott*. London: Karnac Books.
Bion, W. (1967). *Second Thoughts*. Northvale, NJ: Jason Aronson.
Bowlby, J. (1969). *Attachment and Loss*. Vol. I. *Attachment*, London: Hogarth Press.
Goldberg, P. (1995). '"Successful" dissociation, pseudovitality and inauthentic use of the senses'. *Psychoanalytic Dialogues*, 5, 493-510.
Jung, C. G. (1934). 'A review of the complex theory'. *CW* 8.
Kalsched, D. (1996). *The Inner World of Trauma: Archetypal Defenses of the Personal Spirit*. London & New York: Routledge.
Knox, J. (1999). 'The relevance of attachment theory to a contemporary Jungian view of the internal world: internal working models, implicit memory and internal objects'. *Journal of Analytical Psychology*, 44, 511-30.
Liotti, G. (1999). 'Disorganization of attachment as a model for understanding dissociative psychopathology'. In *Attachment Disorganization*, eds. J. Solomon & C. George. New York/ London: Guilford Press, 291-317.
Smith, B. (1989). 'Of many minds: the dynamics of multiple personality'. In *The Facilitating Environment: Clinical Applications of Winnicott's Theory*, eds. G. Fromm & B. Smith. Madison, Conn: International Universities Press, 424-58.
Stern, D. (2003). *Unformulated Experience: From Dissociation to Imagination in Psychoanalysis*. New York / London: Psychology Press.

Winnicott, D. (1954), 'Mind and its relation to the psyche-soma'. *British Journal of Medical Psychology*, XXVII.
– (1960), 'Ego distortion in terms of true and false self'. In *The Maturational Processes and the Facilitating Environment*. New York: International Universities Press, 1965.

Attachment, Sensitivity and Agency:
The Alchemy of Analytic Work

Marcus West

UK (SAP)

Our attachment needs are the most fundamental and powerful elements in our makeup. They can bear little frustration and, if and when they *are* frustrated, they become split off and dissociated, yet remain embedded in insecure and disorganized patterns of relating which can have a defining influence on our lives.

Our attachment comes essentially from our need to relate, connect with others, and to form a secure base, and I will be exploring how this overlaps with the need to develop, unfold and express one's self, which I see as the essence of Jung's understanding of the process of individuation. Expressing ourselves is fraught and difficult because it is essentially an expression of our sensitive core self which opens that self up to rejection and narcissistic wounding; it is for good reason that Fordham called such self expression a 'deintegration of the self'. I will be looking at the work of Ed Tronick and the Boston Change Process Study Group which I think throws vital light on these relational processes.

In this paper I will describe my work with 'Eleanor' and explore her disorganized attachment pattern and, in particular, the way that her unmet attachment needs led her to extremely chaotic and at times dangerous behaviour such as getting into physical struggles with the police, taking overdoses and other suicidal behaviour.

Eleanor

I am grateful to 'Eleanor' for her permission to discuss our work; the account that follows is necessarily abbreviated with only certain themes drawn out due to constraints of time and space.

Eleanor was the eldest child of very proper middle-class English parents. They were kind, but emotionally unexpressive and distant. Her mother described Eleanor as 'clingy', a description with which Eleanor herself readily agreed. Eleanor was 4 years old when her brother was born; he had severe physical, emotional and intellectual needs and required an enormous amount of care from her parents and healthcare professionals. Eleanor was expected to 'be a big girl now' and to just get on with things as the household came to centre around her brother's care needs.

Eleanor in fact grew very close to her brother, taking a significant role in his care at times, and it was very difficult for her when he was sent away to be cared for when she was 11 years old. Eleanor was very upset by this, but her mother told her 'not to make a fuss'; I do not get the sense of her mother being deliberately cruel, and one can imagine, perhaps, a mother who was herself upset at having to put her son into a home and who, as often before perhaps, had few resources to deal with her daughter's distress. However Eleanor vowed never again to tell her mother, or anyone else, what she was feeling. This vow can be traced back to earlier experiences of rejection, as I will describe, but it was one which had enormous significance on the course of her life.

Eleanor struggled at school; unable to share what was going on for her, she felt isolated and unable to cope. She married young and had two children. She trained in the helping professions, but found work hard as she was terrified she would be found not good enough by her managers. She was able to hold things together, after a fashion, whilst she brought up the children, but in her early 40s she broke down completely. She regularly took overdoses and would frequently run down to the local pier, two or three times a week, where she would hang dangerously off the end until the police would come to rescue her. At this point she would usually resist arrest and struggle with the police until they overpowered her and she achieved the experience she was looking for, as she described it to me, of being taken over and of feeling that she was inside someone else.

After a year in a specialist psychiatric unit, followed by a period of three times per week analytic psychotherapy, which she felt had broken down because her therapist felt flooded by her desperate telephone calls at 11 pm at night, she began twice weekly therapy with me.

In the therapy she was very 'well behaved' at first as she feared a repeat of the breakdown of the previous therapy. This meant that, as in her childhood, she was not expressing what was really going on for her, and she would occasionally take overdoses and regularly run down to the local pier.

I was not too drawn into 'managing' her behaviour – fortunately she had a good psychiatric support system – I concentrated with her on what she was feeling and what it all meant. She told me that she did not want to exist in the world, she wanted to come to exist inside someone else; at first, anyone else would do, as long as they took over, took responsibility, made decisions, were physically present and in control. As we explored this her running down to the pier and taking overdoses became less frequent and, within six months, had stopped completely; although she feared that people, and especially me, might think she was 'alright now' and discharge her.

Eleanor was adamant that she did not want to have to make any decisions or take responsibility in her life – she had no sense of agency and did not want one. Paradoxically this meant that everything, even taking the dog for a walk on a beautiful sunny day, became a chore, as it was something she felt she 'had to do' as she made no choices herself. Consequently she got no enjoyment or pleasure from life. Jean Knox describes someone with a similar aversion to self-agency, although with a different aetiology, in her excellent paper, 'The fear of love: the denial of self in relationship' (Knox 2007).

As we explored making some small decisions – which route to walk the dog, what to do at the weekend – she experienced a remarkable change in her life: she felt stable, that she had a direction and a sense of meaning, and her depression lifted and she began to enjoy things. A tentative sense of agency had developed.

This came crashing down after about a month when, in passing, she said in one session that 'everything felt all right'. Afterwards she had an enormous backlash and was plunged into chaos, confusion and panic again, being unable to think and desperately wishing to be inside someone else. Essentially she feared she would have to do everything completely alone again, without support. Whenever any powerful feelings were triggered Eleanor became profoundly confused and unable to think – something that is well documented in the attachment and neuroscience literature as a state of hyperarousal due to a traumatic flooding of affect that cannot be regulated (see for example, Margaret Wilkinson's book *Coming into Mind*, 2006).

Even though we discussed this whole scenario, and Eleanor could understand it clearly, she was equally clear that she did not want to take any control or responsibility for her life. I began to doubt that we could make much further headway and, after sharing this with a group of colleagues one day, I was struck by a powerful sense of shame, which I subsequently understood to parallel Eleanor's own sense of powerlessness and shame at not being able to affect the world or, one could also say, to be in control of it in the way she would have liked.

Perhaps unconsciously picking up on my feelings of hopelessness, Eleanor began exploring more actively her state of mind with me and told me that she realized that what she had been wanting all this time was to go back to a state before she had any form at all – a point just after conception. Her exercising this thinking had an immediate effect, and her longing to be inside someone lessened due, I believe, to the fact that it was being contained by her own thinking ego-functioning.

I would like to pause briefly here to look at the work of Ed Tronick, as it was through focusing on the moment-by-moment interactions in the therapy that we were able to move further.

Tronick

In the 1980s Tronick and his colleagues made some simple but groundbreaking observations of the interactions between mothers and infants which I think throw a profound light on the significance of the way we interact and how that relates to the way we feel about ourselves.

Tronick described how, if the mother does not respond to the infant, or alternatively tries to engage the infant when they are doing something else (such as sucking their fingers), the infant experiences this as a 'mismatch' in relation to their expectations and desires. He says that such mismatches are entirely 'normal, typical and inherent to an interaction' (Tronick & Gianino 1986, p. 159), although they generate negative emotions.

However, Tronick describes the infant's 'coping behaviours' which can repair the mismatch and turn it into a match, at the same time changing the negative emotions into positive emotions (ibid., p. 156). These coping behaviours are such things as signalling, cooing, making 'pick me up' gestures or making a fuss. If they are successful, it increases the infant's sense of efficacy and mastery, their coping capacities are strengthened and elaborated, and the infant internalizes a pattern of interaction that they bring to interactions with others. In other words the infant gains a sense of agency and feels confident that others will respond to them. Tronick writes (p. 156),

> Indeed, to the extent that the infant successfully copes, to that extent will the infant experience positive emotions and establish a positive affective core.

In other words, the way the mother responds (or not) to the infant's 'coping behaviours' to repair mismatches affects profoundly the way infants feel about themselves. He continues, however, regarding the negative outcome:

> The infant who employs his coping strategies *unsuccessfully* and repeatedly fails to repair mismatches begins to feel helpless. The infant eventually gives up attempting to repair the mismatches and increasingly focuses his coping behaviour on self-regulation in order to control the negative emotion generated. He internalizes a pattern of coping that limits engagement with the social environment and establishes a negative affective core.

> (ibid., p. 156)

This, I believe, is what had happened with Eleanor. In the therapy we kept returning to an incident that pre-figured the time when her mother told her 'not to make such a fuss' when her brother was sent away. On this earlier occasion her mother was sitting dozing in her chair in the living room and Eleanor went up to her wanting a cuddle; her mother had said, 'Not now dear I am trying to have a rest', to which Eleanor had responded 'I just wanted to tell you I love you', to which her mother had said, 'Yes dear, but I am having a rest just now.' This might seem like a small interaction, one that might be repeated in any home, yet for Eleanor it was traumatic and she walked away feeling truly terrible: bad, humiliated, rejected and alone. I believe this was to some extent a screen memory, embodying many similar experiences from her early life.

Eleanor began to dare to let me know about a similar conflict she was having in the therapy with me. She told me that she was afraid of running up to me and hugging me, and that she knew this was 'inappropriate' as her previous therapist had told her so, and that she therefore had no option but to repress all these feelings.

Now my telling her it was all right for her to run up to me and hug me would have been no use as it would have avoided the opportunity to explore what, I suggest, was the core difficulty, namely the intense shame and rejection that she experienced when her expression of her vulnerable, loving self was not met in the way she hoped. This is exactly the kind of mismatch which Tronick describes that generates 'negative emotions' in the infant, which makes them turn away from relationship, as Eleanor had done.

When she ran down to the pier to grapple with the police she experienced herself as having been taken over by split off feelings that she could no longer resist. She did not 'own' these feelings, they 'owned her', as it were. They were not integrated with her core self, so that she did not experience the same threat of shame and humiliation, even though she was being driven, in utter desperation, to take such extreme action in order to get the hugs and the sense that someone else was taking control, in other words, to get some of her attachment needs met.

By paying attention to the moment-by-moment interactions in the analytic sessions, it was possible to see and explore with Eleanor the moments when she was struggling to express her sensitive, vulnerable, core self, and equally to explore those moments when she either feared, or actually experienced, intense shame and rejection if she felt what she was expressing was not going to be heard or met; for example, in telling me about her fear of, and wish to, hug me. My attunement to her emotional state, especially, here, her feeling of shame and fear of rejection, served as a matching response which addressed her core feelings of distress. Had I acceded to her wish to hug me I would simply have reinforced her form of self-regulation, which she used to avoid her emotional distress (see below for a discussion of how what may appear as *interpersonal* regulation may actually be a form of self-regulation).

As we explored these things Eleanor began to be able to own and express more of these core feelings and thus begin to integrate them into herself, so that her life became a lot richer and fuller. As her repertoire of feelings increased so her sense of herself became more substantial; everyday issues such as going shopping or parking the car were no longer troublesome.

I believe that in this way she began to organically develop a sense of agency. Until this occurred her attachment had been 'adhesive', requiring that others take over her ego-functioning and regulate her experience of self (Stern 1985/1998). She was now much more able to negotiate the world and relate to me as a separate other, relatively secure in the sense that I would accept what she said and that we would find a way of helpfully engaging with it; as Beebe and Lachmann (2002) would put it, she had developed more adaptive forms of self-regulation as well as becoming more secure in our interactive regulatory processes. I think previously she had just flipped between rigid self-regulation and an intense desire that I would regulate her. Colman has pointed out however (personal communication February 2011) that this form of regulation by the other, for example, running down to the pier to get 'rescued' by the police, is a form of self-regulation in disguise as Eleanor would remain ultimately in control, having set up the scenario; these kinds of interactions do not allow for relationship with a real other and are thus not ultimately satisfying.

As explained above, I think it was important that I did not try heroically to rescue her, bending myself out of the analytic frame to protect her from narcissistic wounding. In our work together I frequently thought of Edward Edinger's (1972) excellent description of the cycle of narcissistic wounding and the recovery from that wounding that we must all go through in order to live realistic and fulfilled lives in this regularly frustrating and wounding world. The 'wounding' that the analytic frame inflicted on her in terms of offering limits to her sense of agency was both reassuring (that she was not, in fact, all powerful), as well as giving us the opportunity to work through her experience of mismatch, facing the reality of her core complex.

As the Boston Change Process Study Group (2007) describe so well, the answer lay 'on the surface', in the intricacies of relating and in the experiences of acceptance and rejection that naturally occur in every interaction and in every relationship. It was not a matter of a deep defence that needed uncovering. The myriad experiences of rejection of her sensitive core self had left Eleanor feeling intensely bad about herself, unable and unwilling to develop her self-agency and instead trying to obliterate herself; as a result her attachment needs had had no option but to emerge in a boundless and unboundaried way. Working with the shame induced by the rejection was key to helping her relate from her core self, and learning to trust that she could affect me and that I would engage positively with her.

The patient comes to us feeling like shit about themselves and shamefully fearing interaction with others; the real alchemy of analytic work is transforming these shitty and shameful feelings into the gold of self-expression and fulfilling relationship.

References

Beebe, B. & Lachmann, F. (2002). *Infant Research and Adult Treatment: Coconstructing Interactions*. New York & London: The Analytic Press.
Boston Change Process Study Group (2007). 'The foundational level of psychodynamic meaning: implicit process in relation to conflict, defense and the dynamic unconscious'. *International Journal of Psychoanalysis*, 88, 4, 843-60.
Edinger, E. F. (1972). *Ego and Archetype*. Boston & London: Shambhala.
Knox, J. (2007). 'The fear of love: the denial of self in relationship'. *Journal of Analytical Psychology*, 52, 2, 543-64.
Stern, D.N. (1985/1998). *The Interpersonal World of the Infant*. New York: Basic Books, revised edn. 1998.
Tronick, E. & Gianino, A. (1986). 'Interactive mismatch and repair: challenges to the coping infant'. *Zero to Three, Bulletin of the National Center for Clinical Infant Programs, 5,* 1-6. Also in *The Neurobehavioral and Social-Emotional Development of Infants and Children*, E. Tronick. London: W.W. Norton, 2007.
Wilkinson, M. (2006). *Coming into Mind – The Mind-Brain Relationship: A Jungian Clinical Perspective*. London & New York: Routledge.

President's Farewell Address

Hester Solomon

President (2007-2010)

It has been a privilege and an honour to serve as the 14th IAAP President. I am very aware of the giants in whose footsteps I have dared to follow and from whom I have learned so much. Of those whom I have had the pleasure to know personally – Tom Kirsch, Verena Kast, Luigi Zoja, Murray Stein, Christian Gaillard – each one has been truly supportive of this administration and always shared generously of their time and experience. I owe much to one and all.

I also owe *much* to the fantastic team – in particular the members of the Executive Committee and the Officers – and many others besides, members of the three Standing Committees, eight Sub-Committees and five Working Parties – all of whom have participated substantially in the work of this administration. Each and every Officer has been constantly available for consultation; especially I want to mention Paul Kugler, Honorary Secretary, whose good natured and thoughtful weekly phone calls with me constituted the backbone of this administration. Always with her affectionate and efficient quick responses has been our treasured Secretary, Mariuccia Tresoldi. Don Williams, our Webmaster, has been tireless in his efforts on our behalf and, you remember, had the misfortune to have to deal with a catastrophic website crash at the beginning of these three years. I wish to pay special tribute to the contribution of Richard Willetts as Chair of the Ethics Committee and to the members of the Ethics Committee for their thoughtful contributions during this administration. Richard Willetts has been called upon on a number of occasions for advice and consultation and he is greatly valued for his clear thinking and availability as a sterling resource to the President, the Executive Committee and to several Sub-Committees and Working Parties; he also served as our Parliamentarian during the Delegates' Meeting. I have thanked all these individuals in my report to the Delegates' Meeting, and I wish to reiterate this now, for it is *surely* true that this administration would not have advanced in the way that it has without their keen input, willingness to collaborate together in the work of the IAAP and its ongoing development, by assiduously carrying out the tasks for which they were responsible, with the greatest of good will and thoughtfulness. I have every confidence that Joe Cambray will lead an equally excellent team, and I wish him and them Godspeed.

As we enter into the second decade of this millennium, it does us good to reflect that the IAAP is now well into its sixth decade. We are concluding its 18th International Congress. In the last few years, we have had to face many difficult events in the outside world – political, economic, ecological. I am deeply proud of the fact that with the help of dear colleagues and friends, the IAAP has provided a stable framework for our member Societies, our Individual Members, and our routers, a safe place and a secure home, where their professional Jungian identities could develop and grow, the most beneficial environment, as we know, for individuation processes to unfold. Just as the IAAP individuates as an organization, so each administration and each member of an administration goes through their own individuation process.

In Barcelona, in 2004, six years ago, speaking in this same context of the President's Farewell Address, Murray Stein offered us a sustained 'case history' of the IAAP in midlife. Referring to the IAAP as the grandchild of Jung, and the child of parents between whom there were considerable tensions at the time, he concluded that at this stage in its midlife, the 'IAAP is the most responsible and powerful adult in the worldwide Jungian family today, … [capable] of containing a great deal of diversity without falling into confusion and vagueness, or splitting apart, or becoming psychically paralyzed.' I think this was a very true and very important assessment at that time, which continues to hold true today. The IAAP's genetic makeup is good – adaptable and flexible; its vital signs are strong and healthy. Our review of the Constitution showed that the basic principles on which the IAAP is founded continue to be sound, even though revisions in structure are in order. Of course, we need to take care of the state of our health, especially at or around midlife. As an organization, we are facing a plethora of future possibilities and choices about how we can go forward and develop into our future, how we might *go on* individuating. We have put into place a number of organizational vehicles to ensure that we do so as safely, in an organizational sense, as possible. The Committees, Sub-Committees and Working Parties continue to devise and revise their working documents with the overview and agreement of the Executive Committee, thus ensuring good governance characterized by the principles of transparency and accountability. The reliance on the practice of good governance according to these principles has given me throughout this administration a secure sense that the IAAP is functioning in the best ways we have at our disposal – good governance is what I think of as the *ethical health* of an organization. This does not mean that there is not a need for regular revision, to hone and fine tune how the IAAP functions. The new role of the Finance Officer, the regular internal audit, the work that the Governance Working Party undertook to look at possible ways of responding to the needed updating of the IAAP's Constitution, voted on at the Delegates' Meeting; the request from the Ethics Committee to fine tune their working documents, which we also voted on; the addition of further Working Parties; the new vision for an Education Sub-Committee; the stable evolution of a new administration. These are all important health checks and they attest to this ongoing process of review and renewal.

But the IAAP does not exist in a vacuum. We have to monitor not only our internal wellbeing, but also our external environment in order to adapt maximally to new conditions as they present themselves. Are we doing enough to ensure that we go on thriving and not just surviving in the current climate, where local requirements for professional regulation, health insurance dictats, and sheer competition from other depth psychological training bodies can impact on our autonomy and freedoms as a profession and our organizational health overall? And how will such forces impact on our own governance procedures? In what ways will we need to adapt? How can we work to protect our future wellbeing?

One of the most vital of the IAAP's recent adaptations over the last decade or so has been our responsiveness to requests for recognition and help from individuals and groups of professionals in areas of the world where Jungian training or study programmes are very difficult or otherwise impossible to undertake. Organizationally, we have adapted to these calls for a response from the IAAP by putting into place two Sub-Committees – the Individual Membership Sub-Committee, which deals with the training of our Routers, and the Developing Groups Sub-Committee, consisting of professionals interested in pursuing a Jungian study programme. The number of these groups and individuals has gradually increased over this time. I wish to emphasize that the IAAP has not gone out to proselytize or to colonize – we have responded responsibly, with agreed and worked out criteria and procedures, to requests that have come to us. Nor, I think, can we or should we turn our backs on such requests without running the risk of jeopardizing the future of analytical psychology, and revoking our responsibilities to the aims of the IAAP as stated in our Constitution and often evoked by former Presidents and administrations. Some IAAP members who may not have been convinced that we should become involved in such projects, once involved in them, have become enthusiastically engaged participants when they have encountered the quality and depth of those who have turned to us for our expertise.

These projects – there are now 21 Developing Groups and almost 200 routers seeking eventual acceptance as Individual Members – have evolved to the extent that the original two Sub-Committees that appeared to be clearly differentiated in function have now become – to use a term borrowed from evolutionary studies – spandrels, functioning more as by-products of our organizational history but no longer adapted in function according to current conditions. And so, in true Jungian fashion, a third position is emerging as the Education Working Party looks likely to become a Sub-Committee in the next administration, absorbing and adopting the DG and IM functions in a new organizational configuration – truly a dialectical process.

Such perspectives call forth from IAAP members enormous amounts of energy, dedication, thought, and personal and professional organizational investment on the part of a very large number. I think that this investment of energy is archetypal in nature, a manifestation of the movement of the Self archetype to the extent that the IAAP can be said to embody such an archetypal configuration, and as such is itself based on sound organizational dynamics. Married to this archetypal movement is the careful governance procedures which I have already mentioned, where much thought, clarification and discernment are brought to bear on the merits of each situation while overall policies are carefully adhered to. I believe that all this bodes well for the future health of our IAAP.

On my desktop, I have an application called EarthDesk, which our computer genius, François Martin-Vallas, introduced me to when I was Chair of the Developing Groups Sub-Committee during the last administration. It is an application, showing on my computer screen in real time the whole of the globe via satellite pictures that are continuously updated. It shows me what parts of the world are awake and in daylight, and what parts are asleep, in darkness, and dreaming, or located in conurbations electrically lit up in the midst of darkness; where there are fair skies, where there is cloud; and where there are storms, typhoons, hurricanes, rain and snow. It is the first thing I see in the morning and often the last I might glance at night. This changing image brings to my mind, from around the world, the IAAP Societies, the Developing Groups, the Individual Members, the Routers, and good colleagues and friends from around the world whom I have had the privilege and pleasure to meet and to get to know, to admire, respect and esteem. I think of all these people leading their lives, working, practising, training, teaching. I am aware of the vast continents and how we are now so globalized that we are beginning to see a new dynamic, a new IAAP configuration process. For after globalization comes a need for more regional, continental, groupings and patterns. We have seen this happen first in North America, then in South America, then in the China and Pacific hub, and now there is a movement for regional organization in Western and Eastern Europe. The wonderful array of photos of IAAP colleagues from former times and distant lands that Paul Kugler and François Martin-Vallas put together for the start of the Delegates' Meeting attests to our global and regional networks. Again, this is an example of Jungian dynamics, of counterbalancing forces between the global (worldwide) and the regional (continental) coming into a new relationship with each other. This dynamic, I imagine, will go on to be played out in the next administration and beyond.

As I hand over, with great confidence and pleasure – and quite a large sense of personal loss – the IAAP baton to Joe Cambray and the next administration, I will carry on gazing at the globe on my desktop, and think of current and future developments in this vital and creative organization, our IAAP, and of the many friends and dear colleagues with whom I have had the privilege to work during these many years.

I look forward to seeing you all this evening at our closing banquet, and to seeing many of you around the IAAP global campus in the years to come.

Thank you.

Contents (CD)

Tuesday, 24 August 2010

Wednesday, 25 August 2010

Friday, 27 August 2010

Posters 22-27 August 2010, Montreal, Canada

Appendix

(The original Congress Programme is included in a separate pdf on the CD.)

Alphabetical List of Authors (in print)

Author Index (CD)

IAAP CONGRESS PROCEEDINGS

CAPE TOWN 2007
Journeys, Encounters: Clinical, Communal, Cultural
Proceedings of the 17th International Congress for Analytical Psychology
edited by Pramila Bennett
illustrated, 288 pages in print + 1142 pages on CD, ISBN 978-3-85630-728-8

BARCELONA 2004
Edges of Experience: Memory and Emergence
Proceedings of the 16th International Congress for Analytical Psychology
edited by Lyn Cowan
illustrated, 240 printed pages, 1380 pages on CD, ISBN 978-3-85630-700-4

CAMBRIDGE 2001
Proceedings of the 15th International Congress for Analytical Psychology
768 pages, paperback, ISBN 978-3-85630-609-0

FLORENCE 1998: DESTRUCTION AND CREATION
Proceedings of the 14th International Congress for Analytical Psychology,
edited by Mary Ann Mattoon, 620 pages, illustrated
hardbound: ISBN 978-3-85630-584-0 / paperback: ISBN 978-3-85630-583-3

ZURICH 1995: OPEN QUESTIONS IN ANALYTICAL PSYCHOLOGY
Proceedings of the 13th International Congress for Analytical Psychology
edited by Mary Ann Mattoon
752 pages, illustrated, hardbound: ISBN 978-3-85630-555-0
paperback: ISBN 978-3-85630-556-7

CHICAGO 1992
The Transcendent Function: Individual and Collective Aspects
edited by Mary Ann Mattoon
Sixty presentations were made by Jungian analysts from around the world,
and they appear in their entirety. 560 pages, illustrated
hardbound: ISBN 978-3-85630-537-6 / paperback: ISBN 978-3-85630-538-3

PARIS 1989
Personal and Archetypal Dynamics in the Analytical Relationship.
edited by Mary Ann Mattoon
This gathering was controversial, provocative and stimulating. All the papers
are presented, many richly illustrated. 510 pages, illustrated
hardbound: ISBN 978-3-85630-529-1 / paperback: ISBN 978-3-85630-524-6

BERLIN 1986
The Archetype of Shadow in a Split World
edited by Mary Ann Mattoon
The 10th International Congress of Analytical Psychology was held in Berlin,
September 2 – 9, 1986. 456 pages, numerous illustrations and diagrams
hardbound: ISBN 978-3-85630-514-7 / paperback: ISBN 978-3-85630-506-2

JERUSALEM 1983
Symbolic and Clinical Approaches in Theory and Practice
edited by Luigi Zoja and Robert Hinshaw
This handsome volume, drawn from the 9th International Congress of Analytical Psychology in Jerusalem, contains contributions reflecting on the meaning and significance of contemporary analytical work from 25 prominent Jungian analysts from around the world.
375 pages, hardbound, illustrated, ISBN 978-3-85630-504-8

Daniel Hell

Soul Hunger

The Feeling Human Being and the Life Sciences

Daniel Hell

Soul Hunger

The Feeling Human Being and the Life Sciences

Modern psychiatry attributes psychological suffering to functional disturbances of the brain. This approach, based on precise outside observation combined with advanced technology, renders the individual ever more an object of examination and treatment. The author of Soul Hunger adds another dimension by arguing for a differentiated perception of inner experience. His basic hypothesis: the more *high tech* there is, the more important *high touch* becomes.

Daniel Hell explains that many psychological disturbances can be attributed to contradictions between a self-image and actual experience. This tension-filled discrepancy is illustrated in detail with examples from the development of depressive, anxiety and adjustment disorders.

(368 pages, ISBN 978-3-85630-730-1)

Ann Ulanov

Spirit in Jung

Carl Jung is the foremost interpreter of the many interactions of religion, the world of the spiritual and psychological insight into human behaviors. In this book, one of the outstanding Jungian scholars of our time surveys Jung's contributions to a whole series of issues, ranging from the political to the pedagogical to the inner life of a saint, Therese of Lisieux.

Ann Belford Ulanov is Christiane Brooks Johnson Professor of Psychiatry and Religion at Union Theological Seminary in New York City. A Jungian analyst in private practice, she is also the author of numerous books, including "*The Wizards' Gate*", "*Cinderella and her Sisters*", "*The Wisdom of the Psyche*", "*Picturing God*", and "*The Feminine in Jungian Psychology and Christian Theology*".

(320 pages, ISBN 978-3-85630-698-4)

ENGLISH TITLES FROM DAIMON

R. Abt / I. Bosch / V. MacKrell - *Dream Child, Creation and New Life*
in Dreams of Pregnant Women
Ruth Ammann - *The Enchantment of Gardens*
Susan R. Bach - *Life Paints its Own Span*
Diana Baynes Jansen - *Jung's Apprentice: A Biography of Helton Godwin Baynes*
John Beebe (Ed.) - *Terror, Violence and the Impulse to Destroy*
E.A. Bennet - *Meetings with Jung*
W.H. Bleek / L.C. Lloyd (Ed.) - *Specimens of Bushman Folklore*
Tess Castleman - *Threads, Knots, Tapestries*
- *Sacred Dream Circles*
George Czuczka - *Imprints of the Future*
Heinrich Karl Fierz - *Jungian Psychiatry*
John Fraim - *Battle of Symbols*
von Franz / Frey-Rohn / Jaffé - *What is Death?*
Liliane Frey-Rohn - *Friedrich Nietzsche, A Psychological Approach*
Marion Gallbach - *Learning from Dreams*
Ralph Goldstein (Ed.) - *Images, Meanings and Connections:*
Essays in Memory of Susan Bach
Yael Haft - *Hands: Archetypal Chirology*
Fred Gustafson - *The Black Madonna of Einsiedeln*
Daniel Hell - *Soul-Hunger: The Feeling Human Being and the Life-Sciences*
Siegmund Hurwitz - *Lilith, the first Eve*
Aniela Jaffé - *The Myth of Meaning*
- *Was C.G. Jung a Mystic?*
- *From the Life und Work of C.G. Jung*
- *Death Dreams and Ghosts*
Verena Kast - *A Time to Mourn*
- *Sisyphus*
Hayao Kawai - *Dreams, Myths and Fairy Tales in Japan*
James Kirsch - *The Reluctant Prophet*
Eva Langley-Dános - *Prison on Wheels: Ravensbrück to Burgau*
Mary Lynn Kittelson - *Sounding the Soul*
Rivkah Schärf Kluger - *The Gilgamesh Epic*
Yehezkel Kluger & - *RUTH in the Light of Mythology, Legend*
Naomi Kluger-Nash *and Kabbalah*
Paul Kugler (Ed.) - *Jungian Perspectives on Clinical Supervision*
Paul Kugler - *The Alchemy of Discourse*
Rafael López-Pedraza - *Cultural Anxiety*
- *Hermes and his Children*
Alan McGlashan - *The Savage and Beautiful Country*
- *Gravity and Levity*
Gregory McNamee (Ed.) - *The Girl Who Made Stars: Bushman Folklore*
- *The Bearskin Quiver*
- *The North Wind and the Sun & Other Fables of Aesop*
Gitta Mallasz - *Talking with Angels*
C.A. Meier - *Healing Dream and Ritual*
- *A Testament to the Wilderness*
- *Personality: The Individuation Process*
Eva Pattis Zoja (Ed.) - *Sandplay Therapy*

ENGLISH TITLES FROM DAIMON

Available from your bookstore or from our distributors:

AtlasBooks	Gazelle Book Services Ltd.
30 Amberwood Parkway	White Cross Mills, High Town
Ashland OH 44805, USA	Lancaster LA1 4XS, UK
Phone: 419-281-5100	Tel: +44(0)152468765
Fax: 419-281-0200	Fax: +44(0)152463232
E-mail: order@atlasbooks.com	Email: Sales@gazellebooks.co.uk
www.AtlasBooksDistribution.com	www.gazellebooks.co.uk

Daimon Verlag - Hauptstrasse 85 - CH-8840 Einsiedeln - Switzerland
Phone: (41)(55) 412 2266   Fax: (41)(55) 412 2231
email: info@daimon.ch
Visit our website: **www.daimon.ch** *or write for our complete catalog*